THE OXFORD HISTORY
OF ENGLAND

Edited by SIR GEORGE CLARK

THE OXFORD HISTORY OF ENGLAND

Edited by SIR GEORGE CLARK

THE
ENGLISH
SETTLEMENTS

By

J. N. L. MYRES
sometime Bodley's Librarian and
President of the Society of Antiquaries

CLARENDON PRESS · OXFORD

Oxford University Press, Walton Street, Oxford OX2 6DP

Oxford   New York   Toronto
Delhi   Bombay   Calcutta   Madras   Karachi
Kuala Lumpur   Singapore   Hong Kong   Tokyo
Nairobi   Dar es Salaam   Cape Town
Melbourne   Auckland   Madrid

and associated companies in
Berlin Ibadan

Oxford is a trade mark of Oxford University Press

Published in the United States
by Oxford University Press Inc., New York

© Oxford University Press 1986

First published 1986

British Library Cataloguing in Publication Data

Myres, J. N. L.
The English settlements.—
(Oxford history of England; 1B)
1. Great Britain—History—Roman period,
55 B.C.-449 A.D.   2. Great Britain—History
—Anglo-Saxon period, 449-1066
I. Title
942.01   DA145
ISBN 0-19-821719-6

Library of Congress Cataloging in Publication Data

Myres, J. N. L. (John Lowell Linton)
The English Settlements.
(Oxford history of England; 1B)
Bibliography: p.
Includes indexes.
1. Great Britain—History—Roman period,
449-1066.   I. Title.   II. Series.
DA152.M97   1985   942.01   85-15538
ISBN 0-19-821719-6

7 9 10 8 6

Printed and bound in Great Britain by
Mackays of Chatham PLC, Chatham, Kent

ACKNOWLEDGEMENTS

THIS book could never have reached the point of publication without the generous assistance of many friends and scholars working in the same fields who have contributed in different ways to its completion. To a number of these I have expressed my obligation in the text or the notes. But I owe much more than I may realize to personal contacts over more than fifty years with those, both in this country and abroad, with whom I have often discussed the problems of this age. I am also greatly indebted to my son, Dr. M. T. Myres, of the Department of Biology at Calgary University, who was mainly responsible for persuading me to persevere with this task at an age when many authors have had their fill of reading and writing, and may find it more burdensome than they once did to express themselves intelligibly in print. His experience of university teaching in Canada, albeit in a field of study far removed from mine, has enabled me to avoid obscurities of expression and to provide explanations, especially of some technical terms, which may be helpful to students unfamiliar with the historical and geographical backgrounds in which the story of the English settlements must be set.

The welcome decision of the publishers to allow for the first time in this series some illustrations in addition to maps has enabled me to include a few visual aids, to explain the basic sequences in the archaeological evidence for this period which are difficult either to expound or to comprehend without such help. For permission to reproduce for this purpose material already published elsewhere in different contexts I am greatly indebted to Professor V. I. Evison, Mrs. S. C. Hawkes, Dr. M. Welch, and Mr. William J. Roberts IV. They are of course in no way responsible for any unexpected conclusions I may have drawn from the objects themselves.

I am also most grateful to Delia Twamley and Margaret Golby, who have typed at different stages a continuously evolving and often rather messy manuscript with admirable accuracy and precision. Above all my thanks are due to my good friends Jean Cook and Grace Briggs, who have collaborated most generously and efficiently in relieving me of nearly all the tiresome and time-consuming incidentals of authorship. They have identified, checked, and standardized my often wayward references, investigated many queries, and removed minor obscurities, duplications, and errors of all kinds. While any remaining defects are entirely my responsibility, it is due to them that this book has reached a form which makes publication possible. I am most grateful for all that they have done to bring this to pass.

J. N. L. M.

CONTENTS

1. THE NATURE OF THE EVIDENCE:
I. THE LITERARY SOURCES

2. THE NATURE OF THE EVIDENCE:
II. ARCHAEOLOGY AND PLACE-NAMES

CONTENTS

3. THE CONTINENTAL BACKGROUND

4. THE ROMANO-BRITISH BACKGROUND
AND THE SAXON SHORE

5. SAXONS, ANGLES, AND JUTES ON THE SAXON
SHORE

6. THE FORMATION OF WESSEX

7. THE HUMBRENSES AND THE NORTH

CONTENTS

FIGURES

SOURCES

Acknowledgements are due for figures taken from the following sources:

Fig. 1: Fig. 2 *g - h*: Åberg, *The Anglo-Saxons in England* (Uppsala, 1926)

Fig. 2 *a - f*: Welch, *Early Anglo-Saxon Sussex*, BAR 112 (1983); *c* by courtesy of Worthing Museum and Art Gallery, drawing by Mrs P. Clarke; other drawings by N. Griffiths

Figs. 3, 5 and 6: Myres, in *PBA* 56 (1970)

Fig. 4: Myres, *Corpus of Anglo-Saxon Pottery of the Pagan Period* (Cambridge, 1977)

Figs. 7–9: Roberts, *Romano-Saxon Pottery*, BAR 106 (1982)

Fig. 10 *a - f*: Hawkes, in *Archaeologia* 98 (1961); *b* drawn by C. O. Waterhouse and reproduced by permission of the Trustees of the British Museum; other drawings by S. C. Hawkes
g - h: Welch, op. cit.; drawings by N. Griffiths

Fig. 11: Evison, *Fifth-Century Invasions South of the Thames* (1965); after Rigollot, pl. XII

MAPS

ABBREVIATIONS

BIBLIOGRAPHICAL NOTE

For books cited in footnotes and in the Bibliography no place of publication is given for those published in London, nor for the series British Archaeological Reports, published in Oxford.

INTRODUCTION

WHEN Volume I of the *Oxford History of England* was published in 1936 it contained, in addition to R. G. Collingwood's full-length study of Roman Britain, a final section of five chapters in which I endeavoured to summarize the current state of knowledge on the English settlements which took place between the collapse of Roman rule in the fifth century and the emergence of the Anglo-Saxon kingdoms in the seventh. I had been asked to contribute this section in order to fill a gap between Collingwood's account of Roman Britain in Volume I and the massive study of Anglo-Saxon England which Professor F. M. (later Sir Frank) Stenton was to write as Volume II in the series, for neither Collingwood nor Stenton wished to concern themselves in detail with the dark centuries between. It would have been natural for my chapters on this obscure period to have formed rather a prologue to *Anglo-Saxon England* than an epilogue to *Roman Britain*. Their purpose was to look forward to the future and it was in these years that the foundations of England were laid in the collapsing ruins of the Roman world. But Collingwood's *Roman Britain* was to be ready for the press some years before Stenton's *Anglo-Saxon England* and, being shorter than Stenton's book was likely to prove, had more space that could be spared to accommodate what had to be said about the English settlements.

This more or less fortuitous circumstance led to Volume I of the *Oxford History* becoming known to generations of history students as 'Collingwood and Myres'. The implication which the phrase carried, that it was a cooperative product of joint authorship, was entirely erroneous. Collingwood himself was eager to make this clear from the start. The first sentence of his preface reads 'This volume is not a work of collaboration', and it was not in fact until his text was in final draft that I learnt that he proposed to pursue the story of Roman Britain far beyond its generally accepted termination in the early years of the fifth century to include a sub-Roman epilogue in the Arthurian age. That he did so made it difficult to provide any coherent account of Britain in the fifth century in either part of the book. On the one side the collapse of Roman Britain makes little sense without a detailed study of those barbarian forces which eventually overwhelmed it, and on the other the activities of those forces are themselves barely intelligible except against a background of the political and economic changes that were affecting the sub-Roman world in the fifth century. Without more effective collaboration between the mutually exclusive viewpoints provided by the two authors of 'Collingwood and Myres' it may have been difficult for the student of these dark centuries to form a comprehensive and just estimate of all the factors that turned Roman Britain into Christian England.

In spite of these disadvantages, perhaps more apparent to me as part-author than to the general reader, the book was well received and had an unusually long run. Owing to the war and to Collingwood's early death it was never substantially revised and in the course of over forty years both parts of it inevitably became very out of date, and the whole thing is now little better than a period piece. A vast amount of fresh information on every aspect of Roman Britain has become available during the past generation, and this has not only necessitated a radically new approach to almost every aspect of the subject as discussed by Collingwood, but has also made it impossible to cover it adequately except at considerably greater length. For all these reasons it became very desirable for the new Volume I of the *Oxford History* by Peter Salway to be devoted to Roman Britain only, without the need to make space for a revised version of my section on *The English Settlements*. That Salway, like Collingwood, has followed the fading ghost of Roman Britain into final extinction in a Europe dominated by Clovis and the expanding kingdom of the Franks makes it even more desirable that, in spite of the inevitable duplication of background which this chronological overlap entails, my revised account of the English settlements should appear separately as the start of something new.

Stenton's *Anglo-Saxon England* was published in 1943, seven years later than 'Collingwood and Myres'. It was inevitable that he should find it impossible to take up the story at the point at which I had left it, just before the coming of Christianity and the emergence of the Anglo-Saxon kingdoms in the seventh century. In his preface Stenton gave the year 550 as the approximate point from which he proposed to begin. But in fact he found it necessary to trace the major Anglo-Saxon kingdoms back to their misty origins in the fifth century, and thus to cover again in his own way the whole period included in my *English Settlements*. What distinguished his treatment from mine was his concentration on the documentary and place-name evidence to the virtual exclusion of the archaeological material which I had endeavoured to combine with it.

With Salway's *Roman Britain* extending to the early sixth century and with Stenton tracing *Anglo-Saxon England* back into the fifth it might well be thought that the *Oxford History* has no need of any independent study of what might appear a non-existent gap between them. The devotion of a whole new volume, however slim, to the elucidation of matters at least partly considered already by both, certainly requires some explanation. It can be found in the fact that neither the new *Roman Britain* nor the old *Anglo-Saxon England* provides any adequate up-to-date reassessment of the topics to which I devoted my chapters on the *English Settlements* in 1936. At least as much new material of importance has accumulated on these matters in the last forty years as that which has required an entirely new assessment of Roman Britain. Much of this has been due, directly or indirectly, on the Anglo-Saxon as on the Romano-British side, to the development of ideas and the opening up of new research projects whose origins can be traced back to *Roman Britain and the English Settlements*. To take only my own studies, my publication of the major Anglo-Saxon cemeteries of Caistor-by-Norwich, Markshall, and Sancton (1973), *Anglo-Saxon Pottery and the Settlement of England* (1969), *Corpus of Anglo-Saxon Pottery* (1977), and many shorter pieces,[1] all arose from thoughts originally generated while I was writing *The English Settlements*.

[1] There is a full list up to 1976 in the Bibliography to my *Corpus of Anglo-Saxon Pottery of the Pagan Period* (Cambridge, 1977), I. p. xxxii. More recent pieces can be found in the bibliography of my writings included in V. I. Evison (ed.), *Angles, Saxons, and Jutes: essays presented to J. N. L. Myres* (Oxford, 1981).

Both in England and on the Continent very great advances have been made since 1945 in our knowledge of the archaeology of the *Völkerwanderungszeit*, and in our understanding of its historical implications. In 1936 I had little on which to build so far as the English material went except for R. A. Smith's purely descriptive county surveys in the *Victoria County History* published between 1900 and 1912, Baldwin Brown's substantial chapters in *The Arts in Early England* III and IV (1915), and E. T. Leeds' pioneer study, *Archaeology of the Anglo-Saxon Settlements* (1913), all of which, though containing much matter of basic importance, were becoming out-dated by subsequent discoveries. None of these scholars were professional historians, and their work had made little impression on historical writing. The only recent attempt at a synthesis of the archaeological material was contained in N. Åberg, *The Anglo-Saxons in England* (1926) and dealt mainly with the classification of brooches and other metalwork.

On the Continent also most of the important cemeteries in north Germany, the Low Countries, and Scandinavia were still unpublished, and there had been no comprehensive attempt to base historical conclusions on the archaeological evidence since Plettke's *Ursprung und Ausbreitung der Angeln und Sachsen* appeared in 1920. In particular no effective use had been made for historical purposes of the great collections of pottery either in English or in continental museums. It was only after 1936, and particularly after 1945, that this situation began to change on both sides of the North Sea. Karl Waller's publication in 1938 of the great cemetery at Galgenberg bei Cuxhaven began this process just before the war, but the appalling war-time losses of archaeological material in the German museums stimulated a notable drive to publish what was left as soon as conditions made such a programme possible.

One unexpected consequence of the war was the determination of archaeologists concerned with the *Völkerwanderungszeit* on the Continent and in England to resume and develop their common interests in the problems of that age. A most useful forum for this purpose was provided by the enlightened initiative of Karl Waller in the establishment of the Arbeitsgemeinschaft für Sachsenforschung based at first on his own museum at Cuxhaven and continued after his death by Albert Genrich of Hanover. It was at Cuxhaven that the first Sachsensymposion, inaugurating a series of such informal gatherings, took place in 1949. Subsequent meetings held annually not only in Germany but in Holland, Belgium, the Scandinavian countries, and (three times) in England have been most useful in promoting the growth of personal contacts, and the exchange of ideas, publications, and visits between the most active scholars in these fields in all countries bordering the North Sea.[1] Numerous publications, partly stimulated by the Sachsensymposion, have not only made available much of the surviving evidence from pre-war museum collections, but have included the results of important recent excavations on settlement and cemetery sites such as Wijster in Holland, Feddersen Wierde near Bremerhaven, and Liebenau (Hanover), which have produced material directly relevant to the Anglo-Saxon settlements in England. The fresh emphasis on evidence from occupation-sites as distinct from cemeteries, throwing new light on the life-style and domestic economy in addition to the burial customs of the pagan Anglo-Saxon peoples, has been one of the most fruitful developments of the post-war period. In 1936 almost the only village site of this kind that had been excavated in England was that at Sutton Courtenay, Oxon. (formerly Berks.) where E. T. Leeds had explored a number of *Grubenhäuser* and published his discoveries in *Archaeologia* 72 and 76 (1923 and 1927). No example was known in this country at that time of the more substantial halls or long-houses which were a regular feature of the contemporary *Terpen*, or mound settlements, on the marshy coastlands of Holland and north Germany. Since then this gap in our knowledge has been largely filled not only by the recognition of many further groups of *Grubenhäuser* all over eastern England, but by the exploration of major concentrations of such habitations and workshops associated with rectangular hall-houses at, for example, Mucking, Essex, and West Stow Heath, Suffolk. The information which archaeology can now supply towards an understanding of the pagan Saxon age is

---

[1] More detail on the earlier stages of the post-war recovery of archaeological study in Germany and north-western Europe in general can be found in my *Anglo-Saxon Pottery and the Settlement of England* (Oxford, 1969), 8-11.

thus not only vastly greater in quantity but also very much broader in range and quality than it was before 1936.

The discovery and excavation of the ship burial at Sutton Hoo, Suffolk, in the weeks immediately preceding the outbreak of war in 1939, was in time to receive brief mention in Stenton's *Anglo-Saxon England* in 1943. But his account was necessarily composed while the magnificent grave goods from this richest of all princely pagan-style burials of the *Völkerwanderungszeit* were still inaccessible in war-time storage. It needs substantial revision in the light of the definitive publication of the finds by R. L. S. Bruce-Mitford between 1976 and 1984.

Nor is it only in archaeology that there have been notable developments in the non-literary evidence for this age. The study of place-names was already contributing much information relevant to the English settlements before 1936, though it has never been easy to interpret with confidence in historical terms. In the early chapters of *Anglo-Saxon England* Stenton, whose knowledge of the subject as then understood was profound, made a much wider use of place-names than I had done. He was able to draw not only on the ever-increasing material being published in the county volumes of the English Place-Name Society, but on that which he had himself assembled for his presidential addresses to the Royal Historical Society delivered annually on aspects of this subject from 1938 to 1940. Since Stenton's time there have been developments in place-name studies due not merely to the continuing expansion of its published raw material, but to various essays in its interpretation which may have a profound bearing on its value for historical purposes in this period. These will require fuller examination at later stages in this book.[1] They are mentioned here as an indication of the need for a fundamental reassessment of the place-name element in the basic evidence for the course and character of the English settlements.

These are some of the reasons which have made a quite new approach to the problems of the English settlements, radically different from that which I took more than forty years ago, essential, if this basic phase in the history of

[1] Especially pp. 37–43

England is to be discussed with proper reference to the present state of knowledge. It is never easy for an author to judge after such a lapse of time how much of what he then wrote is worth incorporating in a reassessment based on so much fresh evidence. There are aspects of the story on which my own views do not now differ much if at all from those which I then expressed. I have had no hesitation in retaining in such cases passages written before 1936, both long and short, and even single sentences and turns of phrase, with little or no modification even if they appear here in a different context.

But in essentials this is a new book whose general arrangement necessarily differs from that of my chapters in 'Collingwood and Myres'. This is required partly to take account of necessary changes of emphasis caused by the differential growth of knowledge on different topics. But partly also it is needed because more has now to be said about the background of native society in the later days of Roman Britain with which the Anglo-Saxon settlers found themselves confronted. These matters, as then understood, had been covered by Collingwood in his part of *Roman Britain and the English Settlements*, and there was no call for me to go over them again in mine. But in a separate volume such as this some account of this background must be given to achieve a proper understanding of the circumstances in which the settlement took place in various parts of the country. This may involve some duplication of ground covered in the later chapters of Salway's new *Roman Britain*. Such duplication cannot be avoided if due weight is to be given, as it must, to all the evidence, mostly unrecognized in 1936, which suggests a degree of overlap and fusion between the last age of Roman Britain and the earliest Anglo-Saxon settlements which was too little appreciated at that time. It is indeed mainly to allow for a proper discussion of this overlap that a separate volume at this point in the *Oxford History of England* is now required.

One point needs emphasis. Like all its fellow volumes in the *Oxford History of England*, the present book is written primarily for students of history, not for specialists in archaeology, linguistics, place-name studies, or any other related subjects. Their conclusions must of course be utilized, and indeed on occasion criticized, wherever it seems that they have a relevant contribution to bring to the elucidation of this phase of English history. But the plan of this series, and in particular its limited provision of illustrations, has made it, for example, impossible to go deeply into the archaeological discussion of the numerous categories of material artefacts which form the evidence on which the conclusions of that branch of knowledge rest. The significance of these conclusions can only be grasped, and their meaning can only be correctly appreciated, with the visual aids which abundant illustrations can alone supply. It has therefore often been necessary to state the conclusions to which I have come on many aspects of this time without providing the reader with the detailed grounds which have led me to them or enabling him to appreciate visually much of the evidence on which my interpretation rests. In the Bibliography I have given further references to relevant illustrated accounts of the material under discussion. But in the text I have only attempted to describe its more distinctive and significant features in broad outline, and I have done this only where it has been essential to the course of an historical argument. I have made no attempt to provide any general guide to Anglo-Saxon, sub-Roman, or any other relevant category of Dark Age antiquities. This book is intended to be a history book and nothing else.

For somewhat similar reasons I have omitted all technical discussion of the linguistic problems which arise at every turn in the search for material relevant to an understanding of this age. This is not because they are unimportant but because I am not properly equipped to handle them. The material and psychological changes which accompanied the general substitution of a Germanic mode of speech for one based either, as in Gaul, on Vulgar Latin or, as in the Celtic lands, on varieties of the Brittonic tongues, must have had profound consequences for the structure of society in all those parts of the country where it occurred. The most obvious is the transformation or replacement of place-names, and this is the only aspect of the matter on which I have felt competent here and there to comment. But language and history in all societies must always be deeply intertwined, and such traumatic changes in speech as took place in Britain

in the centuries covered by this book should be capable of
providing many clues to the corresponding changes in the
population and its way of life. But linguistic change is also a
factor which directly affected the survival value of all
contemporary literary evidence. How much, for example,
would Anglo-Saxon settlers be able to learn about Roman
Britain if it was true that they encountered 'very few people
who talked any sort of Latin at all' in the parts which they
occupied? And if 'Vortigern, around 450, could not have
understood Aneirin around 600, though Gildas, living
through the first half of the sixth century, could probably
have understood both',[1] what were the chances for the
meaningful survival of any historical, social, or economic
information recorded at this time in the lands where Brittonic
speech prevailed? Considerations of this kind are clearly of
direct relevance to the subject matter of this book, but their
discussion cannot be profitably undertaken by any but those
possessed of a high degree of linguistic expertise.

It may perhaps be thought by some readers that I have
placed too much emphasis on matters, whether archaeological
or historical, that directly arise from the topographical
distribution of the early Anglo-Saxon settlements. To stress
these aspects of the period has, indeed, been my deliberate
intention. I have always felt that an essential prerequisite to
any understanding of this age must lie in an attempt to see
the countryside, and the collapsing ruins of Roman Britain
which it contained, from the same point of view as that
which presented itself to the newcomers from the Continent.
Such an intimate and revealing understanding of the contemporary topography can only be achieved by detailed
personal inspection undertaken on foot or horseback, or by
boat, for in the fifth century no other means of transport
were available. Only in these ways can the extent, varying
quality, and interrelationships of the different parts of lowland Britain be appreciated by the modern student in terms
which correspond, as near as may be, to the impression they
must have made on immigrant folk from the Continent in
early Anglo-Saxon times.

[1] K. H. Jackson, *Language and History in Early Britain* (Edinburgh, 1953),
261 and 690; and see my review of this important book, *EHR* 70 (1955), 630-3.

To this end I devoted much of my leisure, as an under-graduate and a young college tutor in the twenty years before 1939, to extensive travels on foot through the relevant parts of Roman Britain and the principal areas of early Anglo-Saxon settlement. Thus I walked the whole line of Hadrian's Wall and examined the sites of all the late Roman signal stations on the Yorkshire coast between the Humber and the Tees. I visited all the Saxon Shore forts of which traces survive, between Brancaster on the north Norfolk coast and Pevensey in Sussex. I walked the whole length of the Fosse Way from Devonshire to Lincoln, and thence north on the Roman road to the Humber crossing at Brough (*Petuaria*), and on past Sancton and Goodmanham to Malton and the Vale of Pickering. In Wessex, I made myself familiar on numerous occasions with the chalklands of Hampshire and Wiltshire, and came to know very well their main links with the upper Thames Valley, by walking the Oxford to Winchester route, the Berkshire ridgeway across the Wansdyke frontier and the Vale of Pewsey on to Salisbury Plain, and the Roman roads from Cirencester to Silchester and Win-chester. In the south-east, I walked the so-called Pilgrims' Way along the North Downs from Winchester to Canterbury and the tracks along the South Downs from the Cuckmere Valley towards Chichester. I crossed the Weald by the Roman Stane Street from Chichester to the southern approaches of London. North and east of the upper Thames basin, I walked the Akeman Street from Cirencester to St. Albans and most of the Icknield Way route along the Chilterns from the Goring gap towards East Anglia and the Wash.

I once had ambitions to penetrate Britain by boat up all the main water-ways on the east and south coasts. It seemed to me important to obtain a visual impression of how the land looks as one approaches the principal harbours and estuaries from the sea. For this purpose I studied both the lower and the upper reaches of the Thames from below Greenwich past London to Oxford and beyond, and attempted to visualize how the valley would have appeared before the upper part of the river was artificially controlled by locks. I made a fascinating trip up the Humber and the Yorkshire Ouse as far as York, and noted with interest how the principal tributaries from the west all seem to join the main river facing upstream; their mouths are thus not at all obvious to inquisitive mariners sailing by, especially when deeply shrouded in reed beds. I also know the Yare Valley from Great Yarmouth (and its earlier mouth, now blocked by shingle, at Roman Caister) through Breydon Water to Norwich and nearby Caistor (*Venta Icenorum*) on its tributary, the Tas.

But life has not been long enough to carry out as much of this programme as I had hoped. I have never found an opportunity to make such a water-borne study of the Trent, or of the important Anglo-Saxon routes into the Midlands provided by the valleys of the Welland, the Nene, and the Bedfordshire Ouse that flow through the Fens into the Wash. Even so, I can claim to have visited by these old-fashioned means a great majority of the places in this country whose names appear in the index to this book, and I retain a vivid visual memory of the present appearance of a very large number of them and their surroundings. And the fact that I have studied and drawn Anglo-Saxon pottery in some ninety English museums and private collections dotted over all the face of the land[5] has also contributed greatly to such familiarity as I have with the landscape, for on these visits I have generally found time to look at their setting in the surrounding countryside.

I cannot claim a comparable knowledge of the topography of the continental homelands. But I have worked in most of the principal museums in Belgium, Holland, north Germany, and Scandinavia. I have observed from the air, and to a lesser degree by rail and on foot, the lower reaches of the Weser and Elbe valleys, the neighbourhood of Kiel and Schleswig, and much of Denmark. A slow stopping train from Bremen to Cuxhaven once provided me with fascinating glimpses of the numerous *Terpen*, many still carrying modern villages, that are scattered over the marshy coastlands between the Elbe and Weser estuaries, from which so many of our Saxon forbears must have come.

Several of my own friends, and many other contemporaries of my generation, made more extensive and adventurous perambulations on foot, both in this country and abroad,

---

[1] Details are listed in my *Corpus*, I. p. xiii.

often with more ambitious objectives than I set myself. I have mentioned what I personally attempted in this field only to explain how it is that I have come to think of the historical and archaeological problems of this age as set always against the immensely informative background of the English landscape. Without some personal appreciation of the relevant features of that landscape, and of its fading Romano-British contents in the fifth and sixth centuries, no one can hope to achieve an adequate understanding of the course and character of the English settlements.

It is, however, unfortunately true that such an understanding is now far harder to obtain by the pedestrian means which it was natural for me to adopt over sixty years ago. Long-distance walking on the older main roads, and even the minor roads, of England has been rendered almost intolerable by the proliferation of motor traffic. The building of motorways, often sited across rather than along, the natural grain of the country, and the construction of bypasses, specifically designed to divert travellers away from the age-old centres of population, have made it much more difficult to comprehend, in the old way, the traditional patterns of human settlement. My generation of historians was perhaps the last for whom it was comparatively easy to identify and appreciate the meaning of these traditional patterns, unhampered by the physical distortions now imposed on them by the requirements of motor transport.

Christ Church, Oxford J. N. L. MYRES
June 1985

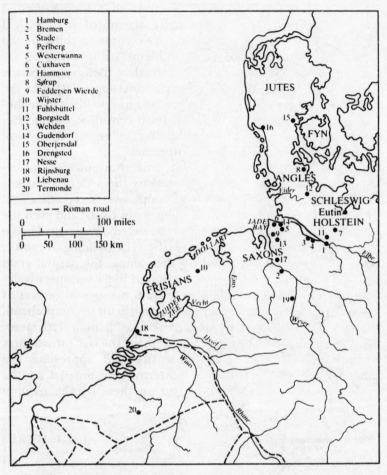

Map 1. The continental background to the English settlements

1	Hamburg
2	Bremen
3	Stade
4	Perlberg
5	Westerwanna
6	Cuxhaven
7	Hammoor
8	Sørup
9	Feddersen Wierde
10	Wijster
11	Fuhlsbüttel
12	Borgstedt
13	Wehden
14	Gudendorf
15	Oberjersdal
16	Drengsted
17	Nesse
18	Rijnsburg
19	Liebenau
20	Termonde

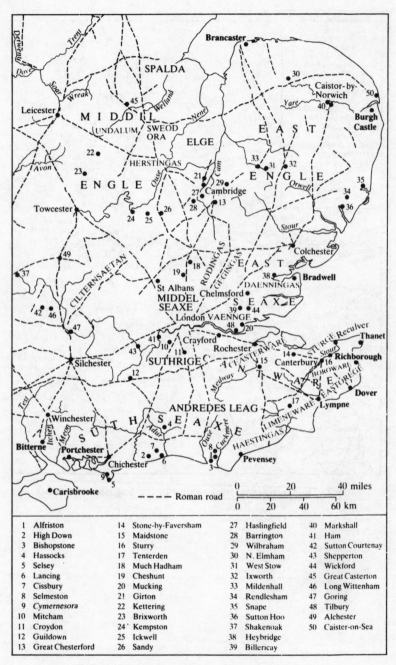

Brancaster

SPALDA

30

Caistor-by-
Norwich   50

Leicester   45   Burgh
                                    Castle
        M I D D I L   40
    UNDALUM   SWEOD
             ORA   ELGE   E A S T
22
        HERSTINGAS   33   31   32
23   21   E N G L E   35
    E N G L E   27 29 Cambridge   34
                              28   13   36
Towcester   24 25   26

                              49   Colchester
37   38   Bradwell
                        19 18   RODINGAS   GEGINGAS   DAENNINGAS
                        St Albans   39 44
42 46   MIDDEL   Chelmsford   S E A X E
            47   SEAXE   48 20
                        London VAENNGE
                    41 10   Crayford   Reculver   Thanet
            43   11   Rochester   CAESTERWARE   STURGE Richborough
        Silchester   SUTHRIGE   14 Canterbury 16
                    12   BOROWARE   Dover
                                                        EASTORE
        Winchester   ANDREDES LEAG   17   Lympne
Bitterne   4   HAESTINGAS
        Portchester   7   8   LIMENEWARE
    Chichester   2   6   Pevensey
        9   5
Carisbrooke   0   20   40 miles
            - - - - Roman road   0   20   40   60 km

1   Alfriston   14 Stone-by-Faversham   27 Haslingfield   40 Markshall
2   High Down   15 Maidstone   28 Barrington   41 Ham
3   Bishopstone   16 Sturry   29 Wilbraham   42 Sutton Courtenay
4   Hassocks   17 Tenterden   30 N. Elmham   43 Shepperton
5   Selsey   18 Much Hadham   31 West Stow   44 Wickford
6   Lancing   19 Cheshunt   32 Ixworth   45 Great Casterton
7   Cissbury   20 Mucking   33 Mildenhall   46 Long Wittenham
8   Selmeston   21 Girton   34 Rendlesham   47 Goring
9   Cymernesora   22 Kettering   35 Snape   48 Tilbury
10 Mitcham   23 Brixworth   36 Sutton Hoo   49 Alchester
11 Croydon   24 Kempston   37 Shakenoak   50 Caister-on-Sea
12 Guildown   25 Ickwell   38 Heybridge
13 Great Chesterford 26 Sandy   39 Billericay

Map 2. The Saxon Shore and its hinterland

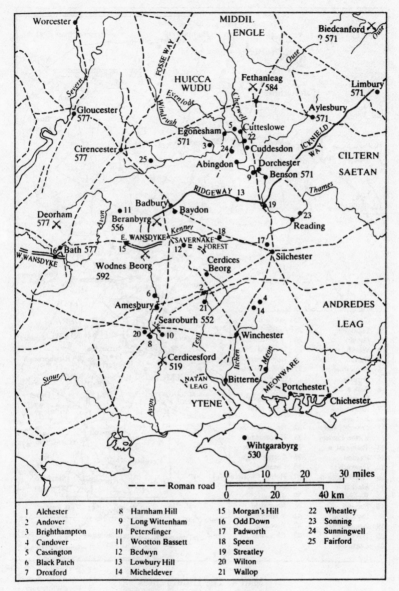

Map 3. The growth of Wessex

1	Alchester	8	Harnham Hill	15	Morgan's Hill	22	Wheatley
2	Andover	9	Long Wittenham	16	Odd Down	23	Sonning
3	Brighthampton	10	Petersfinger	17	Padworth	24	Sunningwell
4	Candover	11	Wootton Bassett	18	Speen	25	Fairford
5	Cassington	12	Bedwyn	19	Streatley		
6	Black Patch	13	Lowbury Hill	20	Wilton		
7	Droxford	14	Micheldever	21	Wallop		

Map 4. The Humbrenses

The following is the legend/key shown within the map:

1	Greetwell	22	Saltburn
2	Elkington	23	Londesborough
3	Fonaby	24	N. Newbald
4	West Keal	25	Driffield
5	Baston	26	Humberston
6	Winteringham	27	Willoughby-on-the-Wolds
7	Winterton		
8	Barton-on-Humber	28	Birrens
		29	Castleteads
9	Kirmington	30	Birdoswald
10	Elsham	31	Carvoran
11	Loveden Hill	32	Great Chesters
12	Kirton Lindsey	33	Housesteads
13	Thurmaston	34	Chesterholm
14	Repton	35	Carrawburgh
15	Heworth	36	Chesters
16	Goodmanham	37	Halton Chesters
17	Market Weighton	38	Rudchester
		39	Benwell
18	Brough (by Malton)	40	Newcastle
		41	Wallsend
19	Almondbury	42	Papcastle
20	Darlington	43	Ebchester
21	Corbridge		

Labels appearing on the map: BERNICIA, Tweed, Lindisfarne, Bamborough, Yeavering, Coquet, High Rochester, Tyne, Carlisle, Jarrow, Wear, Tees, DEIRA, SCOTS DYKE, Catterick, Ure, Swale, Aldborough, Nidd, Flamborough Head, Malton, DERA FELD, DERA, Sancton, WUDU, York, ROMAN RIG, BECCA BANKS, Derwent, LOIDIS, Ouse, Aire, Brough, ELMET, Don, Caistor-on-the-Wolds, Humber, ROMAN RIDGE, LINDSEY, Idle, Lincoln, Horncastle, Newark, Slea, Trent, Sleaford, MERCIA, Ancaster, Soar, Wreak, Witham, Lichfield, Tamworth, Humberstone, Leicester

Scale bars: 0 — 20 — 40 miles; 0 — 30 — 60 km

- - - Roman road

1

THE NATURE OF THE EVIDENCE:
I. THE LITERARY SOURCES

T HE period of some two centuries which lies between the
collapse of Roman government in Britain and the arrival
of St. Augustine in AD 597 has long been recognized as
the most difficult and obscure in the history of this country.
Between Roman Britain and Christian England there is
indeed a great gulf fixed, a void of confusion which remains a
standing challenge to historical inquiry. Within these two
centuries changes more profound and far-reaching than in
any other corresponding period took place: these changes
modified the physical character of the people, altered the
fundamental structure of the language, laid the basis of many
of our institutions, and made possible an economic exploitation of natural resources on a scale scarcely attempted
in prehistoric or even in Roman times. And as the result of
this domestic exploitation came first the possibility and then
the problem of a population expanding towards the limits of
subsistence, and becoming in its turn the centre of expansion
overseas. Many other and later factors have determined the
direction, the character, and the extent of that expansion,
but it is not too fantastic to believe that its beginnings lay in
this period, in the silent and strenuous conversion of the
abandoned arable land and remaining forests of Roman
Britain into the cultivated fields and profitable swine pasture
of countless Anglo-Saxon communities.

At the time, of course, nothing could have been further
from men's minds than such a conception of the meaning of
events. To those brought up in the Roman world the forces
of civilization appeared to be giving way to barbarism, and, in
so far as the civilized attempted consciously to appreciate the
causes of their troubles, they not unnaturally attributed them
to divine vengeance on one another's sins. Nor were the
illiterate barbarians themselves, so far as we can penetrate to

the thoughts which they were themselves unable to express in permanent form, conscious in any way of their destiny. Long after this period was over they were still giving names to places in the forests and fens which show that they regarded them and their contents with superstitious terror, as areas peopled with all the supernatural forces of evil. That not-withstanding they continued to fell the forests and to drain the fens is a fact whose significance only the later historian can appreciate. All that was apparent by the end of the sixth century was the destruction of the whole fabric of Roman imperialism in Britain, the disappearance of its civil and military administration and of many of the arts of life. Instead there was being built up a group of precariously founded barbarian kingdoms whose rulers were still living largely on the spoil of their neighbours, even if many of their dependants, along with the surviving remnants of the British population, were already slowly settling down to the cease-less routine of subsistence agriculture.

The purpose of this book is to inquire by what stages these changes were brought about and how deep they penetrated into the structure of society. In the past, and even in very recent times, the most diverse answers have been given to these questions. Some historians have regarded the destruc-tion of the Romano-British world and of the native popu-lation as virtually total. Others have treated the Anglo-Saxon intruders as imposing little more than the superficial veneer of a new language and a conquering elite on a British popu-lation that remained basically in place, however economically depressed and culturally deprived. How does it come about that such widely different interpretations are possible, and that the changes which certainly occurred should be so diffi-cult to understand?

The best way to find an answer to this question is to look at the sort of evidence on which our knowledge of the period rests, and to contrast it with that on which we rely for an understanding of the times before and after these dark centuries. Our knowledge of Roman Britain is based on an unequal blend of two main groups of evidence. Since Britain became part of the Roman empire, the broad outlines of its history are known from the historians who described at dif-ferent periods the story of that empire. But since Britain was remote from the Mediterranean lands which were the centres of Roman political life, and since the works of few Roman historians have survived, and not one of them after Julius Caesar had certainly visited Britain, these literary sources provide only the barest outline of a story, lacking in all the detail which only local sources of knowledge and understanding could provide. Fortunately, however, that story can be supplemented from the results of archaeological survey and excavation. The character of Roman remains is such that a maximum of historical information can be derived from them. There are three principal reasons for this. Firstly, Roman remains are abundant, easy to recognize, and readily classifiable, so that the evidence derived from individual sites, whether forts, towns, villas, or villages, can be constantly checked by reference to other examples of their own and other classes. Secondly, Roman provincial culture was very well supplied with material goods, in such durable materials as bone, metal, glass, and pottery; many categories of these goods, being more or less mass-produced, are closely datable. Thirdly, it was a literate society operating a money economy, and the occurrence, in some quantity, of coins and inscriptions provides the basis on which such close dating, whether of individual groups of objects or of the buildings and other features in association with which they occur, can rest. Although much more remains to be learnt, and there are still many points of uncertainty in the precise dating of events, a broad and convincing picture of the political, social, and economic history of Britain under Roman rule has been gradually built up from these sources.

If this evidence is compared with that upon which our knowledge of Anglo-Saxon England from the seventh century onwards depends, it is clear that a great change of emphasis has occurred. There has been a notable improvement in the quality and quantity of the literary sources, most of which were written in England and often give detailed and contemporary accounts of the political history and the activities of the most influential personalities, sometimes written from first-hand information. On the social and institutional side the evidence of chroniclers and biographers is supplemented by administrative documents such as the law codes of the kings and the land charters which they granted to churches and laymen. Archaeological evidence, apart from that comprised in surviving buildings, is not on the whole so informative for this age as it is for Roman times. But in recent years excavation in the lowest medieval levels of such towns and ports as York, Winchester, London, and Southampton has revealed much evidence for the renewal of urban life and for the economic developments in trade and industry on which it rested. It can thus be seen that both for Roman Britain and for later Anglo-Saxon England first-hand sources, whether literary or material, are available in sufficient volume to form a reasonably firm basis for the writing of history.

But for the two intervening centuries to which this volume is devoted there are no contemporary sources of either kind approaching in value those available for the periods before and after. Both the literary and the archaeological evidence, moreover, are rendered more difficult of interpretation as a whole by their division into two unrelated groups representing the traditions and the material remains of invaders and invaded. On the literary side the Anglo-Saxons have left no contemporary evidence for the settlement at all, for the very good reason that the invaders were illiterate. It was not until after their conversion to Christianity that they began to record in writing some of the oral traditions that had been handed down from their pagan ancestors. At first these mostly concerned the exploits of their kings, remembered in the form of heroic poetry and authenticated by attachment to the genealogical framework of royal pedigrees. When, for example, the *Anglo-Saxon Chronicle* was compiled in its present form in the reign of King Alfred late in the ninth century, it incorporated three series of annals attached to dates in the fifth and sixth centuries which offer the outline of a traditional story covering the settlement of Kent, Sussex, and Wessex. Claims have been made, no doubt rightly, on philological and other grounds that certain of these annals go back in written form to the seventh century, and thus almost to the living memory of men who took part in the last of these events shortly before the spread of literacy made written record widely possible. Even so, the annalistic format adopted for the *Chronicle* must have required the attachment of dates, which at best are traditional and at worst arbitrary,

to incidents, and groups of incidents, culled from the sagas
of kings and heroes, an art-form notoriously indifferent to
precise chronology.

The point is well illustrated by the fact that the earliest
West Saxon annals appear to contain the remains of two versions of what was essentially the same story whose incidents
are now separated by gaps of nineteen years.[1] This, while it
should make one wary of attaching too much importance to
the exact dates recorded for individual incidents, greatly
strengthens the case for a very high antiquity in the stories
themselves. Such an unconscious combination of two
versions in Alfred's chronicle shows how much had been
done long before his time in the rather unintelligent blending
of what were evidently very ancient tales.

More will need to be said later on about the value of these
tales as historical evidence when the settlement of Kent,
Sussex, and Wessex is considered in detail. Here it is only
necessary to emphasize that their importance is not greatly
diminished by doubts on the reliability of the precise dates
to which they are attached. For this reason there is no need
to pay undue attention to the signs of what has been
regarded in the past as a deliberately artificial arrangement of
some events at intervals of four and eight years, an arrangement which has been thought to derive from the sequence of
leap years noted in Easter tables. Even if this was so—and
there has been a recent tendency among historians to mini-
mize or even deny this kind of apparent artificiality in the
dating[2]—it would do no more than illustrate what is already

[1] See Appendix II and K. Harrison, *Framework of Anglo-Saxon History*
(Cambridge, 1976), 127. The gap of nineteen years is likely to have arisen from
the two versions being dated within two successive nineteen-year Easter cycles, one
running from 494 to 512, and the other from 513 to 531. The duplication is not
obvious from the Anglo-Saxon MSS of the *Chronicle* alone, but it becomes clear
if the annals are compared with Æthelweard's Latin translation. The MS he used
must have had an additional entry at 500 recording the conquest of Wessex which
corresponds closely to the *Chronicle* entry of 519 dating the year when Cerdic and
Cynric 'took the kingdom'. It is very likely that this 500 entry in Æthelweard's
MS was deliberately suppressed by the compilers of the existing Anglo-Saxon
text, who sensed that it must be a duplicate of that for 519. See also K. Harrison,
'Early Wessex annals in the Anglo-Saxon Chronicle', *EHR* 86 (1971), 527–33.

[2] K. Harrison, *Framework*, 147–50; see also C. W. Jones, *Saints' Lives and
Chronicles in Early England* (New York, 1947), 191, who notes that the sequence
of dates at intervals of four and eight years does not bear any fixed relationship
to that of leap years.

obvious. In an illiterate age when past events are handed
down mainly by oral tradition in heroic verse, their exact
dating is of no contemporary consequence, even if means
were available to ascertain it. At best a rough sequence of
memorable incidents may be formed by their association
with personalities whose position in or relation to a royal
pedigree was known.

These difficulties in the establishment of exact dates for
events before living memory were familiar enough to the
Venerable Bede. His profound interest in chronological
systems made him eager to fit some of these tales into a
correct time sequence in the early part of his *Ecclesiastical
History of the English Nation*, finished in 731. But when he
set himself to tabulate in the chronological summary at the
end of his work[1] the most memorable dated events of the
period with which this volume is concerned, he found exactly
nine. These included two eclipses of the sun (useful as pegs
on which occurrences otherwise undated can sometimes be
hung), three matters of ecclesiastical interest in Ireland,
Scotland, and Rome, one which connects the sack of Rome
by Alaric in 410 with the end of Roman rule in Britain, and
two which give imprecise time-signals for the arrival of the
Angles in this country.[2] He notes only one specific event,
and that not without ambiguity, which is directly relevant to
the chronology of the English settlements.[3] For what he
evidently took to be the crucial period of early settlement
between 449 and 538 there were apparently in Bede's considered judgement no datable occurrences to be recorded at
all. In estimating the part which precise dates can be
expected to play in the story it is sensible to recall the
salutary scepticism of Bede.

Nor is this lack of reliable dates in the traditions of the
invaders effectively replaced by the occasional references to

---

[1] *HE* v. 24.

[2] 'The Angles came to Britain in the reign of Marcian and Valentinian who
reigned seven years from 449. . . . When the Augustinian mission reached Britain
in 597, it was about 150 years after the arrival of the Angles in Britain.'

[3] 'In 547 Ida began to reign from whom the royal stock of the Northumbrians
is derived, and remained King for twelve years.' Bede does not tell us whether he
took this event to represent the first Anglian incursions into Bernicia or whether
it interested him only as a fixed point in the genealogy of the Northumbrian royal
family.

the progress of the English settlers which occur either in continental sources or in the works of native writers from the parts of Britain where some degree of literacy was maintained in ecclesiastical circles beyond the reach of the earlier barbarian intrusions. As already mentioned, Bede had information which linked the collapse of Roman rule in Britain with Alaric's sack of Rome in 410, and it was known from the sixth-century Byzantine historian Zosimus,[1] who had good earlier sources, that the emperor Honorius had formally declined a request for Roman military assistance addressed to him by the local urban authorities in Britain in circumstances which implied that the provincial administration was no longer operative. Zosimus goes so far as to say that the Britons 'fighting for themselves freed their cities from the attacking barbarians', and after repudiating external authority 'were living on their own without obeying Roman laws'.[2] Procopius, also writing in the sixth century in reference to these same events, states clearly that from this time the Romans never recovered Britain which continued to be ruled by 'tyrants', the usual term for self-styled local emperors.[3]

As the fifth century progressed, references in continental sources to events in Britain, whether closely datable or not, become rarer and less reliable. Much has been made of the entries in two related South Gaulish chronicles, both of which probably used near-contemporary information. Both purport to record the completion of the Saxon conquest of Britain in the decade or so before 450.[4] These are certainly exaggerated claims, not least because there is near-contemporary

---

[1] Zosimus, ed. L. Mendelssohn (1887), vi. 10.　　[2] Ibid. vi. 5.

[3] Procopius, De Bell. Vand., ed. J. Haury (1905-13), I. ii. 38.

[4] MGH(AA) ix. 661 sub anno 438/9: Britanniae a Romanis amissae in dicionem Saxonum cedunt; ibid. 660 sub anno 441/2 (but probably for 445/6): Britanniae usque ad hoc tempus variis cladibus eventibusque latae in dicionem Saxonum rediguntur. It has been suggested with some plausibility that while it is very unlikely that chroniclers writing in the south of France could have had accurate information on the effective spread of Anglo-Saxon authority over Britain as a whole in the 440s, they could have known from Mediterranean merchants the extent to which the trade routes had been disrupted by piracy and even by the occupation of essential ports and strategic coastlands; for example those hitherto controlled for the Empire by the forts of the Saxon Shore. This could easily have given an exaggerated view of the extent of Saxon power. Harrison, Framework 27. I am not convinced by attempts recently made to discredit the authority of these annals relating to Britain as later interpolations: see M. Miller, Brit. 9 (1978), 315-18.

evidence from Constantius' *Vita Sancti Germani* that the
saint was able to visit Britain as late as the 440s for discussions on theological issues with the sub-Roman authorities.
Although the talks were interrupted by Saxon raiders their
operations are not portrayed as anything like a serious
military take-over. On the other hand such contacts between
Britain and the Continent were evidently becoming increasingly precarious at this time. They must have broken down
almost completely soon after, except in the south-west. From
these parts relations were maintained by substantial, movements of the British population across the Channel which
were probably already beginning the process which soon
converted Roman *Armorica* into Brittany.[1]

The last dated contact between sub-Roman Britain and
the authorities in Roman Gaul is not recorded in a continental source. It is mentioned in a document of which Gildas,
a British priest writing in the second quarter of the sixth
century in these western parts, has preserved a paraphrase
in his *De Excidio et conquestu Britanniae*. It was apparently
a formal appeal for aid against barbarian inroads addressed to
Aetius, ruler of Roman Gaul, and dated between 446 and
453 by a reference to his third consulship. Its failure seems to
have led quickly to a settlement of friendly barbarians as
foederati in the eastern part of Britain, and this in turn
acquired significance for later writers as the moment of the
Adventus Saxonum in Britanniam.[2]

Gildas had no means of dating the third consulship of
Aetius, whom he calls Agitius,[3] and probably had little idea

---

[1] It must be significant that whereas the British Church accepted the change
made in 455 in calculating the date of Easter in the west, it did not apparently
receive any later alterations that were adopted in Gaul on this complicated
matter. A Mansuetus 'Bishop of the Britons' is among the signatories of the Acts
of a continental Council in 461, which suggests that the migration was then recent
and the newcomers had not yet been absorbed into regular dioceses. *Gildas*, ed.
M. Winterbottom (1978), 150, referring to Mansi, *Councils* 7, 941.

[2] In what follows on the *Adventus* I owe much to the penetrating study of
Gildas Sapiens by C. E. Stevens in *EHR* 56 (1941), 353–73. His ideas are discussed and developed in my article 'The Adventus Saxonum' in W. F. Grimes
(ed.), *Aspects of Archaeology in Britain and Beyond* (1951), 221–41.

[3] It is tempting to suppose that the spelling Agitius may be due to a half-
conscious confusion between Aetius and Aegidius who dominated parts of
northern Gaul between 457 and 462. But the document paraphrased by Gildas
cannot have been originally addressed to Aegidius, as supposed by S. Johnson,
Later Roman Britain (1980), 112, for he was never a consul.

who he was, or what the circumstances were in which the letter was addressed to him. He was dimly aware that the stages in the breakdown of Roman rule had been marked by a series of appeals—in Celtic fashion he thought of them as a triad—culminating in the events around 410 already discussed. After this he believed that the Britons had managed for a while on their own to cope with barbarian inroads during what historians have termed a 'prosperity period'. It was thus natural for Gildas to attach the letter to Aetius to the events surrounding the failure of the last appeal known to him, thereby placing it before rather than after the 'prosperity period' which must belong in the second and third decades of the fifth century.

Bede, who used Gildas' book,[1] knew by 731 that the third consulship of Aetius was in 446, and that this appeal was thus some thirty years or more later than Gildas had supposed. But he also knew, probably from his ecclesiastical friends at Canterbury who supplied him with useful information about the early doings of the Kentish royal family, that there had been a settlement of federate barbarians dated to the joint reigns of the emperors Marcian and Valentinian, that is, between 450 and 455. There was obviously no room for Gildas' 'prosperity period', during which in his view kings rose and fell, sporadic raiding continued, and there was progressive corruption of Church and people, between 446 and 450-55. Although Bede conscientiously attempts to allow for a condensed version of it, he had to be content either to treat the *Adventus Saxonum* as an almost immediate consequence of the failure of the appeal to Aetius, that is, 'around 446-7', or to place it in the joint reign of Marcian and Valentinian, between 450 and 455, as his Kentish sources indicated. It is interesting, in connection with the earlier date, that the *Anglo-Saxon Chronicle* (MS E) records under 443 an appeal to Rome, immediately followed on its rejection by a similar appeal to 'the nobles of the Angle race'. This entry, though here dated three years earlier than the letter to Aetius, may refer to the same sequence of events and so preserve a tradition exactly in parallel with that which led Bede to accept the letter as one alternative clue to the date of the *Adventus Saxonum*.

[1] M. Miller, 'Bede's use of Gildas', *EHR* 90 (1975), 241-61.

It is important to understand the origin of these dates because they show how the *Adventus* came to be used by subsequent writers as a peg on which to hang the occurrence of later events. Their use in this way meant that the *Adventus Saxonum* became almost an artificial concept devised for historical purposes and chronological computation largely independent of any intrinsic significance that may have originally attached to the events so dated. This is not to say that they can be disregarded as unimportant. The 'groans of the Britons' to Aetius are of the highest consequence as one of the very few occurrences in British history of this time that can be closely dated, whatever its immediate cause and its effects may have been.

The Marcian-Valentinian date for federate settlement in Kent is also certainly of high antiquity, for this type of reckoning by imperial reigns goes back to an age when the known succession of Roman emperors provided a sure guide to the passage of time. It was familiar, for example, to Gregory of Tours writing his *History of the Franks* at the end of the sixth century. It is worth recalling that not long before his time a literate Frankish princess, Bertha, had come to Kent with a retinue, including a bishop as her chaplain, to be married to Æthelbert before his accession to the Kentish throne in 560. Written records of early Kentish history may well have been compiled in her circle at Canterbury, attached to dates of this type, very much earlier than anywhere else in Anglo-Saxon England, indeed within a generation of the date when Gildas was writing his *De Excidio* in western Britain.

By the time the *Anglo-Saxon Chronicle* was put together in its present form about three centuries later, this type of dating by reference to the regnal years of Roman emperors was long obsolete. This no doubt explains why Marcian and Valentinian appear under 449 at the beginning of the Kentish Annals in the *Chronicle* in the bungled disguise of 'Maurice and Valentines'. This tell-tale corruption of a time-signal whose meaning had long been forgotten is of course not only a proof of the high antiquity of these Kentish annals themselves, but a clear indication that they had followed a line of descent into the *Chronicle* quite independent of Bede. No one basing chronicle entries on Bede could possibly have made such a nonsensical mistake.

It would thus seem clear that the traditional picture of the *Adventus* around the central years of the fifth century has come down to us as the beginning of Anglo-Saxon history, not because these events were necessarily a record of the earliest English settlements that took place, but because they were the earliest such events whose dates were more or less certainly known. It follows that one should be prepared for evidence, of whatever kind, that may suggest different dates or different parts of the country as the times and places for earlier Anglo-Saxon settlement. It may even turn out that, so far from recording the beginning of a process, the traditional *Adventus* stories may be found to be describing the end of it, remembered precisely because these tales were the nearest in time to the days when oral memory could at last be reinforced by written record.

There is one other occurrence in Gildas' generalized account of the Saxon invasions in the fifth century to which he was apparently trying to attach an exact date. This is the *obsessio Montis Badonici*, an event which he emphasizes as the turning-point after which there had been no further Anglo-Saxon advance at least until the time when he was writing. He seems to be trying to say that he knows that this took place nearly forty-four years ago, because it was in the year of his birth and he is now nearly forty-four.[1] Unfortunately a combination of Gildas' tortuous Latinity and a possibly corrupt text makes it not quite certain that this was his intended meaning. Moreover the matter is made more complex by the fact that the manuscript of Gildas used by Bede, which must have been written within two hundred years of his autograph and was at least three hundred years older than any we now possess, apparently dated Mons Badonicus nearly forty-four years after the *Adventus Saxonum*, without any indication that this figure was intended by Gildas as his age at the time of writing. This is, incidentally, a good example of the tendency already noted among Dark-Age historians to use the *Adventus*, however dated, as a peg to which other events can be attached. If Gildas was already

---

[1] *De Excidio* 26, *quique quadragesimus quartus, ut novi, oritur annus, mense iam uno emenso qui et meae nativitatis est*. See Appendix III for a discussion of the date of Mons Badonicus. I have suggested an historical context for it in discussing the formation of Wessex on pp. 152–62.

doing this quite early in the sixth century, as Bede's text implies, it cannot even be certain that his date for the *Adventus* matched either of those employed much later by Bede.

In spite of these frustrating uncertainties it remains true that Gildas is the only contemporary writer who attempted, however inadequately, a general survey of British history from the latter days of Roman rule until the middle of the sixth century.[1] When he was writing, Maglocunus (Maelgwn), the dominant ruler in North Wales who died in 547, was still alive, and, if Gildas was right in his apparent belief that he had himself been born in the year of Mons Badonicus some forty-four years earlier, that makes him on any showing a contemporary witness to the situation somewhere in Britain in the first half of the sixth century. But it is important to appreciate the temporal and spatial limitations of his vision. What he says or implies about the condition of affairs in that half-century is first-hand contemporary evidence, but only for the parts of Britain with which he was personally familiar. What he says about the second half of the fifth century can be based only on what his parents and others of the previous generation may have told him: it may thus be broadly true. But what he says about the century before that, say 350–450, is nothing but hearsay, and of interest mainly as illustrating how little accurate information had come through to educated circles in his generation from even the last years of the Roman past.[2]

For the present purpose it is also important to appreciate the geographical limits of his vision. He displays throughout what may be termed a Highland Zone mentality, which viewed the breakdown of Roman authority from somewhere

---

[1] There is no need to take seriously the attempts that have been made to detach the historical from the hortatory sections of the *De Excidio* and to date them differently. It has been shown convincingly by F. Kerlouégan in M. W. Barley and R. P. C. Hanson (eds.), *Christianity in Britain 300–700* (1968), 151–76, that there is no linguistic distinction between the different sections: syntax, phraseology, vocabulary, figures of speech, etc. are identical throughout, and all fit readily into an early sixth-century stage in the development of literary Latin, appropriate to a region in which it was becoming a learned tongue which had largely ceased to be the common speech.

[2] This approach to the criticism of Gildas as an historical source is very well developed by J. Morris in Barley and Hanson, op. cit. 62–3.

in Western Britain[1] in terms of unsuccessful defence against northern barbarians, the building and loss of frontier walls. He shows little direct interest in eastern Britain, and the part played by Saxons in the earlier stages of the collapse of Roman or sub-Roman authority is virtually ignored.[2] When they eventually appear on Gildas' scene it is not as devastating raiders and invaders of Lowland Britain, but as federate allies settled there by the 'proud tyrant' to defend his lands against Picts and Scots. Gildas thus placed their coming long after the failure of the last appeal to Rome and the ensuing 'prosperity period'. This was the main reason why later writers ignored the possibility of Saxon settlement in the fourth century long before the formalized date attributed to the *Adventus Saxonum* in the central years of the fifth.[3]

In summary, then, Gildas can be treated as a credible and most valuable witness to a broad sequence of events in Britain in the century following the third consulship of Aetius (446-53). His knowledge of a British appeal at that time rests on a dated document and implies a serious barbarian invasion in the immediately preceding years. This disturbance can naturally be taken as reflected also in the news of Saxon penetration which prompted the exaggerated reports of total conquest that found their way into the South Gaulish chronicles. Gildas knew also of a settlement of federate Saxons in eastern Britain about that time, which gave rise to the use by later writers of 446-7 as a date for the *Adventus Saxonum*. He attributed this settlement to the policy of a *superbus tyrannus* or 'proud tyrant', a phrase which seems to be simply a Latin translation of the word 'Vortigern' which

[1] Though he wrote with detailed knowledge of the politics of Wales and Dumnonia and was later associated with Brittany, Gildas probably came from the north-west near the Clyde. The earliest *Life* states that he was *Arecluta regione oriundus*. According to Jackson, *Language and History*, 42, the spelling of this name 'clearly belongs to the sixth century' and 'can only come from contemporary manuscripts'.

[2] The only indication that Gildas was conscious of this earlier Saxon menace is his mention of the Romans providing *turres per intervalla ad prospectum maris* (*De Excidio* 18). Whether this was intended as a reference to Saxon Shore forts or to coastal signal stations is not clear, but in either case he must have been thinking of danger from beyond the North Sea or the Channel.

[3] I have developed this argument further in 'The Adventus Saxonum' in Grimes, op. cit. 222-4.

appeared in his Celtic sources and must have been originally rather a title than a personal name.

There are hints in his language that here too he may have had access to contemporary documents. The most natural explanation of his reference to the Saxons coming in 'three keels' is that this was the number of ship loads specified in the first formal invitation which led to the *foedus* or treaty settlement. Gildas also uses in their correct sense technical terms, *annona, epimenia, hospites,*[1] which most likely derive from official documents relating to the billeting and supply of barbarian *foederati.* In his view this settlement, which he does not precisely locate and was not necessarily in Kent, was followed after a while by further less regulated and less controllable arrivals, and eventually by a general outburst marked by widespread slaughter and destruction. In this episode, whose duration is not specified, Gildas deplores in particular the physical overthrow and ruin of towns, and the massacre of Christian clergy, both decisive in bringing about the liquidation of the most characteristic features of late Roman urban civilization.

Although he writes of all this in melodramatic phraseology employed deliberately to create the maximum impression, Gildas must here be treated as a witness to truth. It would have been fatal to his argument to describe in such terms a situation which his readers knew to have been quite different. Eventually, however, he states that resistance was organized under a leader called Ambrosius Aurelianus, sprung from a family which must have produced one or more of the tyrants, or local emperors, of the first half of the fifth century. After a ding-dong struggle of unspecified duration he reports that a decisive British victory was won at a place called Mons Badonicus, and that this had been followed by something over a generation of comparative peace which was still unbroken, though in Gildas' view seriously threatened, at the date of his writing around 540. In spite of this precarious peace, however, Gildas is careful to point out that the towns were still deserted, and here too his evidence must be accepted as a true description of the situation as both he and his readers knew it.

[1] *De Excidio* 23.

Gildas' sketch of British history in the century before his own maturity is as important for what it does not portray as for what it does. The fate of the 'proud tyrant' is not specified, but he was evidently not thought of as playing any part in the British revival. The whole credit for this is attributed to Ambrosius Aurelianus, whose name and background not only imply an origin in the highest levels of the Romano-British nobility, but suggest a close link of some kind with the Catholic doctrinal circles centred upon St. Ambrose, the very influential Bishop of Milan (373-97), whose father was named Aurelius Ambrosius. This parallel in nomenclature must surely be significant. That Vortigern was afraid of Ambrosius as well as of the Picts and Scots, and of the threat from Roman Gaul is specifically stated in a passage of Nennius' *Historia Brittonum*[1] which must come from a near-contemporary source. I have suggested elsewhere[2] that Vortigern is likely to have been the leader of the Pelagian party among the British notables whose influence the visits of Germanus were designed to counteract, and that, in attributing to Ambrosius the successful resistance to the revolted Saxon *foederati* brought in by Vortigern, Gildas was recording, perhaps half consciously, not only a remarkable military revival on the part of the Britons but the triumph of Catholic over Pelagian ideology. This aspect of the matter is however only indirectly relevant to the story of the English settlements.

What is certainly more significant is that Gildas, in writing the only contemporary narrative of these momentous events, has no mention whatever of Arthur. His silence is decisive in determining the historical insignificance of this enigmatic figure. It is inconceivable that Gildas, with his intense interest in the outcome of a struggle that he believed had been decisively settled in the year of his own birth, should not have mentioned Arthur's part in it had that part been of any political consequence. The fact is that there is no contemporary or near-contemporary evidence for Arthur playing any

---

[1] *Hist. Britt.* 31. *Guerthigirnus regnavit in Brittania et dum ipse regnabat . . . urgebatur a metu Pictorum Scottorumque et a Romanico impetu necnon a timore Ambrosii.*

[2] 'Pelagius and the end of Roman rule in Britain', *JRS* 50 (1960), 21-36, especially 35-6.

decisive part in these events at all. No figure on the border-line of history and mythology has wasted more of the historian's time. There are just enough casual references in later Welsh legend, one or two of which may go back to the seventh century, to suggest that a man with this late Roman name—Artorius—may have won repute at some ill-defined point of time and place during the struggle. But if we add anything to the bare statement that Arthur may have lived and fought the Saxons, we pass at once from history to romance.[1]

This passage was in fact already being made before British scholars collected the materials for the *Historia Brittonum* early in the ninth century, and the later popularity of this curious compilation greatly accelerated it. Nennius' historical method as compiler is best described in his own words. *Coacervavi*, he writes, *omne quod inveni*—'I have made a heap of all that I have found.' Among the scraps in his heap were some Arthuriana, notably a list of twelve battles culminating with Mons Badonicus in which the defeat of the enemy is attributed to Arthur's personal prowess. This list was evidently extracted and condensed from epic matter compiled in Arthur's honour at some unknown date not necessarily long before the ninth century. Much ingenuity has been devoted to attempts at localizing the places mentioned and even to devising intelligible campaigns to account for them. But the conclusions offered by various students cover the whole country from Scotland via Lincolnshire and Sussex to the far west, without establishing any convincing historical basis. It is not even certain that all these battles involved Saxons. That the list culminates with Mons Badonicus at once places it under grave suspicion, for the contemporary evidence of Gildas clearly associates this decisive event with Ambrosius, not Arthur. It suggests in fact that the association of Arthur with all or any of these scenes of real or fictitious conflict may be due rather to wishful thinking by an imaginative panegyrist in possession of a traditional list of battle sites than to historical reality.

[1] To describe the whole period of three hundred years from 350 to 650 as 'The Age of Arthur', as is done for example by J. Morris in his book with that title (1973), shows a total disregard of the valid historical evidence. See my review in *EHR* 90 (1975), 113-16.

The *Historia Brittonum* in its present form dates from an age three hundred years after the time of Gildas. During these centuries there had been much contact between the British and Saxon peoples. Its compiler was thus able to incorporate in it some materials originally of Anglo-Saxon origin and dating to the early stages of the settlement. He had, for example, genealogies of several of the Anglo-Saxon royal families, and some semi-historical memories of the conflict between Hengist and Vortigern that led to the permanent establishment of the Anglo-Saxons in the south-east of Britain. He also had notes of a few otherwise unrecorded incidents, mostly of internal conflict on the British side, which accompanied or followed this settlement. For the final collapse of Vortigern's authority he relied on extracts from a legendary *Liber Beati Germani*, now lost. This seems to have contained a sort of picture-book version of the doctrinal conflict between the Pelagian and Catholic parties among the British notables, personalized as a political struggle between Germanus and Vortigern in which the former finally eliminated the latter, after a series of melodramatic encounters in the mountains of Wales.[1]

Nennius or his sources also had some interesting scraps of information in his heap concerning the early stages of Anglian settlement in the north of England in the sixth century. Some of these relate to tales preserved independently in early Welsh heroic poetry associated with the names of bards such as Aneirin and Taliessin. He was also interested, though in a much less systematic way than Bede, in chronological problems, and included a number of calculations whose significance has given rise to much discussion.[2] In these he appears to be relating various later occurrences to such fixed points in time as he thought he had for Vortigern's reign, the *Adventus Saxonum*, and so on. Very little of value

[1] See Myres, 'Pelagius', 35. I see no reason to follow the opinion of some recent scholars that the *Historia Brittonum* has confused the historical Germanus of Auxerre with an obscure St. Garmon known only from a scatter of church dedications in various parts of Wales. Constantius' account clearly shows that Germanus must have had personal encounters in debate with Pelagian notables in Britain. These discussions could well have been dramatized by exuberant Welsh imagination into the romantic adventures which Nennius paraphrased from his reading of the *Liber Beati Germani.*

[2] *Hist. Britt.* 66.

can be extracted with certainty from this part of Nennius'
heap, although some of the dates are expressed in terms
which suggest that they may derive from sources as early as
the fifth or sixth centuries.

Such then in bare outline are the main written sources
from which the story of the English settlements has to be
deduced. Apart from a few chance references in continental
writers primarily interested in other matters, and that section
of Gildas' narrative that rests on his own experience or his
parents' memory, almost the whole of it belongs in its
present form to much later times. It is thus heavily contami-
nated with accretions and irrelevancies picked up in the slow
progress from these original sources. But here and there some
significant piece of information has come through almost unscathed from the fifth century into these later compilations.
Such is the note in the *Historia Brittonum* of Vortigern's
policy being based not only on the menace from Picts and
Scots, but on his dread both of renewed Roman invasion and
of Ambrosius. Even the most unreliable of the later lives of
Celtic saints may contain shafts of light suddenly illuminating
a dark corner of the sub-Roman scene. There is the tale, for
example, of how St. Tatheus was entertained in a dilapidated
Roman villa near Chepstow whose owner was still trying to
maintain the heating of his bath-house, if only at week-ends.
Then again, St. Paul Aurelian, visiting in Brittany a Roman
town still surrounded by earth ramparts and a lofty stone
wall, is said to have found the only signs of life in it to
comprise a sow, a bear, a wild bull, and a hive full of bees
and honey housed in a hollow tree.[1] Such scenes, like that in
which the anonymous biographer of St. Cuthbert portrays
the saint sight-seeing in 685 in the ruins of Roman Carlisle,[2]
provide dramatic confirmation for Gildas' picture of the
last days of urban and rural civilization in Britain as still
remembered only half a century before his own birth.

But they do nothing to reconstruct even in broad outline
a political history of the centuries covered by this book, or
to explain the social and economic changes that converted
Roman Britain into Christian England. So far as the political

[1] These incidents are both quoted by J. Morris, *Age of Arthur* (1973), 253
and 458.
[2] Anon., *Vita S. Cuthberti*, 37.

story is concerned it is not too much to say that for the sequence and significance of the main events of this time the elements that contribute to historical proof are for the most part lacking. Even when it is certain that an event of importance did occur—say the siege of Mons Badonicus which seems to have marked a temporarily decisive check to the progress of Saxon settlement—it is often impossible, as in that instance, to say exactly when or where it happened, or, for that matter, exactly what took place. Moreover, such events as seem to be reasonably well authenticated frequently display a reluctance to cohere into a single story. There is, for example, no point of contact between the early South Saxon and West Saxon annals in the *Anglo-Saxon Chronicle* and what Gildas has to say about Ambrosius Aurelianus and Mons Badonicus, although the two series of events must have been roughly contemporary and apparently belong to the same quarter of England.[1]

In the social and economic sphere, Gildas certainly provides good evidence for the destruction in the second half of the fifth century of the urban framework which had supported not only the civil administration of the Romano-British diocese but also the Christian organization based until that time essentially on the bishops and clergy of the towns. Gildas may also hint, though less specifically, at the widespread dislocation of rural life brought about both by the physical destruction of villa estates and farmsteads in the countryside, and by the collapse of the money economy on which their viability, as something more than subsistence units, had rested. At any rate this must be the meaning behind his casual mention, almost in an aside, that a time came when the province was deprived of its regular food supply save only for the resources of hunting.[2] But he gives no details under either head and indeed may not have known any.

It is of course especially at the beginning and the end of these two dark centuries that the literary evidence has least of certainty to tell. Thus the first half of the fifth century, after most official contacts between Britain and the world of

---

[1] See *infra* pp. 158–60 for an attempt to find an historical context for Mons Badonicus in the evolution of the West Saxon kingdom.

[2] *De Excidio*, 19.

Rome had broken down, was already beyond the reach of living memory in Gildas' day, and he can tell us nothing coherent or credible about it. What contemporary information has survived from this sub-Roman phase was generated mainly by the ideological conflict between the Pelagian and Augustinian interpretations of basic Christian doctrine. This conflict seems to have bedevilled civilized thought among the Britons just at the time when unity was above all things essential for success in the struggle with Celtic barbarians and Germanic intruders alike.

So it is also at the other end of the period, after the middle of the sixth century, when Gildas' narrative ends with dire and well-justified forebodings of disaster from renewed barbarian onslaughts. Here too contemporary literary evidence largely fails us for the years of decisive Saxon conquest when his prophecies were to be so bitterly fulfilled. For this critical time there is virtually nothing from written sources for southern Britain except a few brief and tantalizing entries in the *Anglo-Saxon Chronicle* mostly culled from a lost saga centred on the exploits of Ceawlin and his contemporaries in Wessex.[1] For the north little literary evidence remains but a few even less coherent incidents derived from similar memories of the wars which established the Anglian dynasty of Ida in the further parts of Northumbria.[2] For the great mass of eastern and central Britain which bore the brunt of Anglo-Saxon conquest and settlement at this time there is no information from literary sources at all, and we are dependent wholly on what archaeology and place-names have to tell.

---

[1] *infra* pp. 162-71.   [2] *infra* pp. 199-201.

2

THE NATURE OF THE EVIDENCE:
II.   ARCHAEOLOGY AND PLACE-NAMES

WITH the archaeological evidence we are at least handling tangible material that comes direct from the years under review. While its quantity in no way compares with that from the Roman period it is, at any rate on the Anglo-Saxon side, impressive both in its range and its quality. But here too, as with the literary evidence, there is a marked contrast between the material remains left behind by the invaders and the invaded. At first sight it might be supposed that the Britons, heirs to the commercialized culture of Rome with its money economy and wide range of mass-produced goods, would be represented archaeologically, even in decline and disaster, by a mass of easily recognizable and informative domestic rubbish. From this one might hope to learn much about the nature and distribution of their surviving centres of power, and about their success or failure in adapting to the simpler economic conditions and declining standards of living that were now their lot.

But this is not so. Apart from a meagre supply of the simplest types of brooches, buckles, belt-fittings, and knives, the sub-Roman Britons of the fifth and sixth centuries appear to have enjoyed—if that is the right word—a culture almost as completely devoid of durable possessions as any culture can be. In Wales and the far west, more or less beyond the reach of Anglo-Saxon penetration in these centuries, their presence can, it is true, be recognized from a considerable number of Christian tombstones and some fortified or refortified hill-top strongholds containing occasionally a scatter of pot-sherds. These may include some from vessels imported at this time by the western sea-ways from the Mediterranean lands. But in the east and centre of lowland Britain even such tell-tale material indications of their presence are almost wholly missing. It has required the development of a highly

specialized technique of excavation that can only be employed
in the most favourable conditions, as in the fields that now
cover the site of Roman *Viroconium* (Wroxeter), to suggest
the presence of a number of timber structures that once
housed the last remaining citizens of the *Civitas Cornoviorum*
almost totally bereft of durable household goods.[1]

It would be natural to draw from this surprising lack of
recognizable archaeological traces the conclusion that the
sub-Roman population of lowland Britain had mostly disappeared. It is difficult in any case to resist the impression
that their numbers must have been very greatly reduced by
the casualties of war, destitution, emigration, and disease,
especially among the urban classes least capable of with-
standing hardship. Gildas clearly implies that this was so. But
before using this negative archaeological testimony as proof
of the once fashionable view that the native population of
lowland Britain was virtually eliminated in these dark
centuries, it is well to consider whether this negative record
may be interpreted differently.

It is probable, indeed certain, that the industries manufacturing mass-produced goods in durable materials such as
pottery, glass, and metal, would be among the first to be hard
hit by the collapse of the money economy, and by the
growing insecurity of transport whether by road or by
water. Later Roman society moreover had become almost
wholly dependent on a copious and cheap supply of consumer
durables. The traditional skills required to replace such
supplies by the local and domestic enterprise universal in
most primitive societies must have been very largely forgotten. As such goods became scarcer through wear, break-
ages, and loss, it would be natural for many of them to be
replaced in less durable materials, wood, leather, and textiles,
which leave little or no trace for the archaeologist. Thus the
place of bronze, iron, glass, and the harder wheel-made
products of the commercial potteries would be taken by
more perishable home-made products requiring less technical

---

[1] P. Barker in P. J. Casey (ed.), *The End of Roman Britain*, BAR 71 (1979),
175–81. There is a rather imaginative portrayal of the centre of post-Roman
Viroconium in P. Barker (ed.), *Wroxeter Roman City Excavations 1966–1980*
(n.d.), fig. 5. It may be salutary to compare this reconstruction with the actual
remains as found. See, e.g., *Brit.* 6 (1975), 106–17 and figs. 3–6.

skill in their manufacture. There might at the same time have been a widespread tendency for ruined buildings that had been constructed in brick and stone, *more Romano*, to be generally replaced in flimsier materials better suited to the simpler needs of a less civilized way of life.[1] It must also be remembered that the latest levels of any archaeological site are necessarily the least well preserved because they are the most vulnerable to interference and destruction in later times.

But when all allowance is made for these factors, it remains difficult, if not impossible, to account for the almost total absence of sub-Roman archaeological remains in lowland Britain on any other hypothesis than a drastic reduction in numbers of the native population and an equally drastic reduction in the standard of living of those who remained. Most impressive in this context is the contrast between east and west. One has only to compare the negative evidence from central and south-eastern Britain with what is found in Wales and the south-west, scanty though this too may be, to realize that the latter was a society still comparatively vigorous and vital, and, however barbarized, still capable of maintaining fortified strongholds, centres of Christian culture, and some contacts with the Mediterranean world. But the natives of lowland Britain have left little or no surviving trace of any of these things, nor were they even capable of retaining their own language or their own place-names in competition with those of their conquerors.

The archaeological remains of the Anglo-Saxons during their pagan phase are of an altogether different order. It is true that most of them come from cemeteries rather than from habitation sites, and that in the absence of contemporary coins and inscriptions nothing is so securely or so precisely datable as one could wish. There is indeed a remarkable contrast in this and other ways with the archaeology of Roman Britain which can perhaps best be appreciated by a

---

[1] This certainly happened at Wroxeter. Verulamium is one of the few Roman cities that has produced evidence of substantial new buildings, involving even some deliberate rearrangement of the street plan, as late as the mid-fifth century. But even there, if Constantius' account of the second visit of Germanus in the 440s can be trusted, the visiting saint seems to have been lodged in a thatched hut, hardly the accommodation for a distinguished bishop from Gaul had anything better been available.

simple comparison. If little but the cemeteries of Roman Britain were available for study and if there were no coins and inscriptions to supply dating evidence, the contribution of archaeology to our knowledge of that phase of British history would be slight indeed.

That however is the position of the Anglo-Saxon archaeologist. Much can certainly be learnt of the course and character of the invasions from the distribution pattern of cemeteries and settlements in relation to the geography and geology of those parts of the country where they are found. Even more significant does that distribution pattern appear when superimposed on that of Roman towns, forts, villas, and villages and of the roads that connected them. In the past Roman Britain and the English settlements were too often treated as mutually exclusive periods of history, each butt-ended against the other with a minimum of linkage or overlap between them. This tendency was reinforced by the contrast between the plentiful range of mass-produced goods evidenced in the excavated ruins of Roman towns, forts, and villas, and the simpler types of hand-made tools, weapons, and pottery that come from the Anglo-Saxon cemeteries. The contrast is certainly real and important, yet the distribution maps indicate that in many areas the Anglo-Saxon shows a marked tendency to follow the Romano-British pattern, in a fashion which suggests a considerable degree of temporal as well as of spatial overlap.

It is at this point that it becomes necessary to consider what means are available for dating the earliest archaeological traces of an Anglo-Saxon presence in Britain. In the absence of associated coins and inscriptions such dating must rest largely on typological considerations, the points in developing sequences of the commoner forms of artefacts at which English examples occur in quantities sufficient to be significant. For this method to be reliable it is essential that the continental sequences on which it rests should themselves be well-established, and tied with reasonable security to the passage of time. In the last resort this means a sufficient number of links, direct or indirect, with deposits dated either by associated Roman coins, of which large numbers were in circulation at this time beyond the Imperial frontiers in Europe, or by historical events whose dates are known. In this way a vast interlocking chronological network has been built up by continental scholars for dating the typological sequences of many sorts of products. While differences of opinion may persist on the position of any particular object in its appropriate sequence, and while the grounds for giving it a rough date may often appear individually flimsy, yet the main chronological framework is now so extensive and so firmly established that it is most unlikely to be overturned, or even to be shifted as a whole either forward or backward by an appreciable period of time.

It must however be recognized that archaeological dating of this kind can never be precise. It may be fairly safe to date the manufacture of an object or a group of associated objects within a bracket of seventyfive or even fifty years. But it is very rarely, if ever, possible to claim that any such objects must have been made either before or after a particular year. For this reason archaeological evidence is very seldom of direct assistance to a historian seeking precision in the dating of events to a year or two, or even a decade.

Further uncertainties may arise in dealing with material mainly derived from cemeteries rather than from the debris of occupation. In the stratified levels of a house or a ditch system it is generally safe to treat most of the material from a sealed *stratum* as roughly contemporary in use, especially when it consists largely of fragile objects such as pottery or glass. These are likely to have had a short working life and once broken serve no useful purpose which would justify their removal to a different context. But grave-goods are a different matter. A much higher proportion of them consist of tools, weapons, or ornaments such as brooches, buckles, strap-ends, and so on, which are not only durable and long-lasting but intrinsically valuable, and thus liable to be reused outside the context for which they were first made. A man may have buried with him objects of value made at every stage of his working life, not to mention the possibility of inherited heirlooms or loot plundered from his enemies. It is well-known, for example, that certain types of weapons, notably swords, were treasured in barbarian society for sentimental or mystical reasons. It might be several generations before a valued object of this sort found a final resting-place in the grave of its last owner, perhaps unrelated by blood or cultural association with its first. An unusual degree of wear and tear or evidence of damage or repair, not to mention the occasional conversion of an object to a purpose other than that which it first served, are all indications of a probable heirloom, or of a more recent acquisition possibly much older than the date of the grave in which it is found. This, to take one example, must be the explanation for the presence of the battered remains of a fourth-century south German brooch in an Angle grave at Londesborough, East Yorks., that is securely dated no earlier than the mid-sixth century by the other objects accompanying the skeleton. Had these other objects not been present it might have been reasonable to date the grave at least a century earlier than its actual period.[1]

It is now normal for archaeologists to pay far more attention than used to be given to the extent to which objects, especially those of high intrinsic value likely to be treasured as heirlooms, exhibit signs of a long or short period of use before burial. The whole chronology of the gold bracteates, which form a crucial element in the dating of the Jutish phase of Kentish archaeology in this period,[2] rests very largely on estimates of the extent to which individual pieces exhibit degrees of wear and tear caused by varying periods of use between the time of their manufacture and that of their deposition in the graves from which they were excavated.[3]

Notwithstanding these complexities, it is largely from the intensive study of metal objects from graves that the chronological framework of Anglo-Saxon archaeology has been built up. The typological sequences of all the main varieties of brooches, buckles, strap-ends, and other belt-fittings, as well as weapons such as spear-heads and shield-bosses, are now reasonably well-established. But for the reasons given they may not be as trustworthy evidence for an absolute time-scale expressed in the passage of the years as could be desired by writers of history. The very durability and intrinsic value of such goods serve to limit their reliability as pointers to an

---

[1]   *Ant. J.* 47 (1967), 43–50.
[2]   See discussion on p. 115.
[3]   See S. C. Hawkes and M. Pollard, *Frühmittelalterliche Studien*, 15 (1981), 316–70.

absolute chronology, and so reduce their value as raw material to the historian.

It should be possible to learn more from the study of successive styles and fashions prevailing in cheaper and more fragile products such as pottery. Here the quantities available for examination are much greater, their turnover in use must have been much more rapid, the individual pieces have little attraction either as loot or as heirlooms, and the likelihood of their transfer, once broken, to misleading contexts is minimal. For all these reasons pottery should provide a much more sensitive tool for the archaeologist, and thus one capable of making a picture much more sharply in focus for the historian. This in fact has been the function of pottery in illuminating the study of most early cultures, and there is no reason why, properly used, it should not provide a similar service in the early Anglo-Saxon age.

As with the metal-work, most pottery of this time comes from graves. Remains of cook-pots and other domestic utensils do of course occur in considerable quantity as household rubbish on occupation sites, but very little of this is sufficiently distinctive to be of much value for purposes of dating. There was very little commercial production of household pottery at this time, so that it is hardly ever possible to study the distribution of output from one workshop. Most families seem to have been content with home-made containers, generally undecorated and in the coarsest of fabrics. Moreover the normal forms which the pots take were designed to serve continuing domestic needs, and thus show little tendency to follow any changing fashions that might have significance for dating.

It is otherwise with the cemeteries. The rituals of inhumation gave scope for the inclusion of food- and drink-offerings for the dead, contained in pottery vessels often of high quality and the latest fashionable style. Where cremation was practised the whole funerary deposit was normally placed in a pottery urn, whose form and decoration similarly reflected contemporary taste. These varied pottery styles are invaluable in providing clues to the parts of the continental homeland from which the different groups of the invaders came. They can also be arranged, like other grave-goods, in typological series which, for the reasons already mentioned, may be easily related to an absolute time-scale. Both the inhumation and the cremation pottery is thus ultimately datable by the same criteria as apply to the metal objects with which they are associated in the graves. It is however worth noting that these associations are less subject to error or mistake in the case of inhumations than cremations. The presence of a particular pot in a particular grave in direct association with the other grave-goods is normally a matter of easily recorded observation. But the association of metal objects, often difficult to identify precisely owing to distortion by heat, with the ashes from a particular cremation urn may sometimes be less certain. Many urns are found collapsed in the ground owing to earth pressure, or broken by other disturbance, and may thus have lost part of their original contents or acquired extraneous objects from the surrounding soil. Moreover there can be no absolute certainty that the original contents gathered from the funeral pyre did not sometimes include objects from two or more cremations of different dates that had taken place on the same spot. This is a contingency most liable to arise in some of the very large cemeteries, which seem to have been equipped with regular burning sites that may have been in use over a considerable period of time.

In spite of such occasional uncertainties, incidental in one form or another to the interpretation of all archaeological remains, there can be no doubt that early Anglo-Saxon pottery, and especially that from the great cremation cemeteries of eastern England, forms an invaluable and highly important source of information, whose potential for historical purposes still remains largely unexplored.[1] It will be drawn upon in detail whenever relevant to the matters discussed in the later chapters of this book. But it may be convenient at this point to draw attention to a few important aspects of this period on which recent study of the pottery has already thrown fresh and sometimes unexpected light.

One such subject is that of the continental origin of the invaders. Bede's celebrated statement that they came from three of the most powerful peoples of Germany, the Angles,

---

[1] Further study of this material should be facilitated by the publication of my *Corpus of Anglo-Saxon Pottery* in 1977.

the Saxons, and the Jutes must be the starting point for this enquiry,[1] and the relevant archaeological evidence will be examined in the next chapter. Another matter on which the evidence of the pottery should throw light is the distribution of the main elements of the invading peoples in England. This too will receive more detailed consideration in later chapters. A third topic of great importance to the historian, and one on which recent study of the pottery has led to some unexpected revision of the traditional chronology, is the dating of the earliest phases of the settlement. This will require further examination in discussing the relation of the newcomers to the collapse of Romano-British society in town and country.

In assessing the contribution that can be made by archaeology to the solution of these problems, the historian has to form his own judgement on these and many additional topics which will be brought up as this narrative proceeds. But however difficult and uncertain of interpretation they may be, these material remains are of great significance, if only because they do derive directly from the years under review, and come to us without any interference or distortion caused by secondary attempts to explain their meaning. First-hand archaeological evidence, unlike most written sources of information about the past, is wholly free from the kinds of error that are so often introduced by subsequent copyists or the well-meaning but sometimes misguided editors of literary texts.

The same unfortunately cannot be said of the evidence of place-names. Here we have to deal with matter that has passed through many hands and been subjected to many possible distortions and transformations on its long and often complex way from the fifth or sixth century to the twentieth. Nearly all the names used by the first Englishmen to identify their dwellings and the natural features among which they were set must have arisen more or less unconsciously in the course of conversation between illiterate folk. In lowland Britain they would have needed great numbers of such names to carry on their lives without confusion, from the very

---

[1] *HE* i. 15. The relevance of ceramic evidence to the interpretation of Bede's statement is more fully considered in my Raleigh Lecture 'The Angles, the Saxons, and the Jutes', *PBA* 56 (1970), 145–74. See also my *Corpus*, i. 114–18.

earliest years of their settlement. More and more would be required as they became increasingly familiar with their own widening surroundings and ever more possessive in their attitudes towards them. But anything up to two hundred years or even more will have passed before, with the coming of literacy in the seventh century, they can have begun to think of these names as written words. In those two centuries sound-changes of many sorts had been taking place in their speech, some old words had passed out of common use, and others were changing their meaning in the face of altered circumstances. It must often have been the case that the clerks who first tried to express in writing the sounds made by illiterate peasants to identify their own and their neighbours' villages will have produced verbal combinations of little obvious meaning to their informants or themselves. They might often bear little relation to the descriptive terms first used to form these names by their ancestors several generations before.

It is moreover salutary, if saddening, to remember how very few written place-names have come down to us from the first century of Anglo-Saxon literacy, and that forms first recorded even in eighth- or ninth-century original documents are still precious rarities. In fact vast numbers of Anglo-Saxon place-names appear in their earliest known written shape in administrative records later than the Norman Conquest, such as Domesday Book, inevitably distorted by French-speaking clerks unfamiliar with the sounds and the sense of what was to them a largely alien tongue.

It is not surprising, in view of the difficulties thus inherent in the correct transmission of these names from early times, that there should be much doubt and disagreement surrounding the interpretation of the first written forms in which they appear. Some of these uncertainties are directly relevant to their proper use in various historical contexts, and will therefore require discussion here as and when these contexts arise. But one general conclusion of great significance emerges at once from this great body of place-name material. That is its overwhelmingly Anglo-Saxon character. Names of British

---

[1] A valuable attempt to assemble the place-name elements for which evidence exists in the oldest written English sources up to 730 can be found in B. Cox, *JEP-NS* 8 (1976), 12-66.

origin are mainly confined in lowland Britain to natural features such as some rivers, prominent hills, and areas of forest, waste or fen, which required immediate identification in terms equally intelligible to natives and newcomers alike. The names of a very few towns, ports, and fortresses of Roman origin mainly in the south-east (London, Dover, Lympne, Reculver, etc.) were taken over more or less unaltered, doubtless because they had long been familiar to seafaring folk of barbarian as well as native antecedents on both sides of the Channel and the North Sea.

Some of the larger Roman towns, whose remains, whether inhabited or not, must always have been as conspicuous features of the landscape as rivers, hills, and forests, retained their names in a barbarously truncated form, combined generally with *ceaster* corrupted from Latin *castra*, to suggest a man-made stronghold.[1] Others, like Leicester or Chichester, lost all trace of their Roman names while still visibly recognizable as fortified *castra*. More significantly perhaps, none, with the possible exception of Canterbury, developed a name based on that of the native tribe or *civitas* of which it had formerly been the administrative centre, as happened almost universally in northern and central Gaul.[2] The names of smaller towns, *vici*, and substantial villages were almost all lost.

Lost also—and this must be a matter of supreme historical significance—were all the names of those Romano-British rural estates whose owners had formed the aristocracy of wealth, society, and culture, certainly as late as the end of the fourth century, perhaps in some cases far into the fifth. Once again the complete contrast with Roman Gaul is illuminating. Countless French villages still retain in their

[1] As in Winchester (*Venta*), Gloucester (*Glevum*), or Cirencester (*Corinium*). Sometimes as at Chester, Caistor-on-the-Wolds, or Caistor-by-Norwich, the word *ceaster* was used by itself, showing that the Romano-British name of the place had been totally forgotten. *Ceaster* was also occasionally incorporated in the names given to Roman villas, as at Woodchester, Gloucs., suggesting that such places may have served a para-military purpose in their final phases. K. H. Jackson, in *Language and History*, 252, has pointed out that *ceaster* as a derivative from Latin *castra* is found in no other Germanic language. It is therefore likely to be a borrowing into Anglo-Saxon from Latin speakers in the Roman towns of Britain; this might have been happening before the final collapse of Roman rule.

[2] As at Paris (*Lutetia Parisiorum*), Reims (*Durocortorum Remorum*), or Amiens (*Samarobriva Ambianorum*).

present names the adjectival form of the *nomen* of the Gallo-Roman family to which the estate from which the present settlement grew had belonged in the fourth or fifth century. Not a single Romano-British villa appears to have left its owner's name incorporated in that of a modern village in this way. Indeed we do not know with any certainty the names of any of the hundreds of Roman villas whose sites and remains are scattered over the countryside of lowland Britain.

This fact must render extremely unlikely the notion some-times proposed that barbarian settlement may have taken place in parts of Britain within the framework of existing estates. Had the method of absorbing barbarian settlers by the legal procedures of *tertiatio* and *hospitalitas*, as practised in Gaul, been followed so extensively in this country, it would most likely have left some such traces in our village names as are found in one form or another all over France.

Even though there was in Britain an almost complete substitution of Germanic for Romano-British rural place-names at this time, recent work has shown that a few of the new names incorporated Latin words which must still have had significant meanings at the time when they came into use. This is an important outcome of place-name study, for it suggests that some at least of the earliest settlers were sufficiently conversant with spoken Latin to adopt words from that tongue to describe things for which they had no appropriate words of their own. The most obvious cases relate to buildings or groups of buildings that had, or appeared to have had, a special function. In addition to *ceaster* already mentioned, the clearest instances are *wic* from Latin *vicus, ecles* from Latin *ecclesia*, and *funta* from Latin *fontana*.

Fontana, giving rise to such names as Fovant, Havant, Cheshunt, etc., is the least significant historically, for it is merely a descriptive term for any structure, large or small, designed to ease the collection of water from a spring or well, whether it were only a simple well-head on a farm or a decorative fountain in a town. The incorporation of *fontana* in a place-name probably implies either the nearby presence of Romano-British buildings whose owners had once provided such a facility, even if its usefulness had long outlasted their own occupation,[1] or a source of water believed to have some unusual virtue or beneficent quality that justified the expense of making it a special architectural feature.

Vicus and *ecclesia* are more interesting. *Ecclesia*, as in Eccles, Eccleshall, Eccleston, etc., seems to imply the survival, or at least the recognizable remains, of a Christian church. The distribution of such names is very distinctive. Of the simple form Eccles there are two examples, both adjacent to Roman roads, in Norfolk and there is one in Kent, adjacent to the site of a substantial Roman villa. This, like the great establishment not far away at Lullingstone, may well have been the property of an aristocratic family which maintained a special building for Christian services. Most of the other Eccles names, including all the compound forms, are away in the north and west Midlands, Cumbria, Lancashire, West Yorkshire, Cheshire, Staffordshire, and Worcestershire, where there was little Anglo-Saxon penetration before the invaders became Christian. They are thus more likely to derive from early forms of Welsh *eglwys* than direct from Latin *ecclesia*, and may not even refer to churches old enough to have survived from Romano-British times. But the three examples in Norfolk and Kent can only be explained as exceptional survivals of Roman churches still sufficiently conspicuous in the early days of Anglo-Saxon settlement to justify specific recognition in this way.[2]

Even more significant may be the combination of *wic* from Latin *vicus* with the early Germanic habitative word *ham*, to produce names now appearing variously on our maps as Wickham, Wykeham, Wycombe, and so on. It is natural to interpret these as indicating a settlement with the special qualities of a Roman *vicus*.[3] In earlier Roman times *vicus* had been a formal designation for the smallest units of local administration in the provinces. It had been used to describe, for example, the lesser towns and some substantial villages, the civil settlements that grew up outside military establishments, and the local sub-divisions of some large centres of

---

[1] Cheshunt, for example, probably means '*fontana* at or near a *ceaster*'.

[2] K. Cameron, 'Eccles in English place-names' in Barley and Hanson (eds.), *Christianity in Britain*, 87–92.

[3] The interest of these names was first pointed out by M. Gelling in *Med. Arch.* 11 (1967), 87–104. See also her *Signposts to the Past* (1978), 67–74.

urban population.[1] It is probable that by the fourth century *vicus* had lost most of what official legal and administrative meaning it may once have had, though it may still have remained in use as an unofficial status symbol. In any case the word was evidently familiar to the earliest barbarian settlers in the Roman provinces. In the form *wic* it was taken over by the Anglo-Saxons and had a long life, acquiring in the process a wide range of special senses for communities engaged in various agricultural and industrial pursuits.

It may be argued that, in view of these later developments, the combination *wicham* need have no unusual significance historically. But there are reasons for thinking that it does mainly belong to the earliest phases of the settlement and may thus have had a special meaning at that time. The mere fact that *wic* was more frequently combined with *ham* than with any other word for a settlement is itself suggestive of an early date. *Ham* belongs, apparently, to the most primitive phase of local nomenclature used by the first barbarian settlers, and is thus less likely to have been combined with *wic* in any of its later senses.

More significant is the distribution of the *wicham* names, which tend to follow a markedly Roman pattern. They are found not merely on, or in the immediate vicinity of, Roman roads, but often in close association with the small Roman towns or other substantial settlements which these roads connected. Many of these were places of a kind that might properly be described as *vici* in Roman times. It has thus been suggested that in calling a place *wicham* the first Anglo-Saxon arrivals were consciously indicating their awareness that it had been a focus of Romano-British population and perhaps of some administrative activity.

It is of course important not to press the evidence too far. These names in themselves do not prove either the continued existence of whatever functions a *vicus* might still be exercising when barbarians first settled in its neighbourhood, or even that any Romanized Britons were still living there. Attempts which have been made to use the *wicham* places which later became parishes as indicating by their boundaries

---

[1] For a discussion of *vici* in lowland Britain see S. Johnson in W. Rodwell and T. Rowley (eds.), *The Small Towns of Roman Britain*, BAR 15 (1975).

the survival of pre-Saxon administrative units, or to argue from the apparent absence of early Saxon settlement near them for the persistence of undisturbed Romano-British communities, are going far beyond the evidence. All that these names can be used to suggest is the possible barbarian awareness of a few still recognizable institutional relics of the last days of rural life in Roman Britain.

It is certainly interesting, and may well be significant, that whereas *vicus* was thus taken over into the small repertoire of Latin words used by the Anglo-Saxons in coining their place-names, *villa*, though it was used in this way extensively in Frankish Gaul, has left little or no trace of similar adoption in Britain. It would thus seem that a group of houses and associated structures, generally sited on a still usable Roman road, might be recognized here and there by early Anglo-Saxons as being, or having once been, a *vicus*. On the other hand the remains of a country house or large farmstead, once the centre of an agricultural estate, whether or not closely associated with a surviving road, would not normally be described by them as a *villa*. This term seems to have had no familiar significance in common speech when the new place-names were being formed.[1] Its disappearance is clearly relevant to the similar disappearance already noted, of *villa* names derived from those of the Romano-British families that had once owned them.

This contrast in survival value between *vicus* and *villa* in the spoken language of pre-literate Anglo-Saxon folk is the more remarkable because, when written Latin records came to be made in the seventh century, both *vicus* and *villa* were once again familiar terms meaning apparently much the same thing in the formal descriptions of rural estates. It has recently been argued[2] that Bede's usage of both was normally to indicate not single tenements but substantial blocks of property. These might include smaller communities and were sometimes distinguished as royal possessions of administrative importance by the use of such phrases as *villa regalis* or *vicus regius*.

[1] It does not appear, for example, among the place-name elements found in English documents earlier than 730, assembled by B. Cox, op. cit. 66; see also F. W. Maitland, *Domesday Book and Beyond* (Cambridge, 1897), 333.

[2] See J. Campbell in P. H. Sawyer (ed.), *Names, Words, and Graves* (Leeds, 1979), 43-8.

It would be tempting to seek the origin of such properties in the Roman period, when *villa* might be a more appropriate description for some of them than *vicus*. But it is well to remember the distinct histories of *vicus* and *villa* in the illiterate age that preceded the Anglo-Saxon use of written record. *Vicus* could then still be used for a recognizable settlement of some kind, though no doubt often for one associated with the personal lordship familiar to the Anglo-Saxons. *Villa* on the other hand seems to have gone out of common speech altogether, and with it no doubt had gone the institution it had once described. Its revival in literate times must have been largely due to influences from the continuing tradition of legal Latin preserved in the courts of Frankish Gaul. If this was so, its later use in this country may have little bearing on the possible survival into Anglo-Saxon times of any rural institution which might have been properly called a *villa* in the last days of Roman Britain.

Most of the new settlement names scattered over the countryside by Anglo-Saxon intruders can be broadly grouped in three main categories, though these are by no means mutually exclusive. There are firstly folk-names of the *-ingas* type, which strictly speaking are not place-names at all but the names of communities living in certain areas, large or small, which had become identified with them. Secondly there are habitative names such as *ham, tun,* and other such words indicative of human settlements or of the farm buildings, enclosures, agricultural or industrial works, and so on which such settlements required. Names of this kind are frequently combined with folk- or personal names, thus serving to identify the addresses of their owners or operators. Thirdly there are names merely descriptive of the locality, by reference to topographical features such as hills, valleys, streams, and so on, or to the different sorts of vegetation, fauna, or flora, which were sufficiently characteristic of the place to be used to identify it. This third category need not be further discussed here, for it is obvious that such descriptive names could arise at any time in the Anglo-Saxon centuries, and need carry no historical implications limited to the earliest period, although their distribution is clearly relevant to the appearance of the landscape at the time they were first used. The folk-names and habitative names, in their widest sense, are, on the other hand, pointers to many aspects of the settlement period, and it is very important to interpret them as correctly as possible, and to extract from them all the historical information which they can properly supply.

Until very recently it was the universal assumption among place-name students that the folk-names in *-ingas* were the earliest group, and that their distribution could be confidently relied on to indicate areas of primary settlement by the Anglo-Saxon peoples in the first century or two after their arrival in this country. This doctrine will be found enshrined not only in the specialist literature but in most of the standard histories of this age. It is implicit in all the early work of the English Place-Name Society, and is accepted without question in the county volumes issued by that admirable body until less than ten years ago.

The origins of this doctrine go back to a very respectable antiquity in the pioneering days of Anglo-Saxon studies before the middle of the nineteenth century. J. M. Kemble, for example, used the evidence of *-ingas* names when he was developing his mark theory of the settlement, which for many years made a powerful impression on historical thought.[1] This view of the *-ingas* names survived more or less unscathed the criticisms which eventually led to the mark theory, at least in its more extreme form, being generally abandoned by historians. There is indeed a great deal to be said for the notion that folk-names of the *-ingas* type are likely to have arisen in the earliest stages of the settlement, when the communities whose names they bear were first imposing themselves on the more or less derelict countryside of Roman Britain. This might well seem the only phase which left room for names to be given which were actually those of the newcomers themselves. The general distribution of the type with its main concentration in the south-eastern counties, Essex, Sussex, and Kent, regions which must have borne the full weight of barbarian penetration in the earliest days, is most naturally explained in this way. Other considerations point to the same conclusion. Thus large numbers of early monothematic personal names were used to form *-ingas*

---

[1] *The Saxons in England* (1849), i. 58–64.

place-names, and a very high proportion of them remained as the centres of substantial estates and large medieval parishes. Others are even referred to as 'regions' or 'provinces' in documents preceding the later administrative pattern of shires and hundreds.[1] All this points to an archaic quality that cannot be readily paralleled in any other type of place-name commonly used by the English settlers.

Yet when the -*ingas* names are plotted on a map that also carries the pagan Anglo-Saxon cemeteries, there is an odd lack of detailed coherence between the two distributions. Both cover in general the same south-eastern quarter of England, with few examples of either to be found north and west of a line from Southampton to Gloucester and thence north-eastward to the Yorkshire coast. But within these limits there are areas such as Essex which have many -*ingas* but few cemeteries, while the neighbouring Cambridge region has many cemeteries but few -*ingas*. In the Thames Valley there is a string of these ancient names following the river all the way almost from its estuary past Sonning and Reading to the Goring gap, with very scanty archaeological counterparts except at Reading itself. But westward beyond the Goring gap the picture is reversed with numerous early cemeteries and very few -*ingas* names to match them.

In commenting on this curious contrast, which became very obvious when the Ordnance Survey's *Map of Britain in the Dark Ages* was first published in 1935, I suggested that the explanation might partly lie in the quite different potential for survival of the archaeological remains and the original names of these early communities.[2] Most archaeological

---

[1] Thus Sonning in the Thames Valley is called *provincia quae vocatur Sunninges* in an eighth-century charter (*CS* 34).

[2] *Antiquity*, 9 (1935), 455–64. A. Goodier has pointed out (*Med. Arch.* 28 (1984), 1–21) what could be a significant link between the location of some pagan cemeteries and the estate boundaries recorded in charters which may preserve very early territorial arrangements. If many early cemeteries were thus placed on the margins rather than near the centres of the territories named after -*ingas* communities, that would help to explain the paucity of obvious topographical links between the archaeological and place-name evidence for these early settlement patterns. Goodier has not mentioned any significant place-names in considering the possible connection between the cemeteries and the estate boundaries recorded in charters. The use of the phrase 'heathen burials' in charter boundaries, generally taken to indicate recognizable prehistoric remains, could have the more restricted meaning of 'pre-Christian Anglo-Saxon cemeteries', which had been disused after the conversion and replaced by more centrally situated churchyards.

remains that have survived for discovery and record in modern times have done so because, being situated in what is now open country, they have been least subject to later disturbance. But for that very reason they are most likely to have belonged to communities which have either died out or were transferred elsewhere, so that their original names have been lost. On the other hand the communities that have retained their early names may have done so just because they have not been thus disturbed. In their case, however, the effect of many centuries of building and rebuilding on the same limited area may either have destroyed piecemeal their earliest remains or have made them inaccessible beneath a succession of later structures. Thus, where early names of this kind are common one should not expect as much archaeological evidence to be available as in those districts where they have mostly disappeared.

It may well be relevant in this context that Essex, Sussex, and Kent, where -*ingas* names are most frequent, suffered on the whole much less from disturbance and devastation by neighbouring rulers in the later Saxon centuries than, for example, the Cambridge region, part of which was for long a vulnerable frontier district of the East Anglian kingdom defended against Mercian attack by massive earthworks. So too the upper Thames Valley, which was continually in dispute between the rival powers of Mercia and Wessex, has few -*ingas* names but a great wealth of early Anglo-Saxon remains. Folk-names of the -*ingas* type, which belonged to groups of people rather than specific places, must have been peculiarly susceptible to disappearance without trace in the fluid conditions that prevailed before a more or less stable pattern of settlement took permanent shape.

Opinions may well differ on the extent to which considerations of this kind help to account for the fact that regions where early settlement is proved by copious archaeological remains do not everywhere correspond in detail with those in which -*ingas* names are most frequent. In recent years some scholars have emphasized the fact that -*ingas* names were certainly still being formed after the spread of Christianity in the seventh century was putting an end to the practice of burial in pagan cemeteries. They have also noted that these names are apt to be found in districts unlikely on geological or other environmental grounds to have been attractive to the earliest settlers, such as the still heavily forested parts of Essex. They have accordingly concluded that, so far from being indicative of primary settlement, the *-ingas* names as a whole belong to secondary phases of colonizing activity. They are thus thought of as spreading out from those parts where the first settlers have left traces of their presence either in the pagan cemeteries or by the use of habitative names believed to be more primitive.[1]

Of these names the most significant is certainly *-ham*.[2] Names in *-ham* occur plenteously in the eastern and southern parts of Britain as a whole. They also show a marked relationship to Roman roads and settlements, and match closely in detail the archaeological distribution of pagan Anglo-Saxon remains. *-Ham* is found compounded not only with terms descriptive of local features, in themselves undatable, but often with personal names that are of early monothematic type. It is commonly linked with the *-inga-* element itself, thus producing names in *-ingaham*. This has given rise to the suggestion that, in place of the generally received sequence of these name-forms in which the *-ingas* were thought to come first followed by *-ingaham* and *-ham*, the reverse order should now be accepted with the *-ham* names as the most primitive, followed by *-ingaham*. Only later would then come the *-ingas* marking secondary settlements in the woodland and waste peripheral to the first centres of immigration.

This theory first took shape on the basis of a detailed study of Kent and the adjacent south-eastern parts. It has been developed and in part modified following examination of the rather different pattern apparently revealed in some regions of East Anglia and the eastern Midlands.[3] Almost

[1] Evidence from some parts of the Continent suggests that the notion that *-ingas* names only represent secondary settlements should be viewed with scepticism. Thus, in the Baltic island of Öland, finds from the Roman Iron Age have been found in close association with no less than nine of the thirteen settlement sites with names in *-inge*, and finds of this period appear only to occur on sites bearing this type of name: see C. I. Ståhle, *Studier över de svenska ortnamnen på -inge* (Uppsala, 1946).

[2] The fullest studies of *-ham* names are by B. Cox in *JEP-NS* 5 (1973), 15-73, and by J. M. Dodgson in *Anglo-Saxon England* 2 (1973), 1-50.

[3] The argument can best be studied in the articles by Dodgson in *Med. Arch.* 10 (1966), 1-29; B. Cox, op. cit.; and K. Cameron in *PBA* 62 (1976), 135-56. See also M. Gelling, *Signposts*, 106-29, and Dodgson in P. Brandon (ed.), *The South Saxons* (1978), 54-88.

certainly more factors are involved in the problem than have hitherto been generally appreciated. It is inherently improbable that the compound form -*ingaham* should precede in time the use of the simpler -*ingas*, since this compound is clearly made up of two elements both of which must have had a familiar meaning before they were combined. Moreover, while it is true that -*ingas* names might be expected to occur more frequently than they do in direct association with pagan cemeteries, there are some notable cases where this direct association is evident, such as Reading (Berks.), Kettering (Northants.), and possibly Mucking (Essex).[1] Some -*ingas* names were certainly formed, or at least came to be attached to specific localities, at a later date than would be expected had this form been used exclusively in the earliest days of the settlement. It clearly had a longer vogue than was at one time supposed, but this has no bearing on the question of the date when these names first began to be used.

More consideration should clearly be given to the factors governing the survival or loss of early names in the confused conditions of the age of settlement. Names of the -*ingas* type, which were essentially the names of people rather than places, would be particularly susceptible to transfer from one place to another while the folk concerned retained any degree of mobility, or indeed to total disappearance in the event of disaster overtaking them. Many of the communities whose existence is now only known from pagan cemeteries of the fifth and sixth centuries may well have been called by -*ingas* names, which either no longer exist[2] or have been transferred to villages elsewhere which only took shape when their people finally settled down or became Christian.

[1] Doubts have recently been raised about the classification of Mucking as an -*ingas* name: since there are no spellings known before the Norman period, the matter must clearly be left open. But one cannot fail to note that the question would never have been raised at all had not the discovery of the very important early settlement and cemeteries at Mucking seemed to threaten the new notion that -*ingas* names were only given to secondary settlements: see Gelling, op. cit. 119–22.

[2] Thus the lost *Nidingham* in Girton parish, Cambs., probably preserves the name of the folk which used the well-known Girton pagan cemetery now generally known by the name of the adjacent village, which is of a type unlikely to be as early as the pagan period: B. Cox in K. Cameron (ed.), *Place-Name Evidence for the Anglo-Saxon Invasion and Scandinavian Settlements* (Nottingham, 1975), 58.

Considerations of this kind are likely to prove significant in evaluating the historical evidence provided by these early names. It is inherently likely that many -*ingas* names now attached to particular villages distant from a pagan cemetery or situated on land unattractive to the earliest settlers, were at first applied to much wider areas which the folk in question had made their own, perhaps as far back as the fifth century or even earlier. A number of such districts bearing names of this kind survived into historic times, where they appear among the smaller units recorded in the Tribal Hidage of eighth-century Mercia[1] or in land charters of that and succeeding centuries. Many others must have lost their original identity by various forms of disintegration, sometimes so completely as to be no longer recognizable at all.

It is not surprising that, as the generations passed, such disintegration should have occurred. The original links that bound the members of such communities together arose from real or imaginary kinship with the eponymous founder whose name they bore, or through original membership of a warband or *comitatus* which had looked to him for leadership. They would inevitably become looser as the founding fathers passed out of living memory and some of their followers hived off to the exploitation of fresh parts of the district. Family connections would eventually be forgotten as the population grew and the degree of cousinship became more distant.

The process of disintegration can be studied in its various stages by examining particular cases. Thus an early stage, which happened to become permanent, may be indicated by the group of Roding villages in Essex, all of which after becoming separate communities retained the original name of the folk from which they all claimed to spring.[2] Two

---

[1] See below, p. 141.

[2] It has been suggested with some plausibility that the Essex Rodingas may have taken their name from the Rodingas who appear as a continental tribe in Widsith, descended perhaps ultimately from the Reudingi of Tacitus. The Reudingi are probably represented archaeologically by the proto-Saxon Fuhlsbüttel culture, discussed by F. Tischler, *Fuhlsbüttel, ein Beitrag zur Sachsenfrage* (Neumünster, 1937). G. Osten (*Niedersächsisches Jahrbuch für Landesgeschichte*, 51 (1979), 102) is mistaken in placing the English Rodingas on what he calls 'the East Anglian Heights': their settlements cover an area of some twenty miles across in the heart of Essex, northwest of Chelmsford, and are thus more likely to derive from a Saxon than an Angle background on the Continent.

adjacent group settlements of this kind in the middle Thames Valley, Sonning and Reading, which both retained their original extensive outlines by becoming enormous medieval manors, illustrate different ways in which development might take place. At Reading, where a group of pagan cemeteries bears witness to the great antiquity of the settlement at the confluence of the Thames and the Kennet, the folk-name became localized at this conspicuous centre. It is not found in any of the subsidiary villages that must have been formed by outlying groups of *Radingas* established in remoter parts of what became the later manor. At Sonning, on the other hand, described as the *provincia quae vocatur Sunninges* in an eighth-century charter,[1] there was no such obvious centre. The folk-name was eventually localized, perhaps not until Christian times, at a spot almost on the border of its original territory, possibly as a deliberate indication that that was where the land which the Sunningas claimed began. But some detached members of this folk left permanent traces of their presence in Berkshire far beyond the compact limits of their main *provincia* at such spots to the east and west respectively as Sunninghill and Sunningwell,[2] suggesting a foot-loose tendency that persisted much longer than was the case elsewhere. So too it might well happen that a subsidiary settlement in the territory of the *Woccingas* might be established at Wokingham earlier than the folk-name itself became localized at Woking, when the process of disintegration had eventually run its full course, and there was no longer any need to retain it for the wider area it had once covered.

By no means all the early -*ingas* communities were of the size to be remembered as *provinciae* in the charters, or to be assessed as separate taxable units by their Mercian overlords when the Tribal Hidage was drawn up. In Sussex, for example, while the *Haestingas* of Hastings were certainly of this substantial character, the numerous -*ingas* names on the coastal plain between the South Downs and the sea in West Sussex present a very different pattern. Here, where several such names may survive within a single parish, it would seem that

---

[1] CS 34.
[2] Perhaps even at Sunbury, Middlesex, where a man with the same name, Sunna, as the founder of the Sunningas, must have had a defensible settlement in early times.

they can represent little more than the holdings of one family group, such as gave rise elsewhere to early names in -*ham*. -*Ham* names are in fact infrequent hereabouts and the fact that compounds in -*ingaham* are also uncommon in Sussex suggests that there was little room here for the kind of expansion that led in other parts to the eventual disintegration of the larger -*ingas* communities.

Such would appear to be the most significant suggestions to be drawn from recent work on the earliest strata of English place-names. The subject is one which cannot be expected to produce many firm and generally acceptable conclusions to assist the historian in his work. Moreover, the present inconclusive condition of these studies is aggravated by uncertainties that bedevil the interpretation of several of what should be the most meaningful elements used in the earliest types of names. Thus the greatest care has to be taken to distinguish among names now ending in -*ing* between those likely to be true folk-names of the -*ingas* type and those containing the singular element -*ing* in any of its less significant meanings. So too it may often be all but impossible to determine from the earliest surviving spellings whether a modern name in -*ham* contains the early element -*ham* meaning a settlement, or the equally common -*hamm* meaning meadow or enclosed pasture. *Hamm* in these senses may have had a much longer life as a descriptive term, and thus carries no such significant information for the historian.[1]

These frustrating ambiguities, which the nature of the evidence in itself often makes it impossible to resolve, may serve as final reminders of the fundamental uncertainties inherent in all English place-name study. These uncertainties have always been recognized by the best scholars in this field, and it may perhaps not be out of place to end this discussion with some wise words which one of its foremost and most learned pioneers used to express his feelings on the matter:

'... it is essential to remember that in the present state of place-name studies these results can only be tentative, and that even when the place-names of all England have been surveyed in the minutest detail,

---

[1] For the element -*hamm* see the articles by M. Gelling and K. I. Sandred in *Namn och Bygd*, 48 (1960), 140-62, and 64 (1976), 71-87.

the conclusions which may be drawn from them will fall far short of scientific precision.'[1]

In spite of the great increase in the volume of available material and in the ever-expanding knowledge and expertise that can be brought to bear on its interpretation, those words are as true now as they were when Sir Frank Stenton wrote them more than forty years ago.

[1] F. M. Stenton, *TRHS* 4th ser. 22 (1940), 21.

3

THE CONTINENTAL BACKGROUND

No discussion of the continental background to the English settlements can start from any other point than Bede's statement that the invaders came from three of the most powerful peoples of Germany, the Angles, the Saxons, and the Jutes.[1] That this should still be so more than twelve hundred years after Bede's day, is a tribute to his remarkable capacity as a historian to express in simple but fundamentally accurate terms the essential facts of a process whose complexity was probably at least as obvious to him as it is to the modern student with a much wider range of evidence to evaluate. And when he goes on to locate the continental Saxons in the lands known in his day as those still inhabited by the Old Saxons, the Angles in a region known to him as Angulus which had been left empty by their migration, and the Jutes in a less well defined area situated somewhere beyond the Angles, he was also providing the essentials for a map of the North Sea coastlands with all the political detail that was strictly necessary for his purpose.

In deriving the Saxons from the districts occupied in his time by the Old Saxons, Bede is certainly pointing to the coastlands between the Elbe and the Weser valleys, where, as J. M. Kemble[2] first demonstrated more than a century ago, the cemeteries have produced much material directly parallel to that found in England. By Angulus, the region that lay between the Saxons and the Jutes, Bede certainly meant Schleswig, where the name is still found on modern maps as the district of Angeln. There has been much difference of opinion over the location of Bede's Jutes. But if, as he implies, they lay somewhere beyond the Angles, he must have thought of them either to the north of Schleswig, in Jutland, or to the east in modern Holstein, where again there

---

[1] *HE* i. 15.
[2] J. M. Kemble, 'On mortuary urns at Stade-on-the-Elbe, and other parts of north Germany', *Archaeologia*, 36 (1855), 270-83.

is a suggestive district name, Eutin, which may indicate the home of some part of the tribe at one time.

Archaeologically speaking, as will be seen later, Bede's Jutes need present no great problem. South Jutland and Fyn have close cultural links in the fifth century with Kent, and throughout eastern England at this time ceramic fashions derived directly or indirectly from East Holstein are conspicuously evident, though without marked concentration in any particular areas. Both Jutland and East Holstein were closely related to the main south Scandinavian *Kulturkreis* that included the Angles of Schleswig, though neither may have developed such recognizably distinctive fashions. It is not impossible that this rather imprecise relationship with the Angles was exactly the impression that Bede intended to convey by the vagueness of his reference to the exact location of the Jutes.

Bede does not in this passage include Frisians among the major peoples settling in Britain, though he does refer to them in this connection elsewhere.[1] This may therefore be the right point to mention that the literary evidence for their presence among the settlers goes back much earlier than Bede. The Byzantine historian Procopius[2] writing in the sixth century, and apparently using information provided by Angles who accompanied a Frankish mission to Justinian's court, understood that in his day the population of Britain, apart from the native Britons, was divided between the Angles and the Frisians. It may well be that the Franks, as their near neighbours on the lower Rhine, took an exaggerated view of the part played by Frisians in the movement to Britain, but their participation was certainly far from negligible. What makes it difficult to evaluate archaeologically is that, as will be seen later, the Anglo-Saxon peoples were themselves infiltrating the Frisian seaboard between the Weser and the Rhine mouths in force at this time, many of them as a preliminary to the short sea passage to south-eastern England. Thus the culture of the Frisians was itself becoming very mixed, and it is scarcely possible to be certain from the archaeological evidence how substantial a contribution the Frisians themselves may have made to the movement in

[1] *HE* v. 9.
[2] Procopius, *Gothic War*, iv. 20.

terms of manpower. Though it may well have been considerable, especially in south-eastern Britain where what has
been termed 'Anglo-Frisian' pottery is especially common in
the cemeteries and settlements,[1] it did not result in the
establishment of any specifically Frisian kingdom or recognizable Frisian institutions. This is no doubt the reason why
Bede did not emphasize Frisian participation in the settlement. But the linguistic similarities that long linked the
speech and dialects of south-eastern England to the Low
Countries suggest that the physical influx of Frisian folk may
have been important.[2] They certainly played a major part in
the recovery of English trade with the Continent, of which
the revival of London, already recognizable in Bede's day as
a focal centre of Frisian merchants, was an early and
conspicuous symbol.

This, however, is to anticipate by two centuries or more
the distant consequences of possible Frisian collaboration in
the early stages of the movement. We need to enquire how it
came about that the Angles, the Saxons, and the Jutes
mentioned by Bede,[3] with or without the substantial Frisian
participation for which Procopius provides near-contemporary
testimony, were in a position to bring about the transformation of what had been the civil provinces of the Roman
diocese of Britannia into a loosely-knit group of hereditary
barbarian kingdoms. It was no part of Bede's purpose in
writing his *Ecclesiastical History of the English Nation*
to describe the detail of this transformation, which was all
but completed while the newcomers were still pagan. He
must have known a great deal about the process, especially
as it affected his native Northumbria, but this knowledge was

---

[1] See my article, 'Some English parallels to the Anglo-Saxon pottery of
Holland and Belgium', in *L'Antiquité classique*, 17 (1948), 453–72.

[2] Certain specifically Frisian words found their way into English place-names
as noted by Stenton, *Preparatory to Anglo-Saxon England* (Oxford, 1970), 269.
The most interesting is perhaps *roth*, a clearing, which occurs in Rothwell and
Rothley, Northants. Ekwall has shown this to be an exact parallel to Old Frisian
rothe: see EP-NS *Northants*. (1933), 119. Its occurrence in Rothwell exactly
matches the finding there (and at nearby Desborough) of two small pots clearly
from the same workshop as that which produced three similar vessels found at
St. Gilles-les-Termonde in Belgium: see my *Corpus*, i. 27 and ii. fig. 143. A Frisian
connection between Northants. and this part of Belgium in the sixth century is
thus implied both by archaeology and by place-names.

[3] *HE* i. 15.

not relevant to the story he wanted to tell, and so is lost. So, too, it is impossible to guess how much or how little he may have known about the continental background of the Angles, the Saxons, and the Jutes, beyond the bare facts of their political geography as he understood it.

There are two main sources from which further information on these matters can be gathered. Roman historians and geographers, notably Tacitus and Ptolemy, were interested in the tribal situation in free Germany beyond the Imperial frontiers in the first and second centuries AD. They had occasion to refer to the peoples mentioned by Bede among many other tribes who had been their neighbours several hundred years before his time. There is also a wide range of archaeological material, extending in date from the earlier phases of the pre-Roman Iron Age in north Germany and southern Scandinavia to the later stages of the Migration period, which can be used to illustrate the cultural changes which preceded, accompanied, and followed the settlement of some of these peoples in Britain.

Much labour and learning has been devoted to attempts to relate the archaeological evidence for the changes, develop-ments, and movements in this cultural background to the activities of particular tribes and confederations of folk recorded in the historical sources. While some of these equations are plausible enough, and can be used with some confidence as pointers to particular historical situations and relationships between the tribes in question, care has to be taken not to overstrain the evidence in identifying any given cultural assemblage of material as necessarily the work of any tribe or group of tribes whose names happen to be known.

Writing towards the end of the first century AD, Tacitus, in his account of the Ingaevones, the group of peoples who then occupied the north-western seaboard of Germany, mentions, among many others less relevant to the present purpose, the Frisians, the Angles, and the Eudoses.[1] The Frisians already occupied the coastland in northern Holland which still bears their name. The Angles and Eudoses, whose precise position at that time was probably no clearer to

[1] Tacitus, *Germania*, 40.

Tacitus than he makes it to us, could at least be described as
'defended by rivers and forests', in an area which made
natural their common participation with other tribes in the
rites of a divinity called Nerthus, centred on an island of the
Ocean. By the Ocean Tacitus probably meant the North Sea
rather than the Baltic. It is thus likely from his account that
the Angles and Eudoses were occupying before AD 100
approximately the regions which Bede many centuries later
seems to have thought appropriate for his Angles and Jutes.

Tacitus, however, makes no mention, in this passage or
anywhere else, of the Saxons. They first appear in the *Geography* of Ptolemy,[1] a writer who lived in the middle of the
second century, though it is generally believed that he
derived much of his information from a source about a
hundred and fifty years earlier. Ptolemy placed the Saxons
'on the neck of the Cimbric peninsula', by which he probably
meant somewhere in the modern Holstein. On the coast
between the Saxons and the Frisians — from the Elbe, that is,
as far as the Ems — Ptolemy and Tacitus agree in locating
the Chauci, an important tribe which, in the time of Tacitus,
could be described as 'the noblest of the German race'. They
seem to have occupied much the same region in the first and
second centuries as Bede's Old Saxons were occupying in his
time. Between these dates it would appear that the Saxons,
moving south-west across the lower Elbe from the base of the
Danish peninsula in Holstein, had somehow replaced, ejected,
or absorbed the Chauci. They seem to have taken over both
their lands and their role as pirates and sea-robbers, soon
making themselves a major menace on the coasts of Roman
Gaul and Britain.

These important changes, of which no details of the
political history are known, seem to have occurred during
the third century. After this the Chauci are no longer mentioned in these coastal regions, though they are referred to in
later Roman sources as participating in disturbances near the
Imperial frontier on the middle Rhine. The archaeological
evidence does not suggest that the changeover from the
dominance of the Chauci to that of the Saxons in these parts
was accompanied by any drastic or sudden cultural change.

[1]   Ptolemy, *Geog.* II. xi. 7.

The two peoples had long been neighbours in the lower Elbe valley exhibiting related styles of decoration in pottery and metal-work, and these fashions continued to develop after the third-century movements without any marked evidence for serious dislocation. It would thus seem likely that the westward extension of Saxon power in the third century, while it broke up the old political hegemony of the Chauci, did not displace the bulk of the population, though some irreconcilable elements may have retained their name and independence by migrating south-westwards towards the middle Rhine.

Much of the archaeological evidence for the culture of the Chauci in these coastal regions before the third century, as for their successors the Saxons later, comes from the numerous *Terpen* or mound-settlements, thickly scattered on the low-lying lands and among the marshes that fringed the sea most of the way from the Elbe estuary in the neigh-bourhood of Cuxhaven to the Frisian settlements in north Holland where much the same conditions prevailed.[1] Roman writers, such as the elder Pliny,[2] were aware of the curious life half-way between the land and the sea which the Chauci had based on these artificial mounds. Pliny's description of them is almost echoed later in the fourth century by Orosius who writes of the Saxons[3] as 'a people of the Ocean settled in pathless swamps and on the sea shore'.

Many of these artificial mounds still carry modern villages; others, which have been excavated by Dutch and German archaeologists, have thrown much light on the social evolution of the communities that occupied them in the centuries be-fore and during the Migration period. Nearly everywhere the evidence points to a growing population, greater elaboration of buildings, and increasing pressure on the habitable area as the mounds were raised and enlarged to accommodate more people and to counter the encroaching sea. At Feddersen Wierde, on the Weser estuary north of Bremerhaven, for example, several small mounds with individual farm-houses

---

[1] A very useful general study of these mounds with plans and illustrations is H. Halbertsma, *Terpen tussen Vlie en Eems*, 2 vols. (Groningen, 1963).

[2] Pliny, *Nat. Hist.* XVI. i. 2-5.

[3] Orosius, *Hist. adversus Paganos*, ed. C. Zangemeister (Leipzig, 1889), vii. 32.

were linked together in the first century AD to form one large *Terp* which soon came to carry as many as thirty houses radially arranged. In the second century a chieftain's house in a ditched and fenced enclosure surrounded by workshops became the focus of some fifty houses, and later still granaries and a large hall were added with industrial installations for bronze- and iron-working. Occupation ceased about the middle of the fifth century, and it is tempting to connect this desertion with the possibility of movement overseas to Britain.[1] In any case the pottery and other objects from the final phase at Feddersen Wierde correspond very closely with those found in such early English settlements as that at Mucking (Essex), a site on the Thames estuary very similar in geographical terms to that of Feddersen Wierde on the Weser.

A village site recently excavated at Wijster (Looveen) in north Holland seems to show a somewhat similar history.[2] It apparently began with a single farmstead in the second century AD which was several times rebuilt. By the third century there were at least three houses and the population was increasing. After a brief decline in the early fourth century there was soon a rapid expansion: many houses were built in rectangular blocks with lanes between, and there was evidence for great activity; but early in the fifth century occupation came to an end. Here too it is very tempting not only to link the final desertion of Wijster with a movement of its people to Britain, but to see in the preceding phase of increased activity the signs of Saxon pressure on the older Frisian population which proved too heavy for the local means of subsistence to support.

It will be necessary to say something shortly about the forces in free Germany and Scandinavia which stimulated this movement westward of the Saxons into the lands of the Chauci and the Frisians. But it was hardly accidental that it should have coincided in time with the increasingly disturbed conditions that troubled the Roman world during the third century. There was great political confusion in Gaul at that

[1] Interim reports by W. Haarnagel are in *Germania*, 34 (1956), 35 (1957), 39 (1961), and 41 (1963).
[2] W. A. van Es, *Wijster, a Native Village beyond the Imperial Frontier 150–425 A.D.* (Groningen, 1967).

time, accompanied by severe inflation and economic weakness. The continuing uncertainties of political control in the Empire were reflected in increasing irresponsibility and local independence among the generals on whom the burden of frontier defence lay. Such conditions proved an irresistible temptation to the restless tribes in movement beyond the frontier on the North Sea coast. It would seem that the Roman authorities attempted to control these movements through the establishment of a virtually independent naval command, based on fortified ports and harbour installations on both sides of the Channel. This policy, however, only increased the political confusion, for the commander in charge, Carausius, soon took advantage of his position in 287 to set up an independent empire of his own.

Carausius was himself a Menapian with a family tradition of piracy based on the Rhine mouths, where his tribe belonged. It is no accident that the coastal installations and fortresses on which his power rested in Britain should have come later on to be known as those of the 'Saxon Shore'. For, as has been seen, it was precisely at this time, in the later part of the third century, that Saxon pressure on the Chauci and Frisians in the coastlands between the Elbe and the Rhine had created an unstable situation, which stimulated the more adventurous elements in all these peoples to seek fame and fortune through plunder, piracy, and even perhaps through settlement overseas. The British side of this situation will require further discussion later on. It is enough here to point out that this is the earliest moment at which conditions on the Continent might have made possible a Saxon settlement on the coast of Britain, sufficient in scale to give rise to the notion of a 'Saxon Shore'.

As the fourth century wore on it would seem that the forces of nature took a hand in increasing the pressure of the Saxon population on the available means of subsistence. It is probable that the whole north German coastline had been slowly sinking for some centuries, and that the widespread practice of living on artificial mounds had arisen as man's natural reaction to the slow advance of the sea. It would certainly appear that the ever-increasing size and height of the mounds, which all the excavations have revealed, is to be explained not merely by the increase of the population but also by the rising level of highwater. There are reasons for believing that this sinkage, which eventually led in the Carolingian age to the formation of the Zuider Zee, the Dollart, and the Jade Bay, was proceeding at an accelerated pace from the fourth century onwards.[1] While all the German tribes bordering on the Roman frontiers were watching with increased restlessness the weakening of its defences, and were themselves beginning to feel the westward pressure of nomad peoples from Asia, the Saxons and Frisians crowded on the German coast were thus faced in addition with local troubles of their own.

Behind these local troubles, however, were the major movements southwards and westwards of Scandinavian tribes, which had forced the Saxons from their earlier homes in Holstein across the Elbe into the lands of the Chauci. They had also stimulated the equally momentous migration of the Lombards up the Elbe valley towards the Alpine passes and their eventual settlement in north Italy. It was this pressure from southern Scandinavia which must have unsettled the Angles from their homeland around Angeln in eastern Schleswig, and their neighbours the Jutes from Jutland and Fyn, perhaps in part from East Holstein also.

German archaeologists have done much in recent years to sort out the various cultural strains which can be identified as contributing, from the pre-Roman Iron Age onwards, to what may be termed the proto-Angle, proto-Saxon, or proto-Jutish phases of Bede's three familiar tribes.[2] It is thus difficult to avoid the use of such literary labels in distinguishing the more significant, for our purposes, of these related cultural groups. Prominent among them in the first and second centuries AD had been the Fuhlsbüttel folk of Holstein, in whom can probably be detected the roots of the

[1] A similar sinkage on the east coast of Britain led to the flooding and abandonment of the prosperous agricultural estates established in earlier Roman times in the Fens. Most of this region had reverted in the fifth century, if not before, to waste and marsh. Low-lying coastal settlements in Essex and in the Thames estuary also became uninhabitable during the fourth century for the same reason.

[2] See especially: M. B. Mackeprang, *Kulturbeziehungen im nordischen Raum* (Leipzig, 1943); F. Tischler, 'Der Stand der Sachsenforschung archäologisch gesehen' in *Bericht der Römisch-Germanischen Kommission*, 35 (1956), 21–215; A. Genrich, *Formenkreise und Stammesgruppen in Schleswig-Holstein* (Neumünster, 1954).

culture later characteristic of the Saxons.[1] To the north, in eastern Schleswig and Fyn, the Angles were already recognizable, and closely associated with them was the Oberjersdal culture of southern Jutland.[2] This was soon to extend all down the west coast of the Danish peninsula, including the North Frisian islands, to form a complex known to German scholars as the *Westgruppe*. Its northern elements probably included the ancestors of the later Jutes, while its southern boundary marched with the Fuhlsbüttel people north of the Elbe estuary.

Increasing pressure from the north and east during the third and early fourth centuries seems to have had the effect of forcing many of the smaller tribes to coalesce into larger combinations whose individual sections became less distinctive archaeologically as they merged. By the mid-fourth century, if not earlier, the western parts of Jutland and Schleswig were occupied by a broadly based *Nordseekustengruppe*. Its characteristic fashions in pottery and metal-work were beginning to spread across the estuary of the Elbe, to mingle with the Saxon complex now occupying in force the lands between the lower Elbe and the Weser and the old territories of the Chauci beyond.

North and east of the lower Elbe, southward pressure from the Angles and possibly some neighbouring Jutish folk in east Schleswig was mingling with and perhaps dominating the remaining tribes in East Holstein, to produce what the Germans appropriately term a *Mischgruppe* incorporating some cultural features from all these elements. Other Angle and Jutish folk evidently joined the Saxon advance beyond the Ems into Frisia. Their presence there can be demonstrated not only archaeologically, in the widespread use of cruciform brooches and pottery of so-called 'Anglo-Frisian' types, but by the literary traditions that link the Jutes with the Frisians in the tales about Hengist and other heroes of which echoes survive in *Beowulf* and the Finnsburh fragment.

It is not possible in this context (and without more numerous illustrations than the plan of this *History* can include) to describe in any detail the characteristic features

[1]   F. Tischler, *Fuhlsbüttel*.
[2]   F. Tischler, *Das Gräberfeld Oberjersdal* (Hamburg, 1955).

of the equipment, in metal goods and pottery, which enable archaeologists to distinguish the various groups of Germanic folk concerned in these movements which took the main part in the settlement of England. There are, however, certain broad differences of fashion which can be mentioned as useful aids in recognizing the presence of one or more of these peoples, or in estimating their relative importance in the various sites of occupation or burial which provide the material evidence for them.

More work has probably been done on the typology of brooches, on both their form and their decoration, than on any other group of metal objects of this age. As the principal items combining both functional use and decorative desirability among the personal possessions of women, brooches were not only indispensable parts of their dress and equipment, but were peculiarly liable to ceaseless development and evolution according to the changing dictates of taste and fashion. Minor differences in form and ornamentation are thus likely to be especially significant, both for dating and for localizing individual styles and even individual pieces. This is not the place for entering into such minutiae, but some appreciation of their existence is necessary to explain the importance attached to the typology of brooches, and to their value as pointers to the relative dates of other less informative objects often found in association with them.

The different types of brooches certainly help to distinguish the cultures and pinpoint the early distribution of the peoples whom Bede knew as the Angles, the Saxons, and the Jutes. Throughout southern Scandinavia, Jutland, the Danish islands, and Schleswig the main fashion at this period was for various forms of long brooch. This was a type whose coiled spring was concealed behind a head-plate at one end, while the pin was held when closed by a catch-plate at the back of the other. Between the two was a bow, varying in size and shape, which lent itself to decorative treatment.

Two main types of long brooches developed in these northern regions. In one the head-plate was square or rectangular in shape entirely covering the spring, while the foot, which similarly covered the catch-plate, was often diamond- or lozenge-shaped and sometimes divided down the centre by a ridge into two parts on slightly different planes.

All three sections, head, bow, and foot, lent themselves to decoration in ways that were fashionable at the date of manufacture. A few early examples show scroll patterns carried out in the chip-carving technique. But the type developed mainly in the sixth century with ever more elaborate zoomorphic decoration. This came to include marginal excrescences around the edges of the head-plate and lobes projecting from the sides and bottom of the foot. These generally carried Style 1 animal ornament of increasing complexity as time went on.[1]

The other main type of these long brooches has a more significant early history. It is known as the cruciform, because the ends of the spring extend beyond the edges of the head-plate and are covered with protruding lateral knobs, whose form is repeated in a third knob on the top edge (Fig. 1). These knobs in the early examples were separately attached and of simple rounded form, but they gradually became enlarged and flattened to form decorative features of the head-plate itself, no longer having any functional purpose. The feet of these cruciform brooches also show a characteristic development. At first narrow and almost featureless, they are soon provided with a small eye on each side and nostrils at the end to become embryo horses' heads. Inevitably the Germanic fondness for animal ornament leads to these simple zoomorphic features being developed and exaggerated in an increasingly elaborate and even grotesque manner to match the exuberant taste of the sixth century.

This very simplified outline of what is in fact a quite complex typological evolution may help to show how these brooches can provide clues of considerable value as historical evidence. Whenever square-headed brooches of the kind with divided foot or any sort of cruciform brooches appear among the grave goods or settlement debris of this period, whether on the Continent or in Britain, one can be reasonably certain that the folk to whom they belonged had links, direct or indirect, personal or ancestral, with one or other of the

---

[1] The most complete study of the square-headed brooches is E. T. Leeds, *A Corpus of Early Anglo-Saxon Great Square-headed Brooches* (Oxford, 1949) which, though now in need of some revision, remains the essential tool required for their understanding. Besides the types of northern origin, it covers also those whose connections are rather with the Frankish Rhineland.

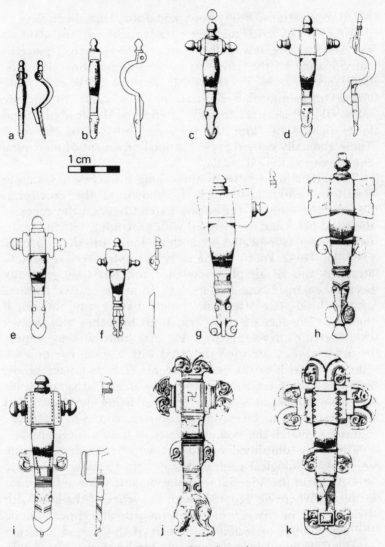

Fig. 1.   Development of the cruciform brooch

a Mildenhall, Suffolk.   *b* Ixworth, Suffolk.   *c* East Shefford, Berks.
d West Stow Heath, Suffolk.   *e* Little Wilbraham, Cambs.   *f* Barrington,
Cambs.   *g* Brooke, Norfolk.   *h* Kenninghall, Norfolk.   *i* Lakenheath,
Suffolk.   *j* Sleaford, Lincs.   *k* Sleaford, Lincs.

Group I. *a,b,c*.   Group II. *d,e*.   Group III. *f,g*.   Group IV. *h,i*.   Group
V. *j,k*.

For sources of figures see p. xiv.

northern peoples comprised in the Scandinavian *Kulturkreis* of this age. The objects themselves may often enable one to go further, to localize their origin or their antecedents in one or other part of this complex, and to date them more or less exactly. When, for example, a number of simple cruciform brooches of early-fifth-century type, similar to others that come from the Frisian *Terpen*, or from cemeteries in Jutland or Schleswig, are found in Kent, they can be used quite properly by historians to set beside Bede's statement that Kent was first settled by Jutes. So too they may be linked with the scraps of tradition that picture Hengist, their leader, as an exile from his Jutish homeland who had since had some not altogether creditable adventures among the Frisians. Similarly the general distribution of cruciform brooches in the rest of England can be treated as a relevant factor in assessing Bede's judgement that the settlers who came to people East and Middle Anglia, Mercia, and Northumbria were Angles.[1]

Quite different, but equally instructive, are the principal brooch types in vogue at this time among the Saxons and their close neighbours in the lands between the Elbe and the Weser. Here also two main types predominate in the cemeteries and settlements of the fifth century. These are the round brooches and the equal-armed brooches, each group appearing in two main forms. Of the round brooches one group comprises those which are cast in one piece, with the circular decorated surface surrounded by a more or less deeply dished upstanding rim, so that they are normally known in England as saucer brooches. In a less common variety of this type, sometimes termed button brooches, the overall size is normally smaller, the rim reduced or omitted, and the whole decorated surface cast to represent a highly stylized human face (Fig. 2).

The other main group of circular form is that of the so-called applied brooches. In these the decoration is carried on a separate thin sheet of metal which is subsequently attached

---

[1] The cruciform brooches of England were first assembled and classified in N. Åberg, *The Anglo-Saxons in England* (Uppsala, 1926). Though many more have been found since he wrote, and some modification is now required in his grouping and dating of them, his classification and chronology are still basic to a correct appreciation of their significance.

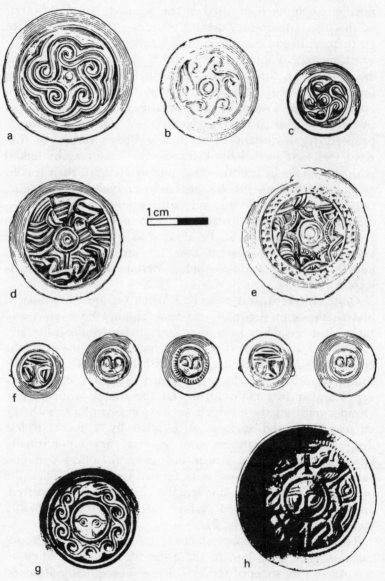

Fig. 2. Circular brooches of various types

a Hastings, Sussex. *b* Kingston-by-Lewes, Sussex. *c* Highdown, Sussex. *d* Alfriston, Sussex. *e* Selmeston, Sussex. *f* Alfriston, Sussex. *g* Fairford, Gloucs. *h* Fairford, Gloucs.

For sources of figures see p. xiv.

by some adhesive to a flat disc forming the back-plate of the brooch. Applied brooches are obviously more fragile than cast saucer brooches, as the sheet carrying the decoration is itself somewhat flimsy and can easily come adrift from the back-plate after some degree of wear or rough handling. Blank back-plates which have lost their decoration, or detached applied sheets, generally in fragments, are often all that may survive of applied brooches. This fragility is no doubt the main reason why the type went out of use comparatively early in this period, whereas the sturdy saucer brooches continued in production throughout these centuries, showing a long sequence of decorative styles more or less parallel with those displayed by the various types of long brooches. Thus the geometrical and scroll motifs in chip-carving technique characteristic of the fifth century, gradually give way to a range of zoomorphic designs becoming ever more elaborate and complex, as Style 1 animal ornament develops throughout the sixth.

The equal-armed brooches form the most characteristic type of bow brooch in the Saxon regions. Unlike the vertical shape taken by the long brooches of the north these have a squarer appearance. This is caused by the head and foot being both extended horizontally above and below the bow to form wide triangular panels, more or less equal in size. The type, which grew out of a simple fourth-century form, the so-called *Stützarmfibel*, of which English examples are known, for example, from Dorchester and Abingdon, Oxon., Luton and Kempston, Beds., and Mucking, Essex, was fully developed by the beginning of the fifth century, but went out of use before 500. It can therefore be an important pointer to the date of deposits in which it is found.[1]

Less than twenty examples of the fully developed form of equal-armed brooch have so far been recorded in Britain, all of them probably imported by the womenfolk of early Saxon immigrants. While they are normally decorated with the scrolls and other motifs in chip-carving characteristic of their date, it is of some interest that they fall into two distinct

[1] The most recent account of these brooch types in England is by V. I. Evison in H.-J. Hässler (ed.), *Studien zur Sachsenforschung* (1977), 127–41. Their distribution in England is almost entirely north of the Thames, mostly in a broad band running from East and Middle Anglia to the Abingdon area: ibid., fig. 6.

groups. There is a simpler form in which the decoration is confined within the wide triangular panels provided by the head- and foot-plates, and a more elaborate style in which the edges of these plates also carry projecting animal figures and other decorative features giving them a much richer and more sumptuous appearance. In the lands between the Elbe and the Weser, where the equal-armed brooches reached their developed form, there appears to be a local difference in the distribution of the two varieties. The simpler type is mainly found west of the river Oste which roughly divides this region in half; it is especially at home in the cemeteries east of the Weser estuary such as Westerwanna near Bremerhaven. The more elaborate ones come chiefly from sites east of the Oste, such as Perlberg in the Elbe valley near Stade. It is significant that a similar pattern seems to be made by the distribution of the two forms of Saxon round brooch, the cast saucer brooches occurring mostly with the more elaborate equal-armed brooches to the east in the Elbe valley, while the applied brooches belong rather with the simpler type in the Weser region.[1]

The English examples of these brooches can thus be used not merely as pointers to the homeland of these Saxon folk in general who took part in the English settlements; they can also provide clues to the local origin of some of them in one or other of the two main centres of Saxon population in the Elbe and Weser valleys at this time. The prevalence in England of the fashion for cast saucer brooches is one of the reasons for thinking that a large part of our Saxon population came rather from the Elbe valley settlements, named after the cemetery at Perlberg near Stade, than from the Weser estuary where the type site is Westerwanna.

These are some of the ways in which a study of brooch-types may be useful to historians. It is also worth noting that the differences such personal articles show in form and use may indicate corresponding differences in the style of dress fashionable among the various tribes and cultural groups.[2] Where, for example, it is usual to find on women's bodies

[1] The distributions are well shown in Tischler, 'Der Stand der Sachsenforschung archäologisch gesehen', Abb. 33 and discussed *ibid.*, 99–101.

[2] See several articles by H. Vierck in C. Ahrens (ed.), *Sachsen und Angelsachsen* (Hamburg, 1978), 231–70.

in the cemeteries a pair of similar brooches, one on each shoulder, sometimes linked by a string of beads or a chain, it is evident that the dress was different in style, and required a different method of fastening, from those cases in which only a single brooch is found centrally placed on the chest, and where the accompanying beads, if present, were worn as a necklace. So too, the use of wrist-clasps, a very common fashion among the Angles, suggests that sleeves of a shape which required fastening in this way were more in vogue among them than among those tribes which rarely seem to have needed such fastenings.

The other main category of household goods that supplies useful clues to the origin of different groups of the invaders is of course their pottery. This is not the place to enter into an exhaustive discussion of the various forms and styles of decoration popular at this time in north Germany and Scandinavia. Nor is there any need to trace the styles prevalent at the turn of the fourth and fifth centuries back into earlier times before the invasions began. But it may be useful to indicate some of the more obvious differences in ceramic tradition which help to distinguish the products prevalent among the Angle, Saxon, and Jutish folk on the Continent, and so to make some of these peoples recognizable among the settlers in this country. The known development of pottery styles on the Continent may also be helpful in suggesting the dates at which they became firmly established in Britain.[1]

Fashions in pottery followed at this time roughly the same cultural divisions that have already been noted in considering the brooches. There is a similar broad distinction between the styles in vogue among the northern group of peoples in eastern Schleswig and Jutland, the Danish islands, and southern Scandinavia on the one hand, and those favoured by the Saxons and their neighbours between the Elbe and the Weser, with outliers eastwards in Holstein and westward in Frisia, on the other. The *Nordseekustengruppe* in western Schleswig and Jutland, with southward extensions across the

---

[1] See my *Corpus* for a rough classification and full illustration of the main forms which this pottery may take, especially the Historical Summary (i. 114-27), where the significance of the relationship between the various groups of the English and continental material is discussed.

estuary of the Elbe, is less clearly distinctive as a ceramic region, being influenced by Anglian fashions on the east and by Saxon on the south; it has, however, some characteristic features of its own.

The whole northern *Kulturkreis*, including for the present purpose Bede's continental Angles and Jutes, favoured what may be termed a rectangular style in pottery decoration. Whatever the forms taken by their pottery, whether tall jars, shouldered or globular vessels, or shallow or carinated bowls, there is a tendency for the decoration to follow much the same pattern, with massed or grouped lines or grooves, horizontal on the neck and vertical on the shoulder or body. This linear or grooved decoration is often continuous, giving a ribbed or corrugated appearance to the surface it covers. The pottery is all hand-made, but is often of high quality technically, smooth in fabric, regular in shape, with well-moulded rims, and finished with a dark grey or black surface burnish, reminiscent of polished metal. Curvilinear motifs in the decoration are rarely used, and mostly confined to finger-tip rosettes, small swags, and roundels of various kinds. Raised slashed collars, and the occasional appearance of vertical and horizontal strips overlaid on corrugated surfaces, lead on to a more extensive employment of plastic ornament in the fifth century. This mostly takes the form of shoulder bosses or long vertical bosses which fit easily into the rectangular designs popular in these northern parts.[1] Stamped decoration is almost unknown, but line-and-dot patterns occur (Fig. 3).

Variants of this kind of pottery, characteristic of the continental Angles, occur also in Jutland and through the territory of the *Nordseekustengruppe* down the west side of the Danish peninsula. So far as Jutland is concerned, particular interest attaches in the present context to the occurrence there of a range of bowls and jars, mostly small and of rather squat appearance, with hollow necks and well-moulded rims. They are decorated with simple grooved designs of Anglian type, but including some chevron and

---

[1] A. Genrich, op. cit. Abb. 2, illustrates thirty standard forms which this pottery of the continental Angles may take. See also E. Albrectsen, *Fynske jernaldergrave*, iii (Copenhagen, 1968), for many others. A full range of the English material is in my *Corpus*, ii. especially figs. 206-7, 219-22.

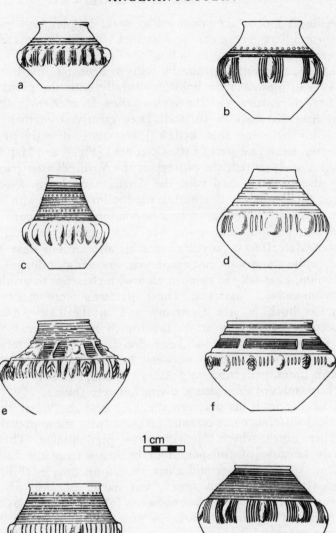

Fig. 3. English and continental pottery of Anglian types

a Bordesholm. b Loveden Hill, Lincs.
c Borgstedt. d Caistor, Norfolk.
e Hammoor. f Caistor, Norfolk.
g Borgstedt. h Newark, Notts.

For sources of figures see p. xiv.

curvilinear motifs accompanied by dots, dimples, and raised slashed collars. These can be matched with similar pots from several sites in Kent, including two pieces from the early *Grubenhäuser* found within the walls of Roman Canterbury.[1] They can moreover be linked culturally with the group of early-fifth-century cruciform brooches from Kent, which also have parallels in Jutland. They greatly strengthen the case for believing that Bede's Jutes came, directly or indirectly, from that part of the Continent (Fig. 4 and Map 5).

As already noted, the pottery of the *Nordseekustengruppe* can also be associated with the Anglian and Jutish *Kulturkreis*. Similar linear decoration predominates here, although the corrugated technique is less common and diagonal or chevron designs are more prevalent, giving less rigidly rectangular effects. Curvilinear motifs also are not unknown and, while stamps are not employed, line-and-dot designs are common, especially in combination with chevrons to produce chevron-and-dot patterns. These patterns were especially popular both in free Germany and in the Late Antique repertoire of Roman art in the fourth and fifth centuries. In Britain this chevron-and-dot decoration is characteristic of the period of overlap between Roman and early Anglo-Saxon times, occurring on pottery,[2] metal, and bone objects on both sides of the cultural divide between them.

The Saxon lands between the Elbe and the Weser show marked differences in ceramic fashions from those prevalent further north where Anglian styles predominate. This is partly because of the persistent influence from the earlier culture of the Chauci and their neighbours long established there from pre-Roman times, and partly because of the intrusive forces from the proto-Saxon folk represented by the Fuhlsbüttel culture of Holstein now extending south and west across the Elbe.

Two pottery forms that arise from these mixed origins seem especially characteristic of the developing Saxon fashions in the years before and after AD 400. One, derived in part from the *Schalenurne* culture of East Holstein, comprises

[1] The English series from Kent is illustrated in my *Corpus*, ii. fig. 279.
[2] e.g. on Group F of the so-called 'Romano-Saxon' pottery: D. B. Harden (ed.), *Dark-Age Britain* (1956), 30, fig. 5, nos. 3–6. Anglo-Saxon examples are illustrated in my *Corpus*, ii. figs. 285–6.

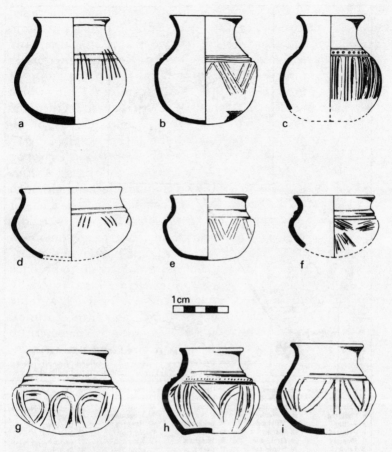

Fig. 4. Jutish pottery
a Beakesbourne, Kent.   *b* Westbere, Kent.   *c* Westbere, Kent.
d Orpington, Kent.   *e* Westbere, Kent.   *f* Hanwell, Mddx.   *g* Sarre,
Kent.   *h* Faversham, Kent.   *i* Howletts, Kent.

For sources of figures see p. xiv.

a wide range of shouldered and carinated bowls, decorated
with linear patterns including curvilinear swags. Some of
these, the so-called *Standfussschalen*, may be mounted on
elegant footstands or pedestal feet, a feature continuing a
tradition that had been common among the Chauci, but in
its earlier form did not last far into the fifth century. Others
are round-bottomed, and this type had a longer period of
development, extending at least to 450. Both sorts are

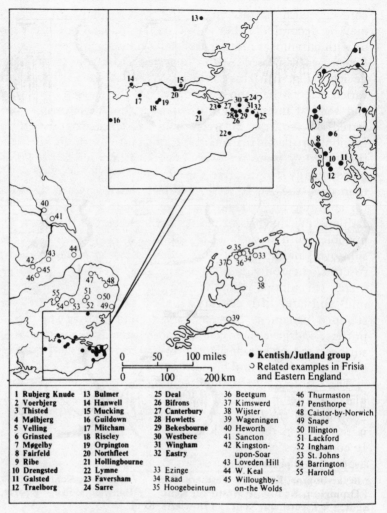

1 Rubjerg Knude	13 Bulmer	25 Deal	36 Beetgum	46 Thurmaston
2 Voerbjerg	14 Hanwell	26 Bifrons	37 Kimswerd	47 Pensthorpe
3 Thisted	15 Mucking	27 Canterbury	38 Wijster	48 Caistor-by-Norwich
4 Mølbjerg	16 Guildown	28 Howletts	39 Wageningen	49 Snape
5 Velling	17 Mitcham	29 Bekesbourne	40 Heworth	50 Illington
6 Grinsted	18 Riscley	30 Westbere	41 Sancton	51 Lackford
7 Møgelby	19 Orpington	31 Wingham	42 Kingston-	52 Ingham
8 Fairfeld	20 Northfleet	32 Eastry	upon-Soar	53 St. Johns
9 Ribe	21 Hollingbourne		43 Loveden Hill	54 Barrington
10 Drengsted	22 Lymne	33 Ezinge	44 W. Keal	55 Harrold
11 Galsted	23 Faversham	34 Raad	45 Willoughby-	
12 Traelborg	24 Sarre	35 Hoogebeintum	on-the Wolds	

Map 5. Distribution of comparable pottery in Jutland and
south-east England

occasionally decorated with a faceted carination, an early
feature which develops later into a continuous row of small
bosses, thus providing one point of origin for the shoulder-
boss bowls common on both sides of the North Sea in the
later fifth century.

The other characteristic ceramic forms common among the
Saxons comprise large urns and jars of rounded or shouldered

contour, with narrow necks and well-moulded rims. They may be decorated either with linear or line-and-dot chevrons, or with curvilinear motifs, especially standing arches, *stehende Bogen*, interspersed with finger-tip rosettes and similar devices (Fig. 5). This style gives rise to looser and more varied effects than those produced by the massed horizontal and vertical lines and grooves which the Angle potters preferred. The contrast between them was accentuated when the fashion for plastic ornament became more pronounced as the fifth century wore on. Curvilinear features lend themselves more readily to the free development of bossed ornament than does the Angle style, whose rigidity leaves little room for anything but straightforward shoulder-bosses. The Saxon fashion, on the other hand, made all sorts of elaboration possible, with designs built up of *stehende Bogen* bosses, split-oval and diagonal bosses, all enriched with finger-tip rosettes, chevron-and-dot patterns, and line-and-groove ornament, to culminate in the extravagant *Buckelurnen* of the mid- and later fifth century (Fig. 6). Before long, moreover, stamped ornament became very popular among the Saxon potters, and gave them yet another means of decorating plain surfaces and of emphasizing the structure of designs built up by the use of lines and bosses.

The whole range of these ceramic developments that took place in the continental lands from which the Angles, the Saxons, and the Jutes sprang in the fourth and fifth centuries is reflected in the pottery of the earlier English settlements. It constitutes a rich and varied source of information on all aspects of the movement, supporting and enlarging in many ways that supplied by the tools, weapons, jewellery, and other personal equipment of the invaders in materials such as metal and bone. Much of the English pottery inevitably reflects, in the mixture of its styles, the tribal confusion already prevalent in the lands from which the invaders came, as well as the dislocation of traditional techniques of pot-making which the movement overseas involved. But it can on occasion identify with unexpected precision the exact continental localities with which some of the English communities were connected. Such links have been noted among the Angles, the Saxons, and the Jutes alike. Among the cremation urns from the Anglian cemetery at Sancton in

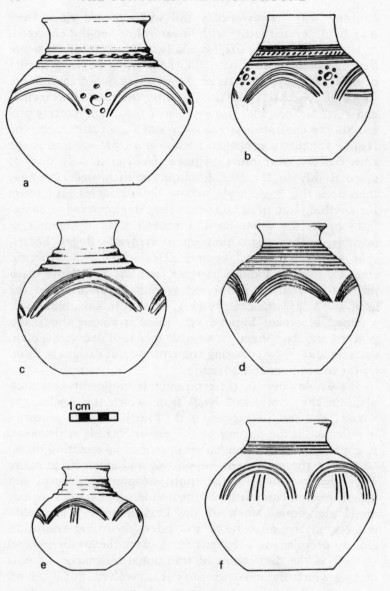

1 cm

Fig. 5. Saxon *Stehende Bogen* pottery
a Zuidlaren.   b Caistor, Norfolk.
c Westerwanna.   d Little Wilbraham, Cambs.
e Westerwanna.   f Elkington, Lincs.

For sources of figures see p. xiv.

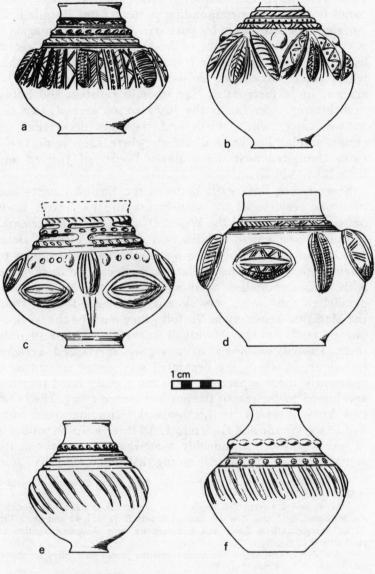

Fig. 6. Saxon *Buckelurnen*

a   Westerwanna.
c   Blumental.
e   Perlberg bei Stade.

b   Sandy, Beds.
d   Luton, Beds.
f   Rushford, Norfolk.

For sources of figures see p. xiv.

East Yorkshire, for example, there are too many close parallels with the corresponding pottery from Borgstedt in Angeln to be explicable by pure coincidence.[1] Then again it is virtually certain that one of the Anglian urns from Caistor-by-Norwich, Norfolk, came from the same workshop as that which made two others, showing the same stylistic idiosyncracies, for cemeteries at Hammoor in Holstein and Sørup in Schleswig.[2] So far as the Jutes are concerned, two tall narrow vases, whose form and elaborate decoration are closely similar, but unparalleled elsewhere, came respectively from Drengsted near the southern border of Jutland and from Bifrons in Kent.[3]

Several such links exist between the English pottery and particular cemeteries or settlements in the Saxon lands between the Elbe and the Weser. Of these the most remarkable are perhaps with Wehden near the Weser estuary. Here, in addition to a number of other pieces markedly similar to English pots, was found an elaborately decorated *Buckelurne* with bosses modelled as human faces. The only known parallel to this—and a very close parallel indeed—came from the Markshall cemetery in Norfolk: they must be the work of one potter.[4] Another Markshall *Buckelurne* is one of only three known examples of a highly specialized ceramic technique, in which the decorated sections of an urn were apparently made separately and subsequently luted together and joined to the rest of the pot in a second firing. The other two known vessels in this unusual technique came from Feddersen Wierde and Gudendorf. All three must be products of one workshop, presumably somewhere among the continental Saxons.[5] It is worth noting that while Markshall is in

[1] J. N. L. Myres and W. H. Southern, *The Anglo-Saxon Cremation Cemetery at Sancton* (1973), 13.

[2] Myres and B. Green, *The Anglo-Saxon Cemeteries of Caistor by Norwich and Markshall*, Soc. Ant. Research Comm. Report 30 (1973), 47 and fig. 3. Urn B2 and the pieces from Sørup and Hammoor are there illustrated together on pls. VIII and IX (a).

[3] See Myres, 'The Angles, the Saxons, and the Jutes', where they are shown side by side on fig. 7, nos. 2 and 4.

[4] These two pieces, Markshall LXX and Wehden 58, are illustrated together in Myres and Green, pls. X and XI. For other links between Wehden and English cemeteries see my *Corpus*, i. 33, 52, 64, 116.

[5] Myres and Green, 255 and fig. 69, no. 84. I am indebted to Dr. P. Schmid for further information about the Feddersen Wierde and Gudendorf pieces and for giving me his views on their method of manufacture.

the heart of Anglian territory in Norfolk, this ceramic evidence links some of its people unmistakably to a Saxon origin, a fact which could not have become known in any other way.

These striking instances of personal contacts between the folk who used particular cemeteries in the Anglian, Saxon, and Jutish regions of the mainland and those who settled in various parts of eastern England, form a natural link between this discussion of the continental background and an enquiry into the British background to the settlements themselves.

4

THE ROMANO-BRITISH BACKGROUND
AND THE SAXON SHORE

I T is no part of the purpose of this book to recount the history of Britain in the later part of the Roman period. Both its political vicissitudes and its changing administrative structure are covered in detail in the relevant chapters of Volume I of this *Oxford History*.[1] The main story can be found better told there, in the context of Britain's place in the declining fortunes of the Roman world. Nevertheless the English settlements with which this book is concerned did not take place in a vacuum. What had so recently been a group of Roman provinces did not suddenly become a *tabula rasa* whose negative character had no effect on the timing or the character of the Germanic settlements. There has been perhaps in the past too strong a tendency to draw a sharp line between Roman Britain and the succeeding centuries, a tendency aggravated by the historical accident that the traditional structure of our educational system has always made the great divide between ancient and medieval history at this point. Historians trained in the classical tradition of Greece and Rome have thus had little incentive to take more than a superficial interest in matters which it was felt could be better explored by those who had grown up in the study of early Germanic literature, antiquities, and institutions. So too, some Dark Age scholars have paid too little attention to the traditions and the social conditions of the later Roman Empire in which the earlier phases of Germanic settlement took place.

In fact however these settlements were made in what had been for some three centuries an integral part of the provincial structure of the Roman Empire. Their character cannot be properly assessed without some idea of the way in which this background may have determined, or at least influenced,

[1] Mainly in Books III and IV, pp. 217–501.

what took place. In particular it is necessary to consider
whether the changeover happened rapidly or gradually, and
in either case when its decisive stage or stages probably
occurred. It is obvious that if the process was sudden and
destructive its results will have been different from the
consequences of a gradual and more peaceful transition. It is
equally obvious that if it took place while the structure of
Romano-British society was still relatively coherent and un-
damaged, the results are likely to have been different from
those that would have followed the takeover of a country
whose people were already in the last stages of political and
economic collapse. Both the date and the speed of the
transition are thus likely to have been significant factors in
determining the nature of the outcome.

It is perhaps best to start this enquiry by considering what
indications there may be of Germanic infiltration into
Romano-British society before the political collapse of
Roman rule. Such infiltration certainly occurred on a
considerable scale throughout the Roman period and by no
means exclusively in its final phases. It is much better documented on the military than on the civilian side. Here indeed
it goes back to the early days of the conquest itself, when
there were eight cohorts of Batavians attached to Leg. XIV
Gemina in the original invasion force under Aulus Plautius
in AD 43.[1] They apparently distinguished themselves by
swimming both the Medway and the Thames in full equipment, a skill which no doubt came easily to tribesmen whose
homeland consisted largely of marsh intersected by water-
courses. Later on, a number of the auxiliary units which for
generations served garrison duty in the forts of Hadrian's
Wall or its hinterland had originally been recruited from
Germanic folk. Thus there was still a mounted cohort of
Batavians posted at Carrawburgh (*Procolitia*) in the third
and fourth centuries, and there were Tungrians at Castlesteads
(*Uxellodunum*) and Birrens (*Blatobulgium*).

Whatever their origin, such units are not likely to have
retained through later generations many obvious links in
blood or culture with their Germanic past. There is little
reason to suppose that they left any sharper racial impression

---

[1] Tacitus, *Hist.* i. 59, ii. 66.

on the population of northern Britain than did the Pannonians or Rhaetians at Great Chesters (*Aesica*) or the Lusitanians at High Rochester (*Bremenium*). It is moreover worth noting that such north German tribes as the Angles, Saxons, or Jutes, who were chiefly concerned with the ultimate take-over of Roman Britain, had either not yet acquired their later individuality, or were too remote from the frontiers in the early days of the Empire to have furnished auxiliary units for the Roman army that can be identified by recognizable versions of their later names.

But even the contingents from the more accessible Germanic tribes whose names do appear among these units would not long retain close cultural or even strong physical links with their continental roots. It was normal for such units, which often remained for several generations posted in the same fort, to be recruited largely from their own children. These must have been mainly the offspring of native British women of whom there is likely to have been a plentiful supply in the *canabae* or *vici*, civilian settlements which soon sprang up round the forts to cater for the miscellaneous requirements of the garrisons. Certainly by the third century, if not earlier, the troops were no longer expected to live wholly in the barrack blocks within the fort walls, and more or less permanent and regular unions led to the proliferation of domestic establishments outside.

There must have been an even more rapid and complete dilution of the material culture familiar to the tribesmen recruited during the first and early second centuries into the auxiliary cohorts of the Imperial army. They would be supplied on enlistment with the standard military equipment of their time. Those of Germanic background would draw not only their weaponry but also their domestic stores such as pottery and other utensils from the same depots and contractors as furnished the needs of cohorts whose ethnic origins were quite different. Archaeologically speaking, it would be difficult if not impossible to determine from the material relics excavated in the barrack blocks and other regimental installations of first- and second-century auxiliary cohorts whether the unit had been recruited originally from Spain, Pannonia, or the Rhineland.

But as time went on the capacity of the Roman army to

absorb, without trace of their ethnic origin, recruits derived from such varying sources, on or beyond the Imperial frontiers, inevitably weakened. By the third century, if not earlier, the system of auxiliary cohorts, mostly still bearing titles indicating their original tribal derivation, was supplemented by the creation of less regular barbarian units known as *numeri* or *cunei*. Several of these formations that served in Britain were of Germanic origin, and it is significant that, unlike the earlier auxiliary cohorts, they could bear names indicating their recruitment from tribes that afterwards took part in the post-Roman settlement of Britain. Thus there was a *cuneus Frisiorum* or *Frisonum* at or near Housesteads (*Vercovicium*) on Hadrian's Wall, and another at Brough-by-Sands early in the third century, which was later moved to Papcastle.[1] A *numerus Hnaudifridi* (Notfried's troop) is also recorded at Housesteads,[2] in close association with the *cuneus Frisiorum* there. The latter carried the name of Severus Alexander, emperor 222-35, and was thus probably recruited in his time.

The Frisian tribesmen concerned in these dedications are termed *cives Tuihanti*, a name which probably associates them with the Germanic war god Tiw, well evidenced later on as a pagan place-name element in Anglo-Saxon England, and in the weekday called Tuesday. It perhaps survives on the Continent in that of the Dutch province of Twente. It is not impossible that the group of people *ex Germania superiori*, whose apparently Germanic names appear on a tombstone also erected near Housesteads, may have belonged to one or other of these Frisian units.[3]

It has recently been pointed out that the so-called 'Housesteads Ware', a type of coarse pottery found not only at Housesteads but at other Roman forts in northern Britain, has its closest parallels on Frisian sites of the second and third centuries in Holland.[4] It is particularly interesting that the distribution of this 'Housesteads Ware' along Hadrian's Wall includes other forts such as Chesterholm and Birdoswald where there is at present no epigraphic evidence for the

[1] S. Frere, *Britannia*, (1967), 186.
[2] *RIB* 1576.
[3] P. Salway, *The Frontier People of Roman Britain* (Cambridge, 1965), 90.
[4] I. Jobey in *Arch. Ael.* 5th ser., 7 (1979), 127-43.

presence of Frisian units. It suggests not merely that the
influx of Frisians into this part of the Roman frontier in
Britain was larger than would otherwise be known, but that,
since the manufacture of domestic pottery was mainly
women's work, the newcomers could have been accompanied
by their families, who would have been familiar with the
local styles of pot-making traditional in their continental
homes.

A particularly significant group of Germanic burials
directly associated with an important Roman military
installation is that from the cemetery at Norton, adjacent to
the fortress of Malton on the east Yorkshire Derwent. These
were recognizable from the mid-fourth-century cross-bow
brooches, accompanied by a belt-buckle and coins of
Constans and Constantius, found with them. They were
probably German officers buried with part at least of their
uniform equipment. Malton probably became the supply base
for the late fourth-century Yorkshire coastal signal stations,
and it is interesting that the garrison there should have
included, perhaps even earlier than their installation, officers
whose equipment points directly to a Germanic origin.

How far such people were able to retain other cultural
peculiarities, such as their personal nomenclature and the use
of their native languages, must remain uncertain. They would
inevitably soon become familiar with enough official Latin
for the efficient performance of their military duties and no
doubt also with enough of its barrack-room equivalent for
less formal communication with more regular Roman troops.
For all epigraphic purposes, tombstones, inscribed altars, and
so on, formal Latin was in universal use. But it has been
suggested that the name of a girl called Ahtehe, whose tombstone was found at Corbridge, indicates, from its use of a
Germanic diminutive form, that her family, who probably
came from the Rhineland, may have spoken German in the
home.[1] So far as personal nomenclature is concerned, there
are instances such as the Notfried, commander of the irregular *numerus Hnaudifridi* at Housesteads already noticed,
or the Dagualdus, a soldier of the first cohort of Pannonians
buried at the Cawfields mile-castle,[2] of German names

---

[1] Salway, op. cit. 228.   [2] Ibid. 232.

remaining virtually unaltered. One may suspect, on the other hand, that some self-confessed Germans, like the Virilis, who set up *RIB* 1102 at Ebchester, may have had their native names translated into Latin. Others like the Mahudas, who also called himself a German and made a dedication to Coventina at Carrawburgh (*Procolitia*), had so disguised their native appellations that the original forms are barely recognizable.

Apart from such more or less regular army units of German origin, whose members may have had some effect on the population of northern Britain, there is evidence for the official settlement of less directly military groups of similar folk in Britain from the later second century onwards. Bodies of Marcomanni were brought over by Marcus Aurelius following his campaigns against that people.[1] In the third century numbers of Vandals and Burgundians were transported to Britain after their defeat on the Rhine frontier.[2] It has been suggested that some of them may have served as *numeri* or *cunei*, though there is no British evidence for units so named.[3] They are more likely to have been settled as *laeti* or *foederati*,[4] with military obligations in times of need, as was happening in similar circumstances at this period in northern Gaul.

The career of Carausius, usurping emperor between 287 and 293, illustrates the extent to which able men of German stock were coming to play a major role in the politics of Britain before the end of the third century. He was himself a Menapian from the Rhine mouths, and the *Classis Britannica*, on which his authority rested, was no doubt largely manned at this time by barbarian sailors from his own and neighbouring tribes on the North Sea coast. It is known that the army of his successor in Britain, Allectus, included a substantial contingent of German mercenaries, for it was regarded as a notable achievement of Constantius Chlorus, the father of Constantine the Great, who suppressed him, that he had moved with sufficient speed after his victory to

[1] Dio Cassius, lxxi. 16.
[2] Zosimus, i. 68.
[3] Frere, op. cit. 220.
[4] Various terms were used to describe different forms of barbarian treaty settlement within the Empire: for the distinctions between them see R. Günther, 'Laeti, Foederati und Gentilen', *Zeitschrift für Archaeologie*, 5 (1971), 39-59.

prevent these now leaderless barbarian troops from sacking London.[1]

The circumstances which led to the proclamation of Constantine as emperor at York in 306 provide a further illustration of the extent to which tribal leaders of German stock, whose authority with the army must have rested on the presence of substantial forces of their own people, were now playing a major part in Romano-British, indeed in Imperial, politics. This event, of crucial consequence for the future of the Roman world, was apparently brought about by one Crocus, described as King of the Alemanni, who had taken part in Constantius Chlorus' last successful expedition into Scotland before his death at York.[2] The initiative taken by Crocus on this occasion indicates the influence which German chieftains of his type could now have with the army, which was by tradition the source of a new emperor's power. It also suggests that Crocus may have had personal reasons for promoting the succession of Constantine to his father's imperial honours. That would be most naturally explained if he had already obtained the consent of Constantius to the settlement of some of his people as *laeti* in the north of Britain, and realized that this arrangement could be best secured for the future by taking a personal lead in promoting the elevation of Constantine.

However that may be, there is good evidence later in the fourth century for the settlement of substantial numbers of Alemanni in Britain. It is known that in 372 an Alemannic king called Fraomar was sent here, with the rank of tribune, by the Roman government following a successful campaign on the Rhine frontier in Gaul. It has been suggested that Fraomar's appointment was to enable him to take charge of Alemanni who were already settled with military obligations in Britain, either as *laeti* or as one or more otherwise unrecorded *numeri*.[3] But Ammianus appears to suggest that Fraomar's transfer to Britain was due to over-population causing unrest among the continental Alemanni, and that the emperor was trying to relieve the pressure there by moving surplus tribesmen to Britain under the command of a

[1] *Pan. Lat. Vet.* (ed. G. Baehrens (Leipzig, 1911)), VIII. xvi. 2.
[2] Aurelius Victor, *Ep. de Caesaribus*, xxxix. 41-2.
[3] Frere, op. cit. 220.

prominent member of their own royal house.[1] Whichever
view is right—and there may well be some truth in both—
there was evidently a substantial settlement of Alemanni
somewhere in Britain by the last quarter of the fourth
century, if not earlier.

If we ask where this settlement is likely to have been, we
are confronted by a tantalizing lack of really convincing
evidence. For the reasons already mentioned one would not
expect such folk, however numerous, to have left many
archaeologically recognizable traces of their presence in
Britain.[2] Whether organized in more or less irregular military
formations on the northern frontier, or planted out as *laeti*
on agricultural holdings in the civilian regions further south,
they would have been quick to adopt the use of standard
Romano-British equipment and household goods with which,
particularly in the Midlands and the south, the country was
still well supplied in the fourth century.

There are however a few chance finds and other slight
indications which suggest that there could have been
Alemannic settlement in Yorkshire and the Humberside area.
It may be significant that the Alemannic king Crocus was in
or near York at the time of Constantine's proclamation as
emperor in 306. The battered remains of a fourth-century
brooch of south German origin—a form otherwise unfamiliar
in Britain—survived to find a final resting place in a mid-sixth-
century Anglian grave at Londesborough in East Yorkshire;[3]
a spearhead and pottery similar to south German types come
from Driffield in the same area; and the early Anglian settlers
who buried their dead in the great cremation cemetery at
Sancton, not far from Londesborough, seem to have been
unexpectedly familiar with ceramic fashions once prevalent

[1] Ammianus Marcellinus, xxix. 4. He describes the tribe as *multitudine
viribusque ea tempestate florenti.*
  [2] No archaeological trace, for example, has ever been located of the
Burgundian and Vandal irregulars who, shortly after their settlement in Britain
during the reign of Probus (276–82), were concerned in the successful suppression
of a rebellious British governor: Frere, op. cit. 189.
[3] Swanton and Myres, 'An early Alemannic brooch from Yorkshire', *Ant. J.*
47 (1967), 43–50: this interpretation of the Londesborough brooch has been
queried by M. Todd (*Ant. J.* 55 (1975), 384–8), but its south German affinities
and probable fourth-century date are confirmed by T. M. Dickinson in *Med. Arch.*
26 (1982), 54–7.

in Mittelfranken and Württemberg.[1] In all these cases the archaeological evidence is consistent with the possibility that cultural links, however tenuous, existed from that period with related tribes in the Alemannic area. And it is not impossible that the hill-fort near Halifax now called Almondbury still retained a tradition that it had once served as a stronghold of the Alemanni, when it was given by Anglian settlers the name *Alemaneberie* which it still bore when Domesday Book was compiled after the Norman Conquest.[2]

South of the Humber in Lincolnshire, as well as in Middle and East Anglia, there are a number of places where very late Roman and very early Germanic remains have been found in close association, without any clear indication either of the specific tribal origin or the circumstances in which their settlement took place. One example, which would clearly repay more detailed exploration, is an unexcavated site in a strategically significant situation at Kirmington on the Lincolnshire Wolds,[3] not far south of the Humber estuary. It has produced surface finds which include, along with late Roman and Romano-Saxon pottery, one of the very few fourth-century German *tutulus* brooches recorded in Britain, and a zoomorphic buckle of the same date and of a form associated elsewhere with settlements of Germanic *laeti* or *foederati*. *Tutulus* brooches of this kind have a wide distribution on the Continent, ranging from Scandinavia, and even Poland, to the Rhineland frontiers of the Empire. They cannot be used to identify closely the tribal affinities of whoever may have brought them to Britain. But their occurrence here is limited to sites where early Germanic and late Roman material occur together, clearly suggesting continuous if not joint occupation.[4]

[1] Myres and Southern, *The Anglo-Saxon Cremation Cemetery at Sancton,* 22-24: see also Myres, *Anglo-Saxon Pottery*, 75, and *Corpus*, i. 26, 56, 117, for other hints of connections between the Anglo-Saxon antiquities of Yorkshire and those of central and south Germany.

[2] The alternative interpretation, that the name merely indicates a common usage of the stronghold by 'all the men', proposed by Ekwall and Smith, was suggested before the other hints of Alemannic presence in Yorkshire had been noted.

[3] *Med. Arch.* 22 (1978), 123-7. The significance of the Kirmington site is considered below p. 180.

[4] As, for example, on the upper Thames at Roman Dorchester and in the very early Anglo-Saxon cremation cemetery nearby at Abingdon.

It is at this point in the story that the problem presented by the Saxon Shore, the *Litus Saxonicum* of the *Notitia Dignitatum*, has to be faced. It is very unfortunate that the earliest use of this phrase to denote the command of a *comes* in Britain, who was evidently in charge of the coastal defences of the country between the Wash and Southampton Water, cannot be precisely dated. Unhappily the *Notitia Dignitatum*, in the form in which it has come down to us, is a composite, or rather a stratified, document, some parts of which comprise records of military commands that are considerably older than other parts. While some sections include units whose names show that they cannot have taken their recorded form before the early fifth century, the dispositions of troops recorded in other parts were certainly outdated and obsolete long before this time.

So far as the *comes litoris Saxonici per Britanniam* (or *Britannias*)[1] is concerned, it is reasonable to suppose that his post did not exist as such before the early fourth century. It was not apparently until the time of Constantine that military commands of this sort, which overlapped the territories of several provincial governors, were created. On the other hand some at least of the coastal fortresses that covered the estuaries and river mouths most likely to attract raiders or invaders seeking convenient landfalls on the east and south coasts of Britain, were certainly in existence in some form or other much earlier. The *Classis Britannica*, which must have needed such bases, had stations at what later became the Saxon Shore forts of Dover and Lympne as early as the second century. Their functions at that time were more likely concerned with routine servicing of the supply routes between Britain and Gaul than in coping with serious raiders or threats of invasion. But several of the later Saxon Shore fortresses, less obviously placed merely to safeguard the Channel crossings, also go back well before the fourth century. Reculver, for example, clearly designed as a base for naval coverage of the Kent coast of the Thames estuary, was certainly in existence by the early third century, as was the earth fort at Richborough at the south end of the Thanet channel.[2] It was probably first reconstructed in stone

[1] *Not. Dig. Occ.* i. 36 and v. 132.   [2] S. Frere, op. cit. 184, 188.

to serve the needs of Carausius (287-93), and it may well have been Carausius who also had Portchester built[1] and created the main system of these coastal fortresses as a unified command. On the other hand, *Anderida* (Pevensey) cannot be earlier than 335; its construction has been plausibly associated with the visit of Constans to Britain in 343, which may have seen the refurbishing of Portchester and the formal completion of the system.[2]

But even this may be too early for the adoption of the title *comes litoris Saxonici*. Ammianus, in recording the death during the *barbarica conspiratio* of 367 (which included Saxons among its participants) of the general who must have controlled these coastal fortresses, calls him *comes maritimi tractus*, not *comes litoris Saxonici*. This suggests that the latter title, even if already official, was not yet in common use. It has even been suggested[3] that the name may not have been given until Stilicho's reorganization of 397. Although this need not be too late for official inclusion in the *Notitia*, one would expect so important a formal change of status to be reflected in Claudian's panegyric references to his hero's activities in British affairs at that time. While, therefore, it is unfortunately impossible to claim that there was an area of Britain officially designated as the *Litus Saxonicum* at any date much before the closing years of the fourth century, it is very probable that both the command and the title it bears in the *Notitia* go back at least to Constans' visit of 343. Ammianus' failure to use the phrase in connection with the events of 367 does not necessarily exclude this. His wording could be due to unfamiliarity with recent changes in the command structure in Britain, or even to a natural reluctance to employ a freshly coined title which seemed to emphasize unduly the extent of Saxon settlement that had already occurred in Britain.

That Saxon settlement did occur on a considerable scale in the fourth century is certain, and it is particularly unfortunate that, for the reasons just given, the date when it reached sufficient proportions to require official recognition is not

[1] B. Cunliffe, *Rome and the Barbarians* (1975), 429.
[2] Frere, op. cit., 348; Cunliffe, op. cit., 430.
[3] P. Salway, *Roman Britain* (Oxford, 1981), 424.

known.[1] Nor is it possible to be at all precise on the form
which it took. It could have meant the settlement of *laeti*
within the bounds of pre-existing estates or on the territories
directly dependent on important towns. This could have
come about by more or less regular arrangement with the
landowners or the local authorities concerned. Or it might
have involved the more spontaneous infiltration of raiders
and squatters on coastal areas whose inhabitants lacked the
will or the power to keep them out. That it was essentially
a coastal settlement in the early stages is indicated by both
phrases, the 'maritime tract' and the 'Saxon Shore', that were
at first applied to it; neither suggests that in the earliest days
a penetration, whether in mass or in depth, beyond the
coastal areas was contemplated.[2]

There can however be little doubt that barbarian settlement was not long limited to a narrow coastal strip. No
attempt seems ever to have been made to contain it by the
construction of any inland *limes* or frontier works. Apart
from the addition of bastions for use as *ballista* platforms
to many town walls throughout the civilian areas of Britain
during the fourth century, the coastal forts on the shore line
itself remained its only formal defensive arrangements. There
is, however, archaeological evidence, thinly spread but un-
mistakable, for the presence on Roman sites all over the
south-east and eastern Midlands of people whose taste in
metal-work such as brooches or buckles, and in pottery,
reflected increasingly as the fourth century wore on the
fashions prevalent on and beyond the formal frontiers of the
Roman world. Most of this material has·been found sporadi-
cally, whether on villa sites like Shakenoak, Oxon., where it
could well indicate the billeting of German mercenaries, or in

---

[1] There is much relevant material in R. Goodburn and P. Bartholomew (eds.),
Aspects of the Notitia Dignitatum, BAR Suppl. ser. 15 (1976), especially the
chapters by J. S. Johnson and M. W. C. Hassall on the Channel Commands and
Britain in the *Notitia*, 81–117. There is no need to discuss here the once popular
notion that the Saxon Shore was so called because Saxon settlement was not
permitted in it. One might as well argue that the Roman Empire was so called
because no Romans were allowed there.

[2] That the Saxon Shore was specifically regarded as a *limes* or frontier zone is
shown by the inclusion of its *comes* in a list of *comites limitum* in the *Notitia
Dignitatum: Not. Dig. Occ.* v. 125–32. For a further historical possibility see post-
script on p. 103.

small towns and villages (*vici*) such as Heybridge in Essex[1] or Dorchester-on-Thames, where again it may imply some official presence, whether civilian or military. With the increasing knowledge now available on the dating of Anglo-Saxon pottery, it is becoming clear that a number of cremation and mixed cemeteries apparently of purely Germanic character include at least a few urns and accessory vessels whose continental parallels put them firmly back in the fourth century, or even in a few instances earlier still.[2]

Before this material had received the more intensive study that has been applied to its elucidation in recent years, the question was often raised why the official title given by Roman authority to this area subject to increasingly intensive barbarian intrusion was the *Saxon* Shore. According to Bede's later analysis, it belonged (apart from the Saxons of Essex and Sussex) rather to the spheres of settlement which he attributed to the Angles of East and Middle Anglia and Northumbria, and the Jutes of Kent. There is no doubt that in Bede's time, and perhaps from as early as the middle of the fifth century, the Angles and tribes closely related to them, of whom the Jutes were one, were the dominant force in the settlement of most of what became eastern England. But there are good archaeological reasons for believing that they had not had exclusive predominance over most of this area in the early stages of the movement. Many years ago it was pointed out by E. T. Leeds that throughout Middle Anglia and Eastern Mercia, and even in the heart of the later kingdom of East Anglia itself, there was much in the way of brooches and other metal-work in the cemeteries and settlements which indicated Saxon rather than Angle origins for the earlier newcomers.[3] In a well-known passage he recalls

[1] Heybridge, on the Blackwater estuary, is a particularly interesting case for the presence of early fifth-century Saxon *Grubenhäuser* within a late Roman *vicus* that must have had significance both as a port and a road centre on the Essex coast: see Drury and Wickenden in *Med. Arch.* 26 (1982), 1–40 and fig. 1, which gives an up-to-date picture of the relationship between the late Roman and early Saxon distribution of archaeological evidence in Essex. There are signs of the destruction of late Roman buildings at several sites in Essex at this time, e.g. at Wickford: *Brit.* 1 (1970), 242.

[2] Myres, *Anglo-Saxon Pottery*, 62–83, and *Corpus*, i. 121–5.

[3] Leeds, *Archaeologia*, 63 (1912), 159–202: his argument was developed in later papers, notably *History*, new ser. 10 (1925), 97–109, *Ant. J.* 13 (1933), 229–51, *Archaeologia*, 91 (1945), 1–106, and elsewhere.

the surprise and delight with which he recognized a very
early form of Saxon saucer brooch that had been recently
recovered from what had until then been thought of as a
purely Anglian cremation cemetery, adjacent to the walls of
Roman *Venta Icenorum* (Caistor-by-Norwich) in Norfolk.[1]
Many other saucer brooches and other characteristic artefacts
similar to those of the Saxon areas on the Continent were
identified by him, or have since been recognized, among the
predominantly Anglian grave-goods in the cemeteries of
Middle Anglia.

Recent work on the pottery from cremation and inhumation burials in Norfolk, Suffolk, and the Cambridge
region has confirmed the conclusions drawn by Leeds and
others from the distribution of Saxon saucer brooches in
what had been regarded, on Bede's testimony, as essentially
Anglian areas. Cremation urns typical of the continental
Saxons in form and decoration occur not only over East
and Middle Anglia, but also further north in some of the
cemeteries of Lincolnshire and Humberside.[2] Moreover many
of these urns belong, on the evidence of similar forms on the
Continent, to the years between about AD 350 and 450.[3]
The ceramic evidence therefore supports the view that there
had been from quite an early date, and well before the
collapse of Roman rule, folk of Saxon antecedents settled
over much of the area that was included in what Roman
authority termed the *Litus Saxonicum*. It would seem that
in using this phrase the government was being more strictly
accurate than has been recognized by some modern scholars.

The distribution of this early Saxon archaeological
material on the *Litus Saxonicum* and in its hinterland is also
of great interest for the pattern which it seems to present on
the map. It appears to bear a distinct relationship to the
principal centres of Roman authority, especially the fortified
towns and Saxon Shore forts, and to sites of villas and *vici*
on or close to the main roads connecting them with one
another. Thus cemeteries adjacent to Roman York, Cambridge,

[1] Leeds, *Early Anglo-Saxon Art and Archaeology* (Oxford, 1936), 39.

[2] Myres, *Anglo-Saxon Pottery*, map 3, illustrates the occasional occurrence
of one early type of specifically Saxon pottery over all these Anglian areas: see
also *Corpus*, i. 119.

[3] Some dated continental parallels to English urns of the type shown in
Myres, *Anglo-Saxon Pottery*, map 3, are mentioned in my *Corpus*, i. 29.

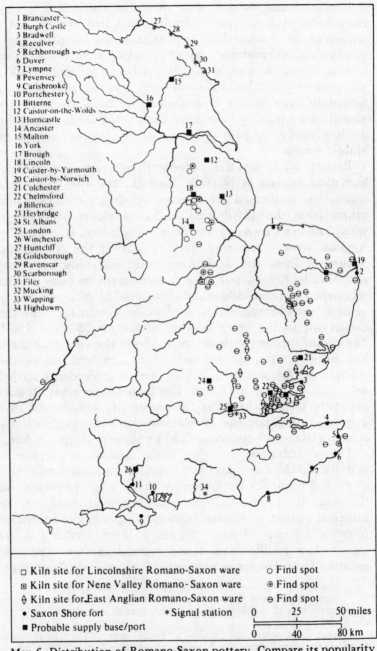

1 Brancaster
2 Burgh Castle
3 Bradwell
4 Reculver
5 Richborough
6 Dover
7 Lympne
8 Pevensey
9 Carisbrooke
10 Portchester
11 Bitterne
12 Caistor-on-the-Wolds
13 Horncastle
14 Ancaster
15 Malton
16 York
17 Brough
18 Lincoln
19 Caistor-by-Yarmouth
20 Caistor-by-Norwich
21 Colchester
22 Chelmsford
 a Billericay
23 Heybridge
24 St Albans
25 London
26 Winchester
27 Huntcliff
28 Goldsborough
29 Ravenscar
30 Scarborough
31 Filey
32 Mucking
33 Wapping
34 Highdown

□ Kiln site for Lincolnshire Romano-Saxon ware   ○ Find spot
◙ Kiln site for Nene Valley Romano-Saxon ware   ◉ Find spot
⌀ Kiln site for East Anglian Romano-Saxon ware   ⊖ Find spot
● Saxon Shore fort   * Signal station   0   25   50 miles
■ Probable supply base/port   0   40   80 km

Map 6. Distribution of Romano-Saxon pottery. Compare its popularity in Essex with the scarcity of normal Saxon pottery there: see p. 130. For the kiln sites and find spots see W. I. Roberts *Romano-Saxon Pottery*, BAR 106(1982).

Caistor-by-Norwich, Caistor-on-the-Wolds (Lincs.), and Colchester, or not far away on roads leading to these walled
towns, have all produced early Saxon as well as Angle
pottery.[1]

It is, moreover, precisely in such contexts that most of the
so-called Romano-Saxon pottery has been found. This
material is of special interest because, while most of it is
technically identical in fabric and finish with the wheel-
made products of Roman commercial industry, it occurs in
forms similar to those familiar in Saxon areas on the
Continent and is decorated with a variety of motifs employed
on the hand-made pottery of those parts.[2] These forms and
motifs also recur among the ceramic material that comes
from many of the purely Germanic cemeteries and settlements used by the earlier Saxon inhabitants of the *Litus
Saxonicum* (Fig. 7).

In view of their source in the Roman commercial potteries
of the fourth century, it is not surprising that these Romano-
Saxon wares had a wide circulation in the principal centres of
population and administration in eastern Britain. They are
found not only in the Saxon Shore forts themselves (e.g. at
Brancaster, Burgh Castle, Bradwell, and Richborough), and in
the principal Roman east coast ports such as Caister-by-
Yarmouth, Felixstowe, and London, but also in other major
Roman towns of the hinterland which no doubt served as their
supply bases, such as Caistor-by-Norwich (*Venta Icenorum*),
Colchester (*Camulodunum*), St. Albans (*Verulamium*), and
York (*Eboracum*). The material also occurs significantly on a

[1] Myres, *Anglo-Saxon Pottery*, map 3 shows many of these sites in relation
to the Roman roads connecting them. Many others could now be added to this
map: see e.g. for Essex, *Med. Arch.* 26 (1982), 2, fig. 1A.
[2] Romano-Saxon pottery was first identified and described by me in D. B.
Harden (ed.), *Dark-Age Britain* (1956), 16–39. Subsequent work has shown that
the types there lettered B–G are the most relevant to the present purpose. A recent
and much fuller descriptive survey of the material by W. I. Roberts (*Romano-
Saxon Pottery*, BAR 106 (1982)) has greatly increased its known quantity and
range and has provided a more comprehensive classification. Unfortunately this
includes a number of types, such as some face-urns, which do not belong to this
category at all. The book is very useful in emphasizing the eastern distribution of
the material in a series of maps which illustrate the various local styles popular on
different parts of the *Litus Saxonicum*. But the commentary is unsatisfactory as
an exposition of the historical significance of these wares, since the author is not
sufficiently familiar with the comparable Germanic pottery fashionable in the last
century of Roman Britain.

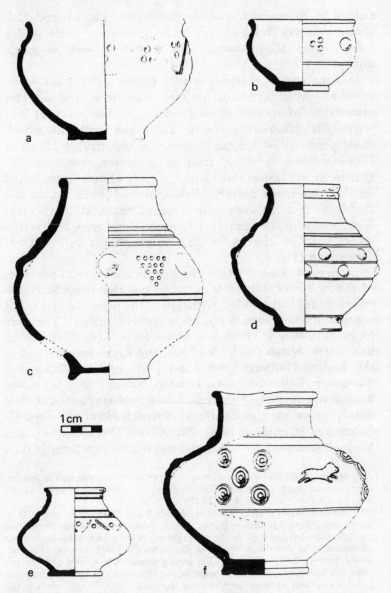

Fig. 7   Romano-Saxon pottery
a Water Newton, Hunts.   *b* Highsted, Sittingbourne, Kent.   *c* Harston, Cambs.   *d* Chesterford, Essex.   *e* Colchester, Essex.   *f* Timworth, Suffolk.

For sources of figures see p. xiv.

number of villa sites,[1] and in the smaller *vici* that lined the Roman road system.[2]

Roman-Saxon pottery is however almost entirely absent south of the Thames Valley except for a few pieces in eastern Kent. This is a fact of some significance for it implies that the earlier phases of Germanic settlement here took a different form, or occurred at a different stage in the breakdown of Roman authority, from what seems to have taken place in the lands bordering the North Sea. The contrast must be directly related to differences in the impact which barbarian raiding and settlement made on the east and south coasts respectively, and to the effectiveness of the Roman reaction to that impact in the two areas in its earlier stages. North of the Straits of Dover it is evident that the eastern coastlands of Britain had been affected by substantial barbarian incursions at least from the early years of the third century, and tentative steps had been taken to meet the danger by about 230 with the building of coastal fortresses at Brancaster and Reculver. But these measures were clearly inadequate to cope with the increasing menace which may soon have led to considerable barbarian settlement on this part of what became the Saxon Shore. Before the time of Carausius (286–93) it had already become clear that communications between Britain and Gaul, as well as the protection of the south coast further west, could only be secured by massive defensive works effectively closing the straits to hostile shipping, or at least preventing pirate fleets which had forced the passage from safely returning with their booty. These works included the building or refurbishing of all the coastal fortresses between Essex and the western borders of Kent by about 275, probably with corresponding bases on the harbours of north-eastern Gaul.

For a while these operations may have secured the essential supply lines between Britain and Gaul and prevented barbarian settlement of the coast between Kent and southern

[1] e.g. at Great Casterton (Rutland), where a complete pot of this type was found in the corn-drying kiln of this villa: Clough, Dornier and Rutland, *Anglo-Saxon and Viking Leicestershire* (Leicester, 1975), 81–2 and fig. 2.

[2] A systematic search of museum stores in the south-east would doubtless reveal much unrecognized and unpublished Romano-Saxon pottery: for the possibilities exemplified by such a search in Essex see Rodwell, *Ant. J.* 50 (1970), 262–76.

Hampshire. But by about 285 it was thought necessary to add Portchester to the western end of the *Litus*, and soon after 335 to fill the gap between it and Kent with a new fortress at Pevensey. Bitterne near the mouth of the Itchen may not have been fortified until about 370.[1]

It would thus appear probable that no substantial settlement of Germanic folk in any way comparable to what had happened a century earlier on the east coast took place in Sussex much before the late fourth century, and even then hardly on a scale to encourage the local potteries to develop decorative fashions of Romano-Saxon type to attract barbarian custom. And within a short time, certainly by quite early in the fifth century, the collapse of the Romano-British economy would have put an end to commercial pottery-making of any kind.[2]

It is of course important not to over-emphasize the significance of this Romano-Saxon material, or to draw from its distribution conclusions that it will not firmly support. Some of the decorative motifs carried by this hybrid pottery, and indeed some of the forms on which it appears, were popular in the fourth century, and even earlier, inside as well as outside the Imperial frontiers. Artistic fashions extended without hindrance across the political limits of the Empire, and it is not always clear whether the source from which they originally arose was among the peoples of free Germany or in Roman provincial society. It has indeed been argued that the inspiration behind some of the decoration popular on Romano-Saxon pottery sprang from the native Iron Age traditions of pre-Roman Britain.[3] In any case there can have been no exclusive use of such designs by folk whose recent origins lay outside the Empire, even if it is possible for archaeologists to point with confidence to the geographical areas in which they had been most at home.

But when all due allowance has been made for these factors it remains true that many categories of this Romano-Saxon

[1] These stages in the growth of the *Litus Saxonicum* are conveniently shown by Cunliffe in *Excavations at Portchester Castle*, Soc. Ant. Research Rept. 32 (1975), 428-31.

[2] The absence of early Anglo-Saxon cremation cemeteries south of the Thames points to the same conclusion that settlement here was both later and less massive than in eastern England at least before the middle of the fifth century.

[3] J. P. Gillam in P. J. Casey (ed.), *The End of Roman Britain*, 103-18.

pottery, whoever may have been primarily concerned in its design and use, were clearly inspired by the corresponding decorated forms popular especially in the Saxon areas of north Germany. Moreover the differences between the two groups largely spring from the technical problems involved in the need to translate designs and decoration appropriate to a hand-made tradition into the wheel-made commercial output of Romano-British kilns. When, however, it is realised that most of this pottery is found on later Roman sites in and behind the *Litus Saxonicum*, it is difficult to resist the conclusion that it was particularly in this part of Britain that there were folk settling who had a traditional liking for pottery formed and decorated in this fashion.

While most of this material whose provenance is known occurs in or above the latest stratified levels of Roman sites, and generally in small and abraded fragments of no individual consequence, a few are larger or more complete pieces found in contexts of special interest in relation to the problems of the Saxon Shore. Two especially, both from Essex, deserve mention here for different reasons. One is a large cremation urn, wheel-made in typical Roman grey ware which came from an extensive and long-used cemetery on the southern outskirts of Billericay, Essex.[1] In spite of its Roman fabric this urn is typically Saxon in form and decoration, with a tall conical neck and twenty-one bosses on the maximum diameter each decorated with a diagonal cruciform motif. Between the neck and the bosses is a zone enclosed by horizontal lines containing line-and-dot ornament, various linear elements, including a probable attempt at a swastika, alternating with groups of dots mostly arranged, rather unsuccessfully, in the form of rosettes (Fig. 8). The vessel contained very inadequately cremated human bones, most being so incompletely burnt as to need breaking up to fit into the pot at all. The burial was conveniently dated not only by its shape and decoration, but by the fact that a Roman stamped colour-coated jar of the fourth century had been inverted over it to act as a lid.

Now cremation had been superseded by inhumation everywhere in the Roman world with the triumph of Christianity

---

[1] Weller, Westley, and Myres, *Ant. J.* 54 (1974), 282–5 and fig. 3.

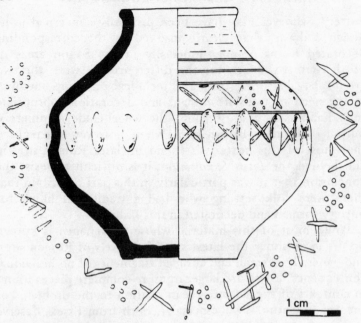

Fig. 8.   Romano-Saxon urn from Billericay, Essex
For source of figure see p. xiv.

at that time, while Germanic paganism still long retained its
ancestral attachment to cremation. It would therefore seem
that this Billericay burial, in its stylistically hybrid urn, must
indicate a Saxon family attempting, not very successfully,
to follow its own burial custom in a land where burning the
dead was now an unfamiliar and difficult ritual. Perhaps it
was not even easy to obtain from the local commercial
potteries what could pass muster as the traditional kind of
container for the incompletely cremated bones.

The second case comes from Chelmsford.[1] It is decorated
on the maximum diameter with two rows of circular bosses,
the upper row alternating with triangular groups of small
dimples, and the lower with large linear six-point stars (Fig.
9). The rim is missing. All the decorative elements of the
design are familiar features of continental Saxon pottery,
especially the hollow bosses, the groups of dimples arranged

[1] Rodwell, op. cit., 262–6 with pl. xxxvii and fig. 2, where it is wrongly
stated to come from Kelvedon: see Roberts, op. cit. 72.

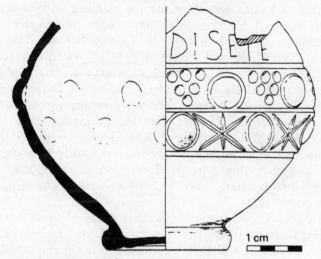

Fig. 9.   Romano-Saxon urn from Chelmsford, Essex
For source of figure see p. xiv.

to form triangles, and the six-point linear stars. But it would
be difficult to find a close parallel on the Continent for their
combination in the arrangement displayed on this piece.
While the potter was evidently acquainted with decorated
Saxon pottery, he shows originality in the use of some of its
commoner features to compose a design of his own.

The most interesting point about this pot is that above
the upper row of bosses it carries a graffito inscription,
incised after firing, which reads DISETE in bold and well-
formed Roman capitals. It cannot be certain that this inscription is complete. Although there are blank spaces before and
after these letters, showing that they form one word, most of
the rest of the pot's neck and all its rim are missing. As it
stands it could be complete and mean 'of (or for) DISETA',
a girl's name in the genitive or dative case, which is recorded
in Roman epigraphic sources, if rarely. But whether the
inscription is complete or not, there is no doubt that whoever
wrote it was well-versed in the use of Roman lettering and
probably had enough Latin to record the association of the
pot with the Latinized form of a girl's name in an appropriate
case. It constitutes firm evidence that the use of at least the
more sophisticated types of Romano-Saxon pottery was not
confined to illiterate German immigrants.

These two pots thus illustrate the blending of two aspects of the cultural life that must have characterized the *Litus Saxonicum* in the last days of Roman Britain. The first shows that wheel-made Roman pottery continued to be available after the influx of Saxon settlers, and could include very plausible imitations of hand-made Saxon urns to satisfy the artistic feeling and the cremation ritual of an immigrant German family. The second proves that these potteries could also produce wheel-made vessels stylishly ornamented with an eclectic variety of motifs in barbarian taste and that this type of decoration could appeal to a literate British family with at least a working knowledge of Latin grammar.

This second pot raises one further point of some interest. Its fragmentary state, and the lack of any record of the circumstances in which it was found, make it impossible to be certain what its original function may have been. It is not out of the question that it was, like the urn from Billericay, a cremation urn, and originally contained the ashes of the girl Diseta, whose name it bears. If the inscription served simply as the label on a cremation urn, the intriguing possibility presents itself that even literate British families of some substance might adopt the Germanic rite of cremation, as some sort of concession to the mixed-up social situation on the Saxon Shore.

It would be possible to illustrate other aspects of this situation by further quotation of particular cases. But perhaps the best way to envisage the characteristics of the Saxon Shore as it developed in the last century or more of Romano-British history is to follow through these years the fortunes of one of the more important centres of its Roman administration, *Venta Icenorum*, Caistor-by-Norwich in Norfolk. Here excavation, both in the town itself and in the Anglo-Saxon cemeteries that adjoin it, has provided a fascinating cross-section of the stages through which this exposed corner of the *Litus Saxonicum* went. Beginning with a Romanized urban centre of an important British tribe, it ended as a deserted ruin almost surrounded by the equally deserted pagan cemeteries of the first Anglo-Saxon settlers, whose Christian descendants soon became part of the newly-formed kingdom of East Anglia under the royal family of the Wuffingas.[1]

Venta Icenorum had originally been laid out in the first century AD with an ambitiously extensive grid of rectangular *insulae*. It was no doubt designed by the Roman authorities as a focus for bringing back the Iceni to more pacific and civilized ways after the traumatic experience of Boudicca's rebellion in 61. But perhaps more than most such Roman attempts to spread the benefits of urban civilization, *Venta Icenorum* seems to have been something of a failure. Apart from the customary provision of forum, basilica, and shops to serve the anticipated administrative and commercial needs in the central parts of the new town, very few substantial buildings were put up. Apparently development was largely confined to small-scale and rather flimsy workshops and other industrial premises designed no doubt to serve the local needs of the neighbourhood. No attempt seems to have been made for a century or more to emphasize the civic status of *Venta* by the building of a circuit of ramparts as a prestige symbol, and many of the outlying *insulae* contemplated in the original scheme seem never to have been built on at all, or at best only with the scattered shacks of a shanty town.

By the middle of the third century, if not earlier, the growing insecurity of what was soon to become the *Litus Saxonicum* was being countered by the building of Saxon Shore forts at Brancaster (*Branodunum*) on the north Norfolk coast, and Burgh Castle (*Gariannonum*) on Breydon Water, a sheltered inlet behind the Roman port at Caister, close to what is now Great Yarmouth. As part of this new system it was obviously necessary to make the unprotected and highly vulnerable cantonal capital inland at *Venta* more defensible, and the present ramparts and flint wall were probably built between 240 and 275. They are strikingly military in layout with almost straight sides and bastioned walls, enclosing a rectangular area of thirty-five acres in the

---

[1] The following pages summarize briefly the story of *Venta Icenorum* and its adjacent Anglo-Saxon cemeteries as contained in Myres and Green, *The Anglo-Saxon Cemeteries of Caistor-by-Norwich and Markshall*, to which reference should be made for the relevant corroborative detail.

middle of the town.[1] There was a gate in the centre of each side. The walls, though roughly on the same alignment, pay no attention to the rectangular grid of roads and *insulae*, so that much traffic would have had to be diverted from the external sections of the existing streets to reach the new gates. Probably as part of the same reorganization of function, the central public buildings of *Venta* were rebuilt, and outlying areas of the shanty town beyond the new defences were largely abandoned.[2]

It was not very long before part of this extra-mural area on the hillside to the south-east was cleared of its remaining shacks and workshops whose debris was spread to make a more or less open space. This soon began to be used as a cremation cemetery for Anglo-Saxon newcomers. Much the same treatment was given to another suburban area at Markshall, just beyond the river Tas north west of *Venta*, which was also developed as a Germanic cremation cemetery clearly related to the town.

Just when these developments took place is not certain. The site of the Markshall cemetery has unfortunately been destroyed by comparatively recent quarrying and building, and nothing remains from it but a large quantity of broken-up cremation urns and some small objects probably associated with them as grave-goods. But at the eastern (Caistor) cemetery, much of which has been excavated in controlled conditions, it is significant that no evidence has been found to indicate continued occupation of the shanty town that preceded it after the end of the third century. Moreover a considerable number of the Germanic cremation urns can hardly be dated any later than the middle of the fourth. It is therefore quite possible that the earliest Anglo-Saxon folk, whose dead were buried in these cemeteries, were established somewhere close at hand, as part of the same programme that had involved the layout of the new defences and the

[1] It is not certain that the bastions are part of the original *enceinte* since the flint construction makes it difficult to tell whether they are butt-jointed to the wall or integral with its construction. The similarity of the defensive layout to that of the earlier Saxon Shore forts makes it probable that they are original features of the plan. See J. S. Wacher, *Towns of Roman Britain* (1974), 235-6.

[2] Myres and Green, op. cit. map 1 shows the relationship of the third-century defences to the earlier street grid and of both to the nearby Anglo-Saxon cemeteries of Caistor and Markshall.

reconstruction of the central buildings of the town. Their arrival cannot in any case be dated more than half a century later. One has thus to envisage a considerable overlap in time between their coming and the final extinction of Romanized life within the walls of *Venta*.

During this overlap the relations between the urban population of the town and their new barbarian neighbours are far from clear, but there is no reason to suppose that they were intimate. The living-quarters of the newcomers have not so far been located but it is reasonably certain that they were not lodged in any numbers within the walls. The fairly intensive excavations of the principal Roman buildings followed the publication in 1930 of a dramatic air photograph displaying in very clear crop-marks the whole layout of Roman *Venta*. Neither this photograph nor the excavations revealed any remains of barbarian occupation in the form of *Grubenhäuser* or areas of post-Roman domestic rubbish, of the kind that have been found in some other Romano-British towns such as Canterbury and Dorchester-on-Thames. The only indications of a possible barbarian presence within the walls took the form of chance finds. They included a number of pieces of Romano-Saxon pottery and some bronze objects, belt-buckles, strap-ends, and so on, of types that were in use in the late fourth and early fifth centuries. These could have been part of the equipment issued to barbarian *laeti* or worn as uniform insignia by civilians in Roman service.[1] Though these must indicate some continuing official occupation, there was hardly enough of such material to prove the presence of a regular barbarian garrison quartered in the town. On the other hand, the existence of the two very early Anglo-Saxon cemeteries so close at hand implies that the communities they served had some official functions in connection with the protection of *Venta* and the maintenance of its services as the main civic centre of this part of the Saxon Shore.

Owing to the unfortunate destruction of much of the evidence from the Markshall cemetery it is difficult to be certain exactly what historical reasons led to the provision of two separate Anglo-Saxon burial grounds, one on each side

---

[1] Ibid., 31–4, 41–2, and fig. 64.

of the Roman town. From what remains it seems likely that
there was no great difference of time between their establishment, for both have produced pottery comparable to wares
in use on the Continent in the fourth century if not earlier.
It may be significant that the fragmentary remains from
Markshall included an unusually high proportion of early
urns of Saxon type, while at Caistor there is a remarkable
collection of purely Anglian forms along with a number of
Saxon vessels. Although it is not possible to claim with confidence that these cemeteries were intended to serve the needs
of two communities of different racial antecedents, it
remains likely that some such distinction is the reason for
their separate establishment in the first place. However that
may be, the cultural distinction between them did not long
persist, for the bulk of the later contents of both cemeteries
consists of the usual stylistic fusion of Angle and Saxon
elements that is normal in the later part of the pagan period.[1]
The two communities, if originally separate, evidently
merged culturally into the same Anglo-Saxon amalgam that
eventually prevailed throughout East and Middle Anglia.
This fusion may have begun before the last flickers of
Romano-British life had been finally extinguished in the
walled town that lay between them.[2]

This story of the latter days of *Venta Icenorum* thus
provides an unusually complete picture of life and death on
the Saxon Shore in the fourth and fifth centuries. It may
well be that, with all allowance made for differences in local
topography, it is typical of what may have occurred at a
number of other centres of Roman culture and administration
in eastern Britain at that time. Several other Roman walled

[1] The point is further discussed in my *Corpus*, i. 119.

[2] It was originally supposed, at the time of the excavations in the Roman
town, that a large deposit of human remains found in one of the latest occupied
buildings represented a massacre pointing to a violent conclusion to *Venta*'s
life. But it has since been shown that these remains did not comprise complete
bodies but *disjecta membra*, including a disproportionately high number of skulls.
They had evidently been removed from the clearance of an earlier deposit elsewhere and had then been used with other rubbish to fill the empty spaces of a
ruined hypocaust. While this gruesome deposit may thus indicate the partial
remains of a massacre somewhere else in the town or merely the clearance of an
earlier cemetery, it cannot be interpreted, as first supposed, as evidence for the
mass slaughter of some of the last Roman inhabitants of *Venta Icenorum* in one
of its latest occupied buildings: see Myres and Green, op. cit. 33-4.

towns in these parts of the country show similar topographical evidence for the close proximity to their defences
of one or more Anglo-Saxon cremation cemeteries. Though
few of these have been explored as thoroughly as the Caistor
cemetery at *Venta*, a number of them have produced
evidence, in pottery or bronze objects, of a probable origin
well before the last days of urban life in the towns with
which they are associated. Thus York (*Eboracum*) has several
early cemeteries, notably those at the Mount and at Heworth
in its immediate vicinity. At Leicester (*Ratae Coritanorum*),
the Thurmaston cemetery is not far off up the Fosse Way,[1]
and other early Anglo-Saxon burials have been found close
to the Roman walls around the East Gate and at Westcote,
with fifth-century pottery in the High Street. At Cambridge,
the St. John's cemetery is only just across the Cam from the
centre of what Bede termed the '*civitatulam quondam
desolatam*',[2] other early pots have been found in the town
itself, and the large cemetery on the site of Girton College is
close at hand on the Roman road to the north-west. Even
at the little walled town of Ancaster (perhaps *Causennae*),
on the Roman road south from Lincoln, and at Great
Chesterford, Essex,[3] there is evidence for early cremation
cemeteries outside their Roman gates.

It will be necessary to defer until the next chapter a discussion of the relationship between the early Saxon settlers
on the *Litus Saxonicum* and the Angles and Jutes, who
eventually became the dominant element in the occupation
of most of eastern Britain. At this point it may be as well
to draw attention to signs of an early Saxon presence at a
few places not so clearly related to the Roman administrative
pattern as those that have been considered so far. There are,
for example, a few pieces of distinctively Saxon pottery that
can hardly be dated much after 400 at various points in the
Thames Valley. Characteristic of these is the pedestal pot, of
the form known to German scholars as *Standfussschalen*,

    [1] P. W. Williams, *An Anglo-Saxon Cemetery at Thurmaston*, Leicestershire
Museum Archaeological Repts., 8 (Leicester, 1983).
    [2] *HE* iv. 19.
    [3] Myres, appendix to V. I. Evison in *Berichten van de Rijksdienstvoor het
Oudheidkundig Bodemonderzock*, 19 (1969), 169-71, discusses five early graves
from the Great Chesterford cemetery.

from the Mitcham cemetery in Surrey,[1] and fragments of similar vessels have come from Ham on Thames-side near Richmond, from Sutton Courtenay and Dorchester on the upper Thames, as well as from the Mucking cemetery and settlement overlooking the Thames estuary in Essex.[2] There is an urn with simple *stehende Bogen* decoration from Shepperton in Middlesex,[3] and a notable group of the same early type from the Abingdom cemetery on the Thames above Dorchester. Urns of this kind can be paralleled at many sites in the homelands of the continental Saxons between the Elbe and the Weser, where most of them appear to date between 350 and 450.[4] It is quite reasonable to treat the occurrence in England, at least of the earlier examples of the type, as a sign of increasing expansion of Saxon influence as it spread from the *Litus Saxonicum* at, or even before, the final collapse of Roman rule in Britain.

This evidence from the pottery is strikingly borne out by that of the decorated buckles and belt-fittings of late-fourth- and early-fifth-century types that have been associated by S. Hawkes with penetration up the Thames Valley from the *Litus Saxonicum*.[5] Such pieces have been found in the coastal fortresses at Richborough (Kent) and Bradwell (Essex), at Mucking and elsewhere on the lower Thames, in London, at Croydon (Surrey), on the upper Thames at Dorchester, and in the Saxon cemetery at Cassington (Oxon.). A few also occur further north in East Anglia. Such equipment indicates an official presence, whether civilian or military, emanating from the last days of Roman rule, and the correspondence of their distribution with that of the earliest groups of Anglo-Saxon pottery found in Britain suggests an obvious connection between them. But to place this early Saxon penetration of the Thames Valley in its

[1]   For its date see Myres, *Ant. J.* 55 (1975), 93–5.
[2]   Myres, *Corpus*, ii. fig. 201: the Thames Valley distribution is shown in Myres, *Anglo-Saxon Pottery*, map 5 and discussed 77–83.
[3]   Myres, *Corpus*, i. 29 and ii. fig. 163. This urn is very like a continental example of the style, Westerwanna 1687, found with a fourth-century brooch.
[4]   Myres in Biddle, Lambrick, and Myres, *Med. Arch.* 12 (1968), 35–41, and Myres, *Corpus*, i. 28–9. For their distribution in England and its relevance to the settlement of the Saxon Shore see Myres, *Anglo-Saxon Pottery*, 44 and map 3.
[5]   *Med. Arch.* 5 (1961), 10–21 and fig. 4 which shows the distribution of the relevant Types IIIA, IV, VA, VI, and VII of this metal-work.

proper context it is necessary to relate it to the evidence for the last phase of the *Litus Saxonicum* on the south coast between the borders of Kent on the east and the Isle of Wight and southern Hampshire on the west. This will be attempted in the next chapter.

POSTSCRIPT

It may be no more than a coincidence that the vast Saxon diocese of Dorchester/Lincoln, which by the late tenth century had come to cover all the eastern Midlands between the upper Thames Valley and the Humber, corresponded more or less closely to what must once have been the internal frontier districts of the *Litus Saxonicum*. In its final form this unwieldy diocese was a product both of the wars between Mercia and Wessex and of the Danish invasions. But it is tempting to think that whatever structural unity it eventually achieved may have owed something to the *limes* of the *Litus Saxonicum* which preceded it over much the same ground in the fourth century. Its development is well shown by the maps in J. Cook and T. Rowley (eds.), *Dorchester through the Ages*, Oxford Univ. Dept. for External Studies (1985), 37. See also p. 85 n. 2.

5

SAXONS, ANGLES, AND JUTES ON THE SAXON SHORE

IN seeking, as has been attempted above, to trace the Germanic settlement of Britain back to its beginnings in the Roman period, it has inevitably been necessary to concentrate attention on the evidence for a substantial Saxon element in the earliest stages of the process. In giving this priority to the Saxons we are doing no more than following the contemporary usage of the Romans themselves. It was, after all, Roman administrators who had given the Saxon Shore its name, and their example was followed by most of the writers within the Empire, such as Sidonius Apollinaris, who had occasion to refer to the barbarian sea-robbers who were still ravaging the coastlands of Gaul and Britain alike in the fifth century.

In this usage a fashion was started which became almost universal, not only among Latin writers but also among the Celtic peoples of the west, whose early contacts with the Germanic invaders would mostly have come through Latin-speaking and Latin-writing officials, whether civilian or military, of the occupying power. This general use of the word 'Saxon' to cover Germanic folk of all kinds has been extraordinarily long-lived. It has led to many difficulties experienced by historians intent on distinguishing the various independent strains of Teutonic people which eventually merged to form the English nation. Thus the Celtic peoples, following in this respect the usage of their Latin-speaking ancestors, continued for centuries to label all the Germanic inhabitants of Britain as Saxons. Even Penda of Mercia, sprung apparently from the purest Angle stock in England, the old royal family of Angeln itself, appears in the Welsh annals as 'Panta the Saxon'. To this day it is rather the Sassenach than the Angle or the Jute whose name is used in Celtic circles to contrast the English unfavourably with the native inhabitants of Wales or Scotland.

However inconvenient this tradition may be for modern scholarship, it was quite natural that a single name should be given in the third or fourth century to the whole group of north German peoples whose homes lay along the coastline beyond the Franks, and whose behaviour was associated in the popular mind with desperate valour and barbarity, and their appearance with a trail of burning farmsteads, wrecked villages, and a panic-stricken countryside. To the frightened provincial the precise ethnology of those who looted his villa was a matter of indifference: Angles or Jutes, they were all Saxons to him.

It is important to appreciate the historical implications of this fact. It means, to begin with, that Saxons, in the restricted sense that the word bore at any rate by Bede's time, must certainly have been a major, and perhaps a dominant, factor among the sea-roving peoples who proved such a menace to the peace of both Britain and Gaul in the last centuries of Roman rule. On the other hand it cannot be assumed that every reference to Saxons in the literary sources for that time should be taken only in that restricted sense. It does not necessarily imply that the folk in question came solely from the coastlands between the Elbe and the Weser, which in Bede's time were known as the home of the Old Saxons. Indeed a writer who used the term may have had no idea where they came from, beyond a general notion that it was far away along the little known and treacherous shores that extended indefinitely east and north into the misty distances beyond the Rhine mouths. For all he knew or cared, they might come from Jutland or from the Baltic lands beyond the Cimbric peninsula. To Roman and Celtic writers alike the word Saxon soon came to lose any precise geographical or ethnic significance; it became not much more than a term of abuse detached from tribal implications, much as Vandal or Hun have become in English usage of more recent times.

None the less, there must be some historical significance in the fact that the Saxons rather than the Angles, the Jutes, or any other group of Germanic tribesmen, achieved this unenviable priority as the prototype of northern barbary. It may well be that as late as the seventh century some more solid memories of the past than mere literary convention would dictate underlay the unexpected use by the Christian

Angles of Northumbria of occasional phrases implying continuing consciousness of a Saxon element in their origins. When, for example, Wilfrid, Bishop of York, an Angle of noble birth, can describe himself to the Pope as *Episcopus Saxoniae*, or Abbot Hwaetberht can address a letter from Wearmouth in Northumbria *de Saxonia*,[1] it can hardly be that they were strangely claiming a Saxon association in any pejorative sense, or even perhaps merely as a literary conceit. It is surely more likely that they were using a term that had been familiar in describing eastern England as a whole since the days of the Saxon Shore.[2] It may even have been intended still to convey a hint of continuity with the far-off days *dum adhuc Romani Britanniam incolerent*. And if this was, even half-consciously, their intention, the archaeological evidence for an early Saxon element in the population of eastern Northumbria, noted in chapter 7, shows that they had grounds for their belief.

The fact remains however that in the long run Roman Britain, in spite of its extensive Saxon Shore, came to be called England and not Saxony. We have still to enquire what historical forces may have been involved in this significant change in nomenclature. There have of course always been regions where the Saxon name persisted, such as those that eventually became Essex, Middlesex, Sussex, Surrey,[3] and parts of eastern Wessex. These, along with Kent, continued to comprise a substantial southern section of the lands covered by the original *Litus Saxonicum*. No direct continuity from Roman times can be proved for the use of these Saxon names, but it is possible that they constitute a link, however tenuous, with the last days of Roman Britain, before other folk such as Angles and Jutes came to dominate

---

[1] Eddius, *Vita Wilfridi*, 30, and Bede, *Hist. abbatum*, 19.

[2] This use of the word Saxonia for eastern Britain goes back at least to the fourth century. It occurs, for example, in a Greek inscription which mentions the military exploits of Count Theodosius in Σαξωνεία: R. Egger, 'Der erste Theodosius', *Byzantion*, 5 (1930), 30, Abb. I. This is an obvious reference to his suppression of the *barbarica conspiratio* of 367 which affected the Saxon Shore in Britain: it has nothing to do with Batavia, as suggested by P. Bartholomew, *Brit.* 15 (1984), 182–4.

[3] Though the word Surrey does not in itself specifically refer to Saxon settlement, it does mean the 'southern region', and this can only imply a very close original relationship with the Saxons of Middlesex and Essex north of the Thames.

the scene and finally put an end to the former military and administrative arrangements of the Saxon Shore.

It is worth noting some factors that contributed to this change. There seem to be no traces of a nominal link with the Saxon Shore persisting in what became East and Middle Anglia north of Essex. It would appear that the belt of heavily wooded country that lies between Essex and these later Anglian regions became before long not merely a geophysical but also a political frontier. Its early importance has certainly left traces on the modern map. Thus several of the main roads that had penetrated it in Roman times went out of use in the Saxon centuries.[1] This break both in nomenclature and in the pattern of communications must imply that a moment came in these dark post-Roman centuries when folk of specifically Angle origin superseded those of Saxon antecedents (however widely the term Saxon might be understood) as the dominant element in the settlement of the country northwards from this area.

Thus when East and Middle Anglia, Lindsey, and Deira came to be regarded, as they were in Bede's time, as the homes of Angles rather than Saxons, there must have been good historical reasons for the change in the name of this part of the Saxon Shore. It has recently been suggested by German scholars that when the main tide of migration to Britain took place in the fifth century, the Angles on the Continent were already becoming the dominant element in the *Mischgruppe* of peoples pressing south-westward into Frisia from all the lands around the lower valleys of the Elbe and the Weser. There is no doubt that this southward pressure of Angles, Jutes, and related tribes was a major force behind the migration to Britain at this time. If in fact the Angles played a leading part in the movement, that might well account for the substitution of their name for that of the Saxons over so much of eastern Britain. It would mean that in the fifth century, as distinct from what had happened in the fourth or the third, the main impetus was now coming

---

[1] I. D. Margary. *Roman Roads in Britain* (1967), 245 and fig. 9. It can be seen that there are long gaps in road 322 north from Colchester to Long Melford, and in the so-called *Via Devana* (road 24) running north-west between Colchester and Sible Hedingham. There is a similar gap in this area in road 33a south-west of Long Melford, and the course of what must have been an original continuation of road 330 south from Bildeston to Stratford St. Mary has never been located at all.

from what German scholars have termed a *Grossstamm der Angeln*.[1] It would have incorporated all the restless peoples on the north German and Frisian coasts under the leadership of Angle or Jutish chieftains pressing down from Jutland, Schleswig, and the Baltic lands beyond the lower Elbe.

For the dating of this movement, so far as it affected eastern Britain, the archaeological evidence is less specific than could be wished. This is partly due to the fact that the cremation pottery of Angeln and Fyn, much of which is closely related in form and decoration to what appear to be the earliest Anglian styles in Britain, is far less easy to date than that from the Saxon areas around the Elbe and Weser valleys. This is because the continental Angles were, for some reason, less accustomed to include brooches and other datable grave goods along with the burnt bones and ashes in their cremation urns. There is thus far less material available for correlating the developing styles in pottery and metal-work, and for relating both to the passage of time by comparison with more securely dated series elsewhere.

Albrectsen, in his massive publication of the pottery of Fyn, was inclined, when the earlier volumes were issued, to date his Period III, which includes many examples of types that can be closely paralleled in Britain, as early as 325–400.[2] Such an early dating, well within the last century of Roman rule in Britain, would make it necessary to envisage a substantial Anglian settlement on parts of the *Litus Saxonicum* some time before the collapse of Roman authority. It remains true that many features of his Period III pottery relate more happily to fourth- than to fifth-century fashions elsewhere. But Dr. Albrectsen is now prepared to agree[3]

[1] e.g. G. Osten in *Niedersächsisches Jahrbuch für Landesgeschichte*, 51 (1979), 77–136. But he overstates the case for Angle dominance south and west of the Elbe in the fifth century by claiming, for example, that the Perlberg culture in this area was rather Angle than Saxon. There is no reason to believe that this was so. Indeed, the prevalence of saucer brooches rather than cruciform brooches, and of Saxon rather than Angle types of pottery, in these parts is clear evidence to the contrary. The close archaeological connection of the Perlberg people with the settlers in the parts of south-eastern Britain that had always been associated with the Saxon name shows that, if they were ever included in Osten's *Grossstamm der Angeln*, this was the outcome of political rather than cultural forces.

[2] E. Albrectsen, *Fynske jernaldergrave*, iii (1968), 303–19, especially 319 and fig. 64.

[3] I am greatly indebted to Dr. Albrectsen for clarifying his position on this point in subsequent correspondence.

that the style may have persisted much longer and that, especially in Britain, its popularity can have centred rather on the early to mid-fifth than on the late fourth century.

If this is so, the main movement of these peoples into Britain, with its change of emphasis from a Saxon to an Anglian basis, seems to fit readily into the historical situation in the first half of the fifth century. There are hints of such a movement in the literary sources. Thus the *Anglo-Saxon Chronicle* (E) records an appeal in 443 (446) from the Britons to the 'chieftains of the Angles', which may well represent a tradition independent of Bede's story.[1] This would seem to be the first dated mention of Angles, as a people likely to be interested in a movement to Britain, to appear in the literary traditions of this time.

Much the same situation seems to be portrayed in the brief notices that have been preserved in various sources regarding the earlier career of Hengist, the traditional founder of the Kentish royal family. He may well have been among those 'chieftains of the Angles' who were in a position to respond to an appeal for assistance in the defence of sub-Roman Britain, whether against Picts and Scots or any attempt at reconquest on the part of the Roman authorities in Gaul. He is portrayed as a man of noble stock from among the Jutish neighbours of the continental Angles who was in exile in Frisia, where he had taken part in activities which apparently breached the heroic code of conduct of the time and made his return home impossible or at least unwise.

Here seem to be hints of a story which could well exemplify, in personal terms, the processes which led to the formation of the *Grossstamm der Angeln*, which archaeology suggests as the dominant force now overrunning the earlier Saxon and Frisian peoples settled on the north German coast. There may well have been many foot-loose chieftains from Jutland or southern Scandinavia like Hengist, or indeed like Beowulf later on. Such men could find plenty of good or bad reasons for leading a mixed band of followers in search of fame or fortune overseas in the fifth century. It only needed an appeal from such sub-Roman rulers in Britain

---

[1] Its independence of Bede is suggested by the fact that Bede's own account of the *Adventus* is itself summarized in the same version (E) of the *Chronicle* under the year 449: see also Myres, *Anglo-Saxon Pottery*, 99.

as Vortigern, like that recorded in the *Anglo-Saxon Chronicle* 443 (E), to set them off on an adventure from which there might well be no return.

The evidence from Britain would suggest that such adventures could take several different forms. The situation that developed out of the earlier Germanic settlements in Kent and the south-eastern sections of the old *Litus Saxonicum*, where relatively orderly arrangements seem to have been made on a federate basis, differed greatly from what took place in the areas of Anglian settlement further north. Gildas is perhaps deliberately vague in locating the lands taken up for barbarian settlement at this time as being in general terms *in orientali parte insulae*. He may have had no more information than has come down to us of the precise arrangements, if there were any such, that led to the settlement of all the regions that Bede attributed to Anglian occupation. Arrangements could have been made, for example, to provide for the special protection of such surviving towns as York or Caistor-by-Norwich by the barbarian garrisons whose early cremation cemeteries adjoin them. If any such *foedera* ever existed, they were evidently lost and forgotten in the turmoil and confusion that followed, as Gildas records, the eventual collapse of Vortigern's scheme for regulated federate settlement.

That there was such a collapse as he describes is certainly a very natural deduction from the archaeological evidence that has survived in Bede's main areas of Anglian settlement. It is in just these parts that the great cremation cemeteries of East Yorkshire, the middle Trent valley, Lincolnshire, Norfolk, Suffolk, Cambridge, Leicestershire, and the other lands around the southern and western margins of the Fens are to be found. Such widespread evidence as these cremation cemeteries provide for the prevalence of a non-Roman, non-Christian, attitude to the problems of death and burial implies a massive settlement of folk whose contact with, and influence by, the surviving Romano-British population was minimal. It is true that this contrast was already evident in the close association of barbarian cremation cemeteries with the Roman walled towns in this part of Britain. But it becomes much more obvious in the development of many other cremation cemeteries which appear less directly related to the Roman administrative pattern of towns and roads.

The siting of several of these cemeteries, such as Loveden Hill or Kirton Lindsey in Lincolnshire, seems to be determined not by any significant features of the Roman landscape but by the presence or proximity of a prehistoric burial mound, whose numinous atmosphere may have appealed to the newcomers as appropriate for their own sepulchral purposes. This was in fact a burial custom which they brought with them from the Continent. Several of the great cemeteries of this period in the German homelands, such as Galgenberg bei Cuxhaven, were centred on burial mounds of Neolithic or Bronze Age date.[1] The transference of this custom to Britain suggests that, in what may be termed the post-federate phase of uncontrolled Anglian settlement, the choice of cemetery sites had ceased to be determined by the administrative topography of Roman authority. It now depended, as no doubt did also the location of most new village communities, on the unfettered will of the invaders.[2]

On the other hand, in Essex, Kent, and all the regions south of the Thames as far west as central Hampshire, the situation in the fifth century seems to have taken a radically different form. However much it may have varied in detail from one area to another it presents one major contrast. Common to all these southern parts is a virtually total absence of large purely cremation cemeteries, and where cremation occurs at all, it nearly always forms a comparatively minor component in cemeteries that consist predominantly of inhumation burials. Even in the upper Thames Valley west of Reading, where there are plenty of signs of fifth-century settlement, cremation forms a significantly large component in only a few cemeteries.[3] Nowhere do the

---

[1] The point is further discussed in Myres, *Anglo-Saxon Pottery*, 121-2.

[2] I have pointed out elsewhere (op. cit. 103) how this decreasing dependence on the administrative topography of Roman Britain can be illustrated from the contrast between the distribution of some early fifth-century types of Anglo-Saxon pottery and those of the second half of the century.

[3] Abingdon with 82 cremations and 119 inhumations from the excavated part (about two-thirds) of the cemetery has the highest proportion of cremations. Long Wittenham has 46 recorded cremations and 188 inhumations. No other upper Thames cemeteries show such a high proportion of cremations: see Biddle, Lambrick, and Myres, *Med. Arch.* 12 (1968), 35, and J. R. Kirk in D. B. Harden (ed.), *Dark-Age Britain*, 123-31.

numbers of cremations exceed, or even approach, those of inhumations in any substantial burial ground that has been sufficiently explored for the figures to be statistically reliable. In all this region the links with Middle Anglia were evidently close and persistent. Mixed cemeteries are normal there also, outside the main cremation area of Norfolk, Suffolk, Cambridge, and parts of Leicestershire and Northamptonshire.

Cremation, wherever it occurs in massive numbers, is a clear sign of Anglo-Saxon settlement in sufficient density, or so well organized, as to be uninfluenced by the native culture of Romano-British society. On the other hand it is much less easy to interpret with confidence the meaning of·the mixed cemeteries. Inhumation was not unknown as a burial rite in the German homelands. It is particularly common in those parts most open to Roman cultural influence, whether from proximity to the frontiers, from recruitment of the local tribesmen into Roman service, or from the development of trade. Wherever Christian influence had begun to infiltrate German society one of its first consequences had been to induce what E. T. Leeds termed a 'flight from cremation'. It may well be, therefore, that the mixed cemeteries of the upper Thames Valley and the southern Midlands as a whole are evidence, not so much for the continuing strength of Romano-British cultural influence as for a higher proportion among the newcomers of folk who had already adopted, or were ready to adopt, inhumation as their normal burial rite.

A great deal more information than is at present available on the comparative dating of these different rituals in the mixed cemeteries is needed to settle this question. Without this information it is not possible to be at all certain whether the 'flight from cremation' had already occurred among many of these intrusive folk before their arrival in this country, or was mainly brought about by a process of assimilation to the habits of the sub-Roman Britons among whom they settled. Wherever there was already a considerable, even if patchy, degree of barbarian settlement, as on the *Litus Saxonicum*, before the total collapse of Roman authority, such a process of assimilation becomes much easier to understand.

In the south-eastern corner of Britain, especially in Kent,

the adjacent parts of Surrey, and beyond the Thames estuary in Essex, this cultural assimilation was in any case most complete. There are many obvious reasons for this. This region must always have been the centre and focus of the Saxon Shore, with its principal ports and harbours dominated by the massive fortifications at Reculver, Richborough, Dover, and Lympne, on which the crucial section of the system rested. So long as any Roman authority remained active in Britain, whether civilian or military, this corner of the country covered its lifelines to the centres of Imperial power in Gaul and Italy. Any barbarian settlement on this part of the Saxon Shore must have been effectively controlled from the beginning, and such control must have been maintained longer and more thoroughly than on any other part of the coastline. For this reason the date, nature, and extent of its earlier phases are especially difficult to ascertain. Germanic burial customs in these parts would be rapidly adapted to contemporary British models, and material equipment of every kind would take on forms hard to distinguish from those prevalent in the Romanized towns, villas, and villages of the Kentish countryside.[1]

It is against this background that the problem of the Jutes has to be set. It must be expected that the earliest Germanic settlement in the regions of Britain where Bede located the Jutes—Kent, the Isle of Wight, and the parts of Hampshire around Southampton Water—will be very difficult to identify. Cremation as an intrusive burial custom is likely to be in evidence only in the initial stages. The material equipment found either in inhumation cemeteries or in domestic contexts may not be easy to distinguish from what would be expected anyway in a late or sub-Roman phase of native British culture. Moreover the close proximity of Kent to Gaul would be likely to result in an early admixture of all kinds of objects of continental manufacture or artistic fashion with the cultural equipment both of the Germanic newcomers and of the Romano-British folk among whom they settled. The

[1] The most significant pieces of personal equipment likely to indicate the presence of such people are the Quoit Brooch Style buckles discussed by V. I. Evison, *Ant. J.* 48 (1968), 231-46, which may have been regarded as more or less official indications of civilian or military employment. Their distribution seems directly related to the south-eastern sections of the Saxon Shore.

earliest literary sources portray the settlement hereabouts
as resulting in the first place from arrangements agreed
between such barbarian chieftains as Hengist and sub-Roman
authorities like Vortigern. Such a situation adds point to the
difficulty of distinguishing culturally between native and
intruder in those parts of south-eastern England in which
the most extensive and effective of such treaty settlements
most probably took place.

The origin and identity of the Jutish people themselves
have in the past been tangled up in these uncertainties. Bede
is here the primary authority, and it must be remembered
that he was singularly well-informed on the early history of
Kent. He had very close contacts with ecclesiastical sources
in Canterbury, where, alone in Britain, there were probably
written records going back to within a generation or two of
the settlement itself.[1] Although the early place-names of
Kent have not so far produced any direct reference to Jutish
settlement, there is good place-name evidence, independent
of Bede, which corroborates his statement that there were
also Jutes established in southern Hampshire. It is not impossible that the Jutes of Kent and the Jutes of Hampshire
may both have originated from related treaty settlements on
the *Litus Saxonicum* in the final or sub-Roman phase of its
functioning in the fifth century.

It has been noted earlier[2] that Bede himself may have been
in some doubt as to the precise continental origin of the
Jutes. In placing them somewhere beyond the Angles,
whether to the north in Jutland or to the east in Holstein,
he was at least clearly implying that it was with the Angles
that they were primarily to be associated. This close association is borne out both by the archaeological and by other
literary evidence. It is remarkable, for example, that the early

[1] Bede (*HE* i. 15) says that there was a monument to Horsa, inscribed with
his name, in the eastern part of Kent. If this was really Horsa's gravestone, and
not just a misread Roman inscription of earlier date, the fact is of considerable
interest. It would imply that the first generation of federate settlers was here
sufficiently in touch with Roman ways to understand the practice of setting up
inscribed memorial stones. If so, some of them were either literate themselves, or
at least were able to make use of literate sub-Roman craftsmen in inscribing such
monuments. For other views see E. Wadstein, *On the Origin of the English*
(Uppsala, 1927), 28-9.
[2] p. 10.

kings of the Cantware never seem to have referred to themselves and, so far as is known, were never referred to by
others, as kings of the Jutes; they are always described
as kings of the Angles.[1] Whatever their precise tribal origin,
it was as rulers of a part of the *Grossstamm der Angeln*
that they thought of themselves and expected others to
think of them. Archaeologically, too, their links with the
Angles were very close. Whether the bulk of the Jutish people
were based at this time in what later became Jutland or were
settled east of the lower Elbe in Holstein, there were no
major cultural frontiers between them and the Angles of
Angeln.

None the less it is possible to recognize in the fifth-century
archaeology of Kent clear signs of folk whose closest continental connections are as much with Jutland as with other
parts of the Anglian *Kulturkreis*. The most distinctive, because most strictly localized of these links are in the sphere
of pottery. There are at least fifteen sites in north-east Kent,
mostly in Thanet and on Thames-side east of the river
Medway, where a series of small pots that can be closely
matched from a dozen or more sites in Jutland have been
found.[2] From this same area, and scattered more widely in
the cemeteries of east Kent, have come a number of the
earliest (Group 1) type of cruciform brooch, which on the
Continent would be as much at home in Jutland as in
Angeln.[3]

Jutland is moreover the source from which the Kentish
series of gold bracteates derives its inspiration. These very
decorative, and valuable, circular gold pendants became
something of a status-symbol in the jewellery of high-ranking
families in sixth-century Kent. They seem to have owed their
attraction in part to a distant resemblance to Byzantine gold
coins, in part to some prophylactic associations of their
mysterious zoomorphic designs, and in part to their monetary
value as gold bullion. Whatever the main cause of their
popularity, the fashion for their use at this time is one of the
firmest bonds linking the immigrant culture of Kent to its

---

[1]   e.g. Gregory the Great, in the letter to Æthelbert of which Bede gives the
text in *HE* i. 32, addresses him as *regi Anglorum*.

[2]   See Map 5. Myres, *Corpus*, ii. fig. 279 shows a number of these pots.

[3]   Åberg, *Anglo-Saxons in England*, figs. 35–7.

immediate origins in Jutland, the closest part of the barbarian world where it was equally prevalent.[1]

Just as significant of such an origin are the earliest square-headed brooches of Leeds Class A1.[2] These owe their form to Denmark, even if much of their decoration, including the beginnings of Style 1 animal ornament, may be based on the late classical models which would have been familiar to Romano-British craftsmen in Kent in the late fourth and early fifth centuries. These models underlie what has come to be known as the Quoit Brooch Style of decorative metal-work, as displayed on annular and penannular brooches, buckles, strap-ends, and so on. They are of great importance, not merely to the art student seeking the origins of barbarian zoomorphic decoration at this time, but to the historian as exemplifying the final vivid flashes of late classical crafts-manship in the dying embers of Romano-British culture.

Illustration is necessary to provide a visual impression of the Quoit Brooch Style of decoration. It is otherwise difficult to make manifest its lively and vigorous nature as an art-form and its relationship to the classical models from which it sprang in the late fourth century. Nor is it easy to appreciate its position as a source from which much of the zoomorphic art of the Germanic Migration period derived its inspiration.[3] Thus it retains from its Roman background a fondness for a wide range of animal forms, often portrayed in rapid motion—hunting scenes with hounds pursuing hares, stags, and other game—or set in linear procession or as opposing pairs. The animals and birds, though often drawn with lively imagination and including mythical creatures such as hippo-camps from the decorative repertoire of the classical world, are mostly coherent and recognizable. They have not yet disintegrated into the *disjecta membra* with which the

[1] There is a large and rather confusing literature on gold bracteates. I have followed in the main S. C. Hawkes's full account in *Frühmittelalterliche Studien*, 15 (1981), 316–70, which has a very useful distribution map, fig. 1. See also M. Axboe, *Acta Archaeologica* 52 (1981), 1–100.
[2] E. T. Leeds, *Corpus of . . . square-headed brooches*, 7–11.
[3] A good general account of the Quoit Brooch Style is in Evison, *Fifth-Century Invasions South of the Thames* (1965), 46–78, figs. 26–30, and pls. 10–18. The term seems to have been first used by E. Bakka, *On the Beginnings of Salin's Style 1 in England* (Bergen, 1959), 7–14, to distinguish this decorative fashion from the subsequent Style 1, especially in Kent.

succeeding Germanic Style 1 tended to fill every available space, from an apparent *horror vacui* in the barbarian mind. The Quoit Brooch Style, on the contrary, retained from the formality and realism of classical art a sense of proportion and balance in the arrangement of decoration. This is true not only of its portrayal of animal forms but of such incidental detail as tendrils and border patterns, running scrolls, the dot-and-triangle and ovolo motifs, in fact of all the incidental repertoire of late Roman decorative art (Fig. 10).

It is not at all surprising that artistic styles of this general character should have sprung up in and around the fringes of the Roman world. They were a natural outcome of trade contacts with Germanic barbary. The Imperial frontiers were increasingly subject to penetration at this time by Teutonic folk, whether these were being recruited into Roman service or, before long, operating independently under their own leaders. Britain in its last Roman phase was not alone in developing, through its close contacts in peace and war with the encroaching barabarian world, the art-forms characteristic of the Quoit Brooch Style. Something very similar occurred at much the same time in Denmark and southern Scandinavia, here no doubt stimulated mainly by trading contacts rather than mass migration of people. A closely comparable artistic development accompanied or preceded the spread of Visigoths and Burgundians across the Danube and the expansion of the Franks over the Rhine frontier and across northern Gaul.[1] In all these regions their material culture was soon thoroughly permeated by artistic influences very similar to those exemplified by the Quoit Brooch Style in Britain.

A good deal of confusion over the origin of the style and its significance in Britain has resulted from these very natural developments. On the one hand, those seeking to find archaeological links between the Jutes of Jutland and the Jutes of Kent have been tempted to use the parallels between the Kentish Quoit Brooch Style and the somewhat similar artistic developments in Denmark as another argument for bringing the Kentish Jutes from Jutland. It has thus been

---

[1] See the very suggestive map of the distribution of chip-carved belt-fittings in Europe in *Med. Arch.* 5 (1961), 12, fig. 3.

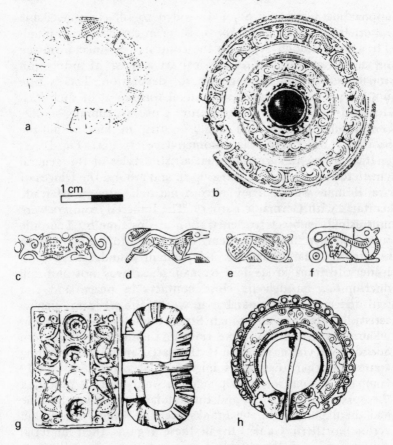

Fig. 10.   The Quoit Brooch Style
a Lyminge, Kent.   *b* Faversham, Kent.   *c* Howletts, Kent: detail.
d Howletts, Kent: detail.   *e* Sarre, Kent; detail.   *f* Alfriston, Sussex:
detail.   *g* Alfriston, Sussex.   *h* Alfriston, Sussex.
For sources of figures see p. xiv.

proposed to label all this kind of zoomorphic art wherever
it occurs as a Jutish Style A. [1] On the other hand, there are
those so impressed by the similarities between the examples
of the style found in Frankish contexts in northern Gaul and
Belgium and those from the Kentish cemeteries that they are
prepared to regard the whole style as basically Frankish, and
to use its occurrence in Britain as one of the main arguments

[1]   e.g. S. C. Hawkes, *Archaeologia*, 98 (1961), 29-74.

supporting the notion of a massive Frankish invasion of Kent and other parts of southern Britain in the sixth century.[1]

It will be necessary to consider later this idea that Kent and south-eastern Britain as a whole were more or less taken over by the Franks as a by-product of the conquest of Gaul by Clovis.[2] But if this kind of zoomorphic art was a natural by-product of the close contacts that developed between the Roman and barbarian worlds in the fourth century, wherever those contacts were sufficiently close and abrasive to generate it, then it is surely reasonable to consider its various manifestations, whether in Britain, Scandinavia, or Gaul, as parallel and more or less independent phenomena. This is in fact much more likely than that they should stand to one another in a closer relationship of cause and effect. If this is so, there may be little ground for using the prevalence of this attractive late Roman art-style either as an argument for linking the Jutes of Kent directly with Jutland (an argument which in fact hardly requires such additional support), or as a ground for believing in a Frankish conquest of south-eastern Britain in or after the time of Clovis.

There are in fact good reasons for believing that the Quoit Brooch Style was in vogue in Britain well before the Frankish expansion began in the second half of the fifth century. Many of its characteristic features are found on objects whose associations are rather with Roman contexts in the late fourth century than with any part of the barbarian world in the late fifth.[3] One of the most remarkable examples of such an association is an object, first recorded in the seventeenth century, which is now in the Treasury of the Bibliothèque Nationale in Paris.[4] It is a circular bronze plate engraved with an elaborate pictorial design which shows two lines of Roman soldiers facing one another and labelled respectively LEG. XX. VV and LEG. SECUNDA AVGVS. Centred

[1] e.g. Evison, op. cit. 46–78.
[2] pp. 126–8.
[3] The distribution of objects in the Quoit Brooch Style is very closely related to the parts of the Saxon Shore south of the Thames. In addition to north and east Kent it is virtually confined to coastal Sussex and the Isle of Wight: there is a convenient map, based on Evison, in C. A. Arnold, *Roman Britain to Saxon England* (1984), 104.
[4] Evison, op. cit. 54 and fig. 25. I am grateful to Professor C. F. C. Hawkes for telling me of its present whereabouts.

between them is an eagle and on each side are the legionary standards and their respective badges, a boar and a hippocamp, together with the name AVRELIVS CERVIANVS. Below the soldiers of the Twentieth legion is the injunction VTERE FELIX ('Make happy use of this'). This shows that the object was a formal piece of presentation plate, presumably given to Aurelius Cervianus by the combined officers' messes of the two legions. The lower half of the design includes a lively hunting scene featuring a lion, two peacocks, and hounds pursuing a stag and a hare, all drawn in the characteristically vigorous manner of the Quoit Brooch Style (Fig. 11).

The find-spot of this remarkable object is unknown. It was first published as long ago as 1698 in France. The incident it was designed to celebrate must have directly concerned

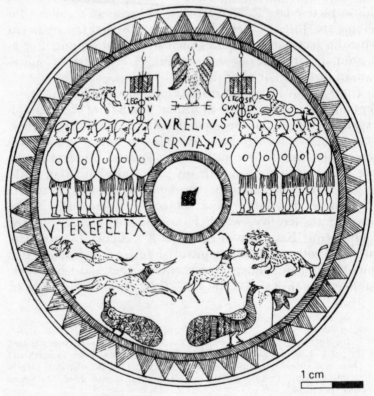

Fig. 11.   Engraved bronze plate
For source of figure see p. xiv.

the last days of the Roman army in Britain. Both the legions involved had been part of the permanent British garrison since the first century. Leg. XX V(aleria) V(ictrix) had its base at Chester until the late fourth century, and Leg. Secunda Augus(ta) was at Caerleon until it was moved to Richborough some time before that Kentish fortress appears as its headquarters in the *Notitia Dignitatum*. There is no reason to suppose that the two legions were ever quartered together, except possibly in the circumstances surrounding their final evacuation. It is therefore very tempting to associate the presentation of this piece of plate, in which both legions were concerned, with the ceremonies surrounding the evacuation itself.[1] Little is known of the future of these two legions after they had left Britain, and it may well be that this was the last, perhaps the only, occasion on which such a joint celebration could have taken place.

However that may be, the historical and artistic interest of this object in relation to the subject matter of this chapter could hardly be greater. Not only does it present a unique impression of the visual appearance of a group of legionaries at this late date, but it does so in a strictly Roman context, without any indication whatever of direct influences, artistic or cultural, from the barbarian world. The lettering of the inscriptions, if a trifle slapdash, is quite clear and in no sense barbarous, and the depiction of the legionary uniform, military equipment, and badges, if somewhat sketchy, shows a realism much closer to classical than to Germanic notions of representational art. The same is true of the vigorous treatment of the hunting scene. Though the inclusion of peacocks and lions may arise from artistic imagination, this may well be intended to convey an idea of the rural recreations that could still compensate Roman officers for the rigours of military life on the collapsing frontiers of the civilized world.

If this interpretation is convincing, it suggests that the origins of the Quoit Brooch Style must be sought in the

[1] Professor Hawkes has suggested to me that, since there is no evidence for the presence of the Twentieth Legion at Chester after 383, both it and at least part of the Second Legion were probably withdrawn then by Maximus. If the object was found, as is probable, somewhere in France, such a provenance would strengthen the suggestion that it might have been made for an evacuation party, probably in Kent. It would naturally have been included in the recipient's baggage which accompanied him on his last Channel-crossing from Britain.

declining years of the Roman occupation of Britain, long before the period when Frankish fashions became a major influence on the culture of Kent. As the fifth century wore on the style displays increasing signs of a barbarian overlay on a surviving basis of late Roman art-forms. That is exactly what might be expected from the known historical situation in Kent at that time. It was here, far more than in other parts of Britain, that the procedures of federate settlement would have cushioned the impact of Germanic intrusion, so that it could be absorbed with a minimum of disturbance to the existing structure of society. It was here too that the culture of the newcomers was most profoundly affected by that of the Romano-British natives among whom they settled.

It is thus interesting that in association with the earliest Jutish material, which, as has been seen, underlies the Germanic settlement of Kent, there is some evidence for the practice of cremation in the cemeteries. This suggests that at the start of their settlement in the fifth century, some of the new federate settlers were not yet wholly assimilated to Roman funerary customs. But they very quickly became acclimatized to local custom for in all the later developments of Germanic culture in Kent cremation is virtually unknown.

In this and other ways it is possible to detect in Kent much clearer signs of some genuine continuity with the social conditions of the Romano-British past than are evident in most other parts of the country. Memories of the great days of Empire still lingered in Kent in the eighth century. Thus it was natural for Bede to speak of Canterbury in Æthelbert's time as *imperii sui totius . . . metropolis*[1] and for Alcuin a little later to describe Kent as a *regnum imperiale.*[2] Such phrases could hardly have been used of any other part of what had once been Roman Britain. Even if Germanic settlement had not occurred on a large scale in late Roman times on this strategically significant section of the *Litus Saxonicum,* there is every reason to believe that substantial treaty settlements did take place hereabouts around the middle of the fifth century.

The kingdom of the Cantware, with its traditions going back to the Hengist/Vortigern story, thus grew directly out

[1] *HE* i. 25.   [2] *MGH (AA) Ep.* iv. 191-2.

of the ruins of Roman Kent. That had been a region whose social structure, with its towns, ports, and numerous villa estates, linked by an effective system of roads, was one of the most highly developed in the provinces of Britain. That structure was still based primarily on those relatively dry and easily cultivable soils beloved of prehistoric man, but it had already extended beyond them into the richer and heavier lands of natural forest. To this pattern in general that of the federate settlement conforms, although here and there it may be possible to catch glimpses of a temporary return to more primitive conditions in some of the naturally forested areas that had yielded in part to the intensive cultivation of Roman agricultural estates. Thus the marked abundance of villas and other settlements which had lined the Medway valley from Rochester as far south as Maidstone in Roman times is only faintly echoed in the early Germanic distribution. There are here no large Jutish cemeteries far south of the Downs, and only a trickle of early place-names suggests that some advantage would soon be taken of the wide clearings of good land which presumably remained from Roman times.[1]

On the other hand, there is a striking concentration of early Germanic remains in the open country of east Kent, both in Thanet, the traditional home of the first *foederati*, and thence thickly up the valleys of the two Stours towards Canterbury and Watling Street. Here the village of Sturry still preserves in its name the memory of the 'province of the Stour men', and in its remarkable early cemetery the relics of the men themselves. Between Watling Street and Richborough a group of cemeteries and a scatter of early place-names centre similarly on Eastry, the *villa regalis* of the early 'eastern district' of the Cantware. The Watling Street and its immediate neighbourhood, forming the great highway of Roman communication from the Channel ports to London and beyond, is likewise marked by cemeteries and

---

[1] It is worth remembering that the primary clearance of natural forest may present fewer problems for early farming communities than the secondary clearance required after a period of neglect in the continued cultivation of such naturally wooded ground. This is because the high canopy afforded by forest trees often reduces or inhibits scrub growth below them, whereas once the big trees have gone there is nothing to prevent the unrestricted spread of tangled undergrowth.

early place-names all the way from Dover to the borders of Surrey. Moreover it is especially interesting, in the light of barbarian behaviour elsewhere in eastern England, to find that the proximity of each important Roman centre on this route—Dover, Canterbury, Faversham, and Rochester—is marked by considerable Germanic settlement. Three of the four—Canterbury, Faversham, and Rochester—became centres of lathes, the early administrative districts under the kings of Kent. On the south coast, another of these early administrative districts took its name, Lyminge, from the Roman Saxon Shore fortress of *Lemanis* (now Lympne), which became its centre, and may well perpetuate the governmental pattern of this part of Kent in late Roman times.

Indeed, the whole administrative structure of pre-feudal Kent, so brilliantly reconstructed by Jolliffe,[1] may well retain the outline of the Romano-British system, within which Hengist and his Jutes were permitted by such sub-Roman rulers as Vortigern to make their federate settlements. It was normal in Gaul for such arrangements to take the form of a *tertiatio*, or division into thirds, of existing properties. Where this was done either directly or with any modifications dictated by local circumstances, the framework of the old estates would remain as the recognizable background to the new pattern of landholding. That is no doubt the reason why in many parts of France village names— especially those ending in -ac, -ecque, -gnan, and -gny—are obviously derived from the adjectival forms of the names of their former Gallo-Roman proprietors. No certain examples of this type of place-name have so far been recognized in Kent, a fact which must warn one against too ready an acceptance of the idea that events in this corner of Britain followed a course exactly parallel to the developments in Gaul. It would however be only natural for any fifth-century settlements of *foederati* to pay some regard to the existing structure of land tenure.

The pattern made by the lathes of Kent certainly suggests that this happened there. The use of the Saxon Shore fort of *Lemanis* as the territorial centre of what became the lathe of

---

[1] J. E. A. Jolliffe, *Prefeudal England: the Jutes* (Oxford, 1933). His conclusions are developed and to some extent modified in K. P. Witney, *The Kingdom of Kent* (Chichester, 1982), Appendix C 236-8, and elsewhere.

the *Limenewara* has already been noted. The lands directly dependent in Roman times on the cantonal capital, the *territorium* of *Durovernum Cantiacorum*, are no doubt represented by the lathe of the *Borowara*, the folk based on the *Cantwara burh*, which became Canterbury. Alone in England this would appear to be an example of the process by which in northern Gaul the tribal capitals mostly lost their urban names when Roman rule ended, while retaining the name of the tribe or canton of which they had been the focus.[1]

Further west, at the point where Watling Street crossed the Medway, the other main Roman town in Kent kept its administrative importance as the centre of *Cesterwara* lathe. Here, in becoming *Hrofesceaster* (and eventually Rochester), it retained in garbled form only the second syllable of its Roman name *Durobrivae*, which must have been stressed in the late Roman pronunciation of the word.[2] Of the other Kentish lathes, that centred on Faversham is of special interest. Though it lost whatever name it may have borne in Roman times, it retained an important semi-urban built-up area on Watling Street. It was marked both by a considerable concentration of late Roman buildings and a very rich and extensive Germanic cemetery, the combination clearly implying a significant continuity of occupation through both periods.[3] Moreover its name appears to bear the meaning of 'the smith's *ham*', the first element being probably derived more or less directly from Latin *faber*. This would certainly be a very appropriate designation, for Faversham was in this period a major centre of metal-working. As an Anglo-Saxon loan-word from *faber*, this element is apparently otherwise unrecorded.[4] Its use in Faversham, if unique, may thus be directly due to the presence there of a conspicuous group of bilingual craftsmen, some of whom could have been

[1] See p. 31, n. 2, for such examples as *Lutetia Parisiorum* becoming Paris, *Durocortorum Remorum* becoming Reims, or *Samarobriva Ambianorum* becoming Amiens.

[2] British *Durobrivae* probably means 'walled town with bridges'; the form *Hrofesceaster* is not likely to contain a personal name (B. Cox, *JEP-NS* 8 (1976), 36), but it is probably as early as the fifth century (Jackson, *Language and History*, 647).

[3] See B. Philp, *Excavations at Faversham* (Crawley, 1968) for a recent account.

[4] E. Ekwall, *Oxford Dictionary of English Place-names* (1936), s.v. Faversham.

Latin-speaking Britons, already known locally to their Jutish neighbours as the *fabri*.[1] The centres of several other early Kentish lathes have produced evidence of very late Romano-British activity, and present almost as clear an indication of continous significance through these centuries of transition.

The place-names of Kent are also remarkable for retaining more examples that are little altered from Romano-British forms than any other part of eastern or central England. While, as has been noted, Canterbury, Rochester, and Faversham all lost their pre-Saxon town names, the Saxon Shore forts of Dover (*Dubris*), Reculver (Regulbium), and Lympne (*Lemanis*) retained theirs virtually unchanged. So did the Isle of Thanet, whose people also perpetuated their identity in the name of their appropriated share of Wealden forest at Tenterden. The virtually unchanged British names of Kent are however mostly related to prominent features of the coast-line. Like the word Kent itself,[2] they probably owe their survival from very early times as much to the conservative requirements of navigators, retaining the traditional names for ports and other coastal features, as to any exceptional degree of survival in the population or of continuity in its institutional arrangements. It may thus have been geography rather than history that determined the unusual degree of survival of Romano-British names in Kent.

By the early sixth century however, if not before, a change was coming over the culture of post-Roman Kent. This had been based essentially on a fusion of sub-Roman survivals (represented artistically by the Quoit Brooch Style) with the forms of metal-work and pottery introduced by Hengist and his federates from Jutland and Frisia. It was now being increasingly overlaid by a much more elaborate and spectacular range of equipment inspired from Frankish Gaul. This was a natural consequence of the military expansion which had brought the Franks, under the vigorous leadership

[1] It may also be worth noting that the ruined church of Stone-by-Faversham appears to incorporate the remains of a rectangular mausoleum of Roman date. It must have been a conspicuous feature of the adjacent Romano-British cemetery, and still in sufficiently good shape to be made part of a new church when Christianity returned to Kent early in the seventh century: see A. C. Thomas, *Christianity in Roman Britain to AD 500* (1981), 183-5.

[2] It has been suggested that *Cantii* probably signifies 'the hosts, the armies': K. H. Jackson, *JRS* 38 (1948), 55.

of Clovis and his family, from the lower Rhineland into the parts of northern Gaul from which Kent was most accessible.

So dominant did this Frankish influence on the culture of Kent become in the sixth and seventh centuries that, as has been noted already, some scholars have found it impossible to explain except by postulating a massive influx of immigrant Franks into south-eastern Britain.[1] It is certainly difficult to understand how Frankish influences could have penetrated the culture of Kent so thoroughly until their conquest and settlement of northern Gaul had exposed the Channel ports to the unobstructed passage of Frankish merchants and their goods. But whether such trading links need have involved any substantial permanent settlement of Franks in Kent is another matter. There is no convincing evidence for anything like a political or military take-over by Frankish power. Had anything of this kind taken place it could hardly have escaped the notice of contemporary or subsequent chroniclers and historians. Bede, for example, has no suggestion of any political contact between the Franks and Kent earlier than the marriage of Æthelbert to the Frankish princess Bertha late in the sixth century. In view of his close personal contacts with the affairs of Kent, Bede could hardly have avoided recording a Frankish conquest, or even an intrusion on any large scale, instead of attributing, as he does, the settlement of Kent entirely to the Jutes.

Moreover, a Frankish conquest would surely have involved a political upheaval, most likely leading to an interruption of the traditional descent of the Kentish royal family from Hengist and his Jutes. It could also be strongly argued that any Frankish conquest of Kent early in the sixth century would certainly have involved the introduction of Christianity. The Franks had been converted at the start of their expansion in the time of Clovis, and their success owed much to the support of the Catholic bishops in Gaul, who would certainly have been eager to take advantage of any extension of their authority to Britain. But in fact, as Bede makes very clear, the royal house of Kent remained both independent and pagan even after Æthelbert's marriage to the Christian Bertha. It was eventually papal rather than Frankish initiative

---

[1] The case is most fully argued in V. I. Evison, op. cit.

that inspired the introduction of Christianity through the Augustinian mission at the very end of the sixth century. Thus the earlier Frankish influence on the culture of Kent, while no doubt accompanied by the appearance of merchants and traders in the Kentish ports and towns who stimulated a taste for continental goods and artistic fashions among the local nobility, was evidently not the result either of a fresh invasion or of a political conquest. Procopius, in the sixth century, certainly had some odd tales about the relations between the Franks and the Angles of Britain, no doubt derived from Frankish visitors to the Byzantine court. But while they reported Frankish ambitions to the overlordship of Britain it is clear that the Angle rulers were quite independent. Indeed the Franks with whom Procopius spoke appear to have been strangely ignorant of the situation and topography of Britain.

The conclusion must therefore be that the remarkable flowering of Kentish culture in the seventh century sprang initially from the grafting of Jutish and Anglo-Frisian federate settlers upon the basic stock of late Romano-British society. The latter was here much less deranged than elsewhere in eastern Britain owing to its more complete and successful absorption of earlier Germanic elements already long established on this part of the Saxon Shore. This promising mixture was then fertilized by a powerful top-dressing of cultural influences from Frankish Gaul. It was also stimulated economically by the facts of geography, which made Kent the natural channel through which trade could increasingly build up by the exchange of British raw materials for luxury goods imported from Gaul and soon manufactured in Kent itself.

The position of London was clearly crucial to this process and its status between the fifth and seventh centuries has been much discussed. The last literary reference to it as a Roman city is in the *Anglo-Saxon Chronicle* under the year 457, which records that after their defeat by Hengist at the battle of Crecganford the Britons of Kent fled to London in great terror. Its revival as a major commercial centre by the seventh century is vouched for by Bede.[1] Early Kentish royal

---

[1] *HE* ii. 3.

charters purport to indicate similar developments at this time both in London itself and at various points lower down the Thames estuary. But there is no direct record of what happened to London or, for that matter, to the other major cities of south-eastern Britain, such as Verulamium and Camulodunum, in the two hundred years between the collapse of Roman rule and the seventh century.

The position of London itself must always be important when political and commercial links between Britain and the Continent are as close and active as they were both in Roman times and after the establishment of more or less settled Saxon regimes in south-eastern Britain in the seventh century. But between these dates it can have had little role to play owing to the collapse of the Saxon Shore system and the breakdown of trade using the Thames Valley route into the southern Midlands.[1] Here for a long while political confusion must have reduced commercial activity to a trickle. Beyond the Goring gap the conflicts between rival Anglo-Saxon forces pressing up from Hampshire and down from the Fens, and of both with surviving British communities in the Chilterns, the Silchester region, and in Wiltshire, must have prevented the growth of stable political conditions in which trade between London and the interior could develop.

Whether London can have survived in spite of these adverse factors as more than a shrunken and barbarized ghost of its former civic splendour has been much debated. The case for its remaining as something of an independent political force through the fifth and sixth centuries was most forcibly made by R. E. M. Wheeler.[2] He pointed to the lack of evidence for early Saxon settlement in and around the city, and to the existence of various undated earthworks in the Chilterns and elsewhere in its vicinity which might indicate the limits of its former *territorium*, from which for a while barbarian invaders could have been barred. He also claimed that certain features of medieval custom in the city's later

[1] That these two events were closely linked is suggested by the distribution throughout the Thames Valley between east Kent and the Dorchester area of the types of buckles and belt-fittings characteristic of Roman military equipment in the late fourth century. Traffic up the Thames was evidently not obstructed until the Roman military withdrawal soon after 400: *Med. Arch.* 5 (1961), 16 and fig. 4.

[2] R. E. M. Wheeler, *London and the Saxons* (1935).

constitution were more likely to have had Roman than
Germanic origins.

Most of these considerations are susceptible of alternative.
and less dramatic explanations than Wheeler gave them, and
some of his conclusions are certainly ill-founded.[1] There are
also factors which make it difficult to accept the idea of any
effective continuity in London's political or social life. It has
been pointed out, for example, that the chaotic street-plan
of medieval London bears no relation to the rectangular layout of the Roman *insulae*, except for the continuing use of
some approach roads to the original gates. This radical
change, involving the wholesale alteration of property
boundaries, is not likely to have come about without a
complete breakdown of civic discipline.

Moreover, if British authority survived in any substantial
fashion through the fifth and sixth centuries in London, it is
difficult to account for the disappearance of the Christian
episcopal organization, for this, as happened in many parts of
Gaul, might be expected to form an essential element in its
social continuity. In fact, as Bede points out,[2] the attempt
by the Augustinian mission to establish a bishop's seat in
London had to be abandoned owing to opposition by the
pagan royal family of the East Saxons, who evidently controlled the city. There is no suggestion here of any surviving
sub-Roman authority in London at this time.

The scarcity of early Anglo-Saxon archaeological remains
in and around London certainly requires explanation. It
should be noted however that this scarcity is by no means
confined to the lands that may have been included in the
territorium of London itself. As Wheeler himself pointed
out,[3] it is a feature characteristic of the whole northern part
of what he termed the 'sub-Roman triangle', a region which
covers most of Essex and Hertfordshire, together with the
Chiltern area to the west. It thus includes what might be
supposed to have comprised the *territoria* of Verulamium and
Camulodunum as well as that of London.

Wheeler did not directly associate the apparent scarcity of
Saxon remains in what he took to be these sub-urban *territoria*

---

[1] *Antiquity*, 8 (1934), 437–42 and my review in *JRS* 26 (1936), 87–92.
[2] *HE* ii. 5.
[3] Wheeler, op. cit., fig. 2.

with conditions likely to have arisen from the early Germanic settlement of the Saxon Shore. Yet this seems a very probable explanation. On this central section of the *Litus Saxonicum* the settlement of *laeti* from the fourth century onwards is likely to have been dense, but to have left little archaeological trace owing to their early and complete assimilation to Roman cultural conditions. Thus it might be only on sites that were for some reason of special significance that continuity can be easily detected between late Roman and early Saxon occupation.[1]

One such site is that above the present village of Mucking on Thames-side east of Tilbury. Here continuity both of cemeteries and of settlement between the two periods has been clearly and abundantly demonstrated by the recent excavations.[2] It is highly significant that this continuity should occur on a site which has a magnificent visual command of the Thames estuary, so that its people were ideally placed to detect and monitor the movement of shipping in the lower reaches of the river. It is hard to resist the conclusion that this place, which may well have lain on the eastern borders of the *territorium* of London, could have been deliberately chosen by the urban authorities to provide early warning of danger from strange vessels sailing up the river with possibly hostile intent.[3] The position and purpose of the Mucking installations may thus be compared with those of the Yorkshire coastal signal stations and the High Down establishment behind the Sussex coastline at Worthing.

The high ground above Mucking continued to be occupied by Saxon folk throughout the sixth century until the settlement was moved downhill to the site of the present village. This probably followed the coming of Christianity early in the seventh century. It cannot be assumed that its people continued to serve what seems to have been its original

---

[1] See also pp. 149–52 for a somewhat similar situation in Wessex.

[2] One of the earliest datable Saxon graves (no. 987) contained a late Roman buckle of Hawkes Type IB and two Saxon brooches of the early fifth century: S. C. Hawkes, *Brit.* 5 (1974), 387. For a discussion of the early Anglo-Saxon pottery from Mucking and its association with Romano-Saxon pieces see Myres, *Ant. J.* 48 (1968), 222–8 and fig. 5.

[3] The fourth-century signal tower recently located on Thames-side at Wapping east of London could well have been part of the same early-warning system: *Brit.* 6 (1975), 269, and 7 (1976), 351.

purpose all that time, and it would be unwise to suppose that they were still providing intelligence to a surviving sub-Roman London until they eventually moved downhill to be near the river.

A good deal of information on conditions in and around the Roman city in the fifth and sixth centuries has come from recent archaeological and topographical work both inside and outside its defensive walls.[1] It has been shown, for example, that there is a marked contrast in late Roman and sub-Roman times between the eastern and western parts of the walled area which are roughly separated by the course of the Walbrook. To the west of the stream there is comparatively little evidence for late or sub-Roman activity. This part of the city had never been so densely built up as the eastern area, and much of it seems to have become gardens or open ground, evidenced by the presence of deep soil surrounding and sometimes covering the foundations of earlier buildings. It was in the heart of this comparatively unencumbered area that a central site was chosen in the early seventh century by the Augustinian mission for the building of their church of St. Paul and the establishment of the new bishop's seat.

East of the Walbrook on the other hand and especially in the south-eastern quarter along the river frontage, close to the site of the later Tower of London, there are indications of much greater activity in the last days of the Roman city. Most remarkable is the construction of a new and very well-built riverside wall whose foundations cut through deposits containing coins dating from 388 and 402. It cannot therefore have been laid before the early fifth century. That some Roman administrative centre was still operating at this late date on or near the site of the Tower is shown by several discoveries there of silver ingots, some associated with gold coins of Honorius and Arcadius, a type of deposit characteristic of the official donatives made on special occasions at that period to the armed forces.[2] The discovery at different dates of more than one such group in this very limited area

---

[1] For an excellent summary of this work see R. Merrifield, *London* (1983), especially 236–55, on which I have drawn heavily in the three following paragraphs. P. R. V. Marsden, *Roman London* (1980), has also been useful.

[2] Late Roman silver ingots of this kind are listed and discussed by K. S. Painter in *Ant. J.* 52 (1972), 84–92.

suggests strongly that the building which had housed them
had been abandoned in a hurry, for such valuables would not
have been left lying about had there been time to remove
them to safe keeping.

A recent excavation in the same part of the city in Lower
Thames Street has revealed the remains of a late Roman bath-
building of so substantial a kind as to raise the possibility
that it too served an official purpose. This building was
certainly in occupation up to the end of the fourth century,
and perhaps later, for a scattered hoard containing coins as
late as 394-5 had found its way into the furnace stoke-hole
while it was still in use. Eventually however the tiled roof of
the building collapsed, and that this probably happened
during the fifth century is suggested by the presence among
its debris of a Saxon applied brooch of that date. Whether
this brooch had been lost by its owner while scrabbling over
the broken tiles in a half-blocked street or while he was himself engaged in demolition work on the roof of the building,
cannot be known. But certainly no one ever bothered to clear
up the tiles, which remained as they had fallen until found in
the recent excavation.[1] No incident could point more clearly
to a lack of continuity in the fifth-century occupation of
what had been apparently the busiest quarter of the city in
the last phase of Londinium.

It has always been difficult to reconcile such evidence for
a more or less complete breakdown of civic consciousness in
London at this time with what is known from Bede and other
sources of its apparently flourishing condition as a commercial centre in the seventh century. The explanation of this
difficulty seems to lie in the recognition that the main focus
of this new activity lay not inside the Roman walls but in
the extra-mural suburb to the west in the area part of which
is still significantly known as Aldwych, 'the old *vicus*'.[2]
This extended on both sides of the main Roman road along
the Strand which bordered the river frontage towards what is
now Westminster. It is here rather than in the city itself
that there are many signs of immediately post-Roman
occupation, especially between the road and the river,

[1] Merrifield, op. cit. fig. 56 and pp. 23-7.
[2] As has been pointed out by M. Biddle, *Popular Archaeology*, 6 (1984),
23-7.

including seventh-century coins and contemporary pottery of types that are hardly found at all within the walls.

It would thus appear that the problem of London's continuity can be resolved by the recognition that its survival, or more properly revival, included a temporary change in the main focus of its commercial life. It also adds greatly to the significance of the choice of site made by the Augustinian mission for St. Paul's. Its establishment in the more or less deserted western part of the walled city, though at first less than wholly successful for political reasons, had long-term consequences of great significance. It must eventually have played a major part in reuniting as a single community what was left of sub-Roman London to the east with the new Saxon and Frisian commercial developments around Aldwych to the west.

Between the western limits of Kent and the borders of what became Hampshire there sprang up on the south coast the rather isolated and apparently fragmented kingdom of the South Saxons, which consisted essentially of the southward-facing lands that lay between the chalk escarpment of the South Downs and the English Channel. Hemmed in thus by the Wealden forest on the north and the sea to the south, it formed an obvious geographical entity which might have been expected to develop a strongly unified political structure, especially as it must have formed in late Roman times a naturally delimited section of the *Litus Saxonicum*. But, in fact, the series of southward-flowing rivers that carry the drainage of the Wealden forest into the sea through breaches in the chalk escarpment of the Downs seems to have had the effect of dividing up the whole region into more or less self-contained blocks of territory each with its coastal plain, its high downland, and its claim to adjacent stretches of woodland in the Weald to the north. Thus in early Roman times there was no natural centre to the whole area, which at first seems to have been administratively dependent on *Noviomagus Regnensium*, now Chichester, in the far western section of its tribal lands. Both these names suggest a certain artificiality. *Noviomagus* probably implies a recently created centre for commerce and administration, while the *Regnenses* seem to have been called after the client kingdom created by the Romans to reward the loyalty of the native chieftain

Cogidubnus whose support was useful to them in the first days of their conquest.

It is interesting, and probably significant, that neither name survived in any form into Saxon times, and both may have gone out of use before the end of the fourth century. Roman Chichester has produced no certain sign of urban survival between the fifth and the ninth centuries. This break in its continuity must be the reason why Wilfrid made no attempt to establish his bishop's seat there in the seventh century, in spite of his own strong links with Roman ecclesiastical traditions. There is no other obvious explanation for his choice of rural Selsey as the main centre for his missionary activity among the pagan South Saxons.

This early disappearance of Roman Chichester, and the cantonal structure of which it had been the centre, was probably due not solely to its own artificiality. It may also have been brought about by the administrative changes involved in the creation of the Saxon Shore. The defence of what eventually became the Sussex coast must have been based in the last days of Roman Britain on the Saxon Shore fortress later known as *Andredesceaster* at Pevensey Castle. This was itself the latest and most irregular of the whole series of these coastal fortifications. It must be highly significant of its administrative importance at this time that the whole of the Sussex Weald forming the hinterland of this western section of the *Litus Saxonicum* continued to bear its name as the *Andredesweald* throughout the Saxon centuries. Such a usage must imply that *Andredesceaster* had superseded *Noviomagus Regnensium* as the administrative centre of the whole region. It was evidently now playing a part in the Saxon Shore system similar to that which the next fortress to the east (*Lemanis* at Lympne) came to play in giving its Roman name to the *Limenewara*, the most south-westerly of the lathes of Kent.

There are few certain archaeological traces on the Sussex section of the defended 'maritime tract', which became the *Litus Saxonicum*, to illustrate the final phase of its transition from Roman to Saxon control. The most significant is the cemetery at High Down behind Worthing.[1] This probably

---

[1] M. G. Welch, *Early Anglo-Saxon Sussex*, BAR 112 (1983), i.219 and ii.461-84 and figs. 87-124; for the excavation report on High Down see E. H. Read in *Archaeologia*, 54 (1895), 369-82.

began by serving an isolated community of mercenaries established towards the close of the Roman period in or near a prominent prehistoric hill-fort on the Downs, a defensible position with excellent visual command of the shore line and coastal shipping for many miles both to the east and the west. It could have served much the same purpose in the late fourth and early fifth centuries as was served by the signal stations on the Yorkshire coast. Such a usage would provide the readiest explanation for the presence among the burials there of Quoit Brooch style metal objects similar to early fifth-century Kentish types,[1] together with a fine late Roman glass decorated with a procession of animals portrayed in the same style and a Latin inscription.[2] That the site remained in occupation for some time after the collapse of Roman rule is shown by the presence of a normal range of Saxon inhumations accompanied by late-fifth- and sixth-century brooches and weapons.

Three entries in the *Anglo-Saxon Chronicle*, plausibly dated between 477 and 491, associate the transition from Roman to Saxon authority on this section of the *Litus Saxonicum*, with the exploits of a chieftain named Ælle.[3] They are evidently derived from a lost saga recalling the more memorable events in a career of conquest which put Ælle in control of what became Sussex. He is said to have landed in 477 with his sons at *Cumenesora*, a place probably now represented by the Owers Banks off the low-lying Selsey peninsula, and drove the surviving British defenders of the area to take refuge in the *Andredesleag*. In 485 he is recorded to have fought them again near an unidentified river called the *Mearcredesburna*, a name which has been plausibly interpreted to mean 'the stream of the agreed frontier'. It may thus relate to a boundary based on one of the river valleys which, as noted above, serve to divide the Sussex coast plain and its hinterland into naturally self-contained sections. There is, however, no means of knowing which valley was so called in early Saxon times or what political circumstances gave rise to the name.

[1] Welch, op. cit., figs. 91a, 93b, 97b and c, 100c, 101a, 105a, 115d, 116a and b. There are also a number of small fifth-century carinated bowls: figs. 91c, 124b, d, and e, which belong to the same chronological horizon.
[2] Ibid. fig. 103c.
[3] For the South Saxon annals see Appendix I(b).

The last and most significant of the South Saxon entries in the *Anglo-Saxon Chronicle* records that in 491 Ælle and his son Cissa beset *Andredesceaster* and carried out a total massacre of its last British garrison. This dramatic event is the most clearly recorded conflict focussed on the attempted defence of a Roman stronghold on the Saxon Shore. If any one moment could be taken to symbolize the final loss of Roman Britain to the forces of barbarism it could well be this unsuccessful attempt by its sub-Roman defenders to hold what by 491 must have been almost the last section of the *Litus Saxonicum* to remain in British hands. It is perhaps equally symbolic that they were trying to hold it against an invader recorded by Bede as the first barbarian chieftain to deserve the title of Bretwalda.[1] Ælle was evidently remembered in the days of Bede as the first dominant figure to establish a supremacy, however transient, over most of the barbarian forces now overrunning southern Britain on the final collapse of the Saxon Shore's defensive system.

Nothing is known of Ælle's ancestry or antecedents and in the absence of a reliable genealogy for the South Saxon royal family, his relationship to any of the mysterious rulers who figure in Sussex charters purporting to record grants of land in the seventh century is also unknown. Even his three sons, noted in the 477 entry in the *Anglo-Saxon Chronicle* as Cymen, Wlencing, and Cissa, have been suspected of deriving their names, and perhaps their existence, merely from antiquarian attempts to explain such place-names as Cumenesora, Lancing, Cissbury, or Chichester. None of them is certainly ancestral to any of the later kings, *subreguli* or *duces* who figure in what claim to be seventh-century Sussex charters.

None the less Bede must have had some grounds of historical tradition for placing Ælle at the head of his list of bretwaldas. Since he did not think it essential to his purpose to specify the reasons for his acceptance of Ælle's primacy, it is necessary to consider whether the tradition can be supported by other than literary evidence. The Saxon settlements and cemeteries of Sussex have produced a wide range of archaeological material, some of which goes back at least as early as the traditional date of Ælle's bretwaldaship in the

[1] *HE* ii. 5.

last quarter of the fifth century. Such material comes from all sections of the Sussex littoral, with a special concentration in the country between the Cuckmere and the Ouse west of Beachy Head.[1] Here the substantial cemetery at Alfriston, among others, has produced a number of fifth-century graves and some examples of Quoit Brooch Style jewellery as at High Down.[2] At least five other cemeteries, including those at Bishopstone and Selmeston, confirm the presence of early Saxon settlements in this area, which, perhaps significantly, does not appear to contain any Roman villas. It may thus have been available even before Ælle's time as a base for friendly mercenaries or *laeti* employed for the protection of the *Litus Saxonicum*. The absence of large cremation cemeteries from the whole South Saxon area strongly suggests that the initial settlement took place at a time and in conditions when the cultural influences of late Roman life were still powerful, indeed dominant.

Characteristic of South Saxon jewellery in and shortly after the time of Ælle are saucer brooches with five running scrolls and button brooches decorated with a stylized human face. The distribution of these types or of forms influenced by them may provide a clue to the extension of Ælle's authority as bretwalda beyond the Sussex coast plain. However little early Saxon settlement may have taken place in the Wealden forest itself, some at least of the Roman roads that ran through it certainly remained open and gave access to the Thames Valley and beyond. Thus the Stane Street that had linked Chichester to London does not appear to have gone out of use. It is significant that it approaches the Thames not far from the early Surrey cemeteries of Mitcham and Croydon which have produced some of the closest parallels in glass and brooches to material from Alfriston and High Down. Another Roman road (Margary 150) passes directly through Croydon on its way from London to the Roman and Saxon settlement at Hassocks under the South Downs. Other early remains in Surrey, such as those from Guildown where the river Wey intersects the chalk escarpment of the North Downs, illustrate parallel fashions in

---

[1] Welch, op. cit. fig. 9. 24.
[2] Ibid. i. fig. 9. 13 and ii. figs. 7a, 8c, 27c, etc.

brooches and pottery with those of Hassocks, Alfriston, and other Sussex sites.[1]

It seems clear therefore that the apparent absence of pagan Saxon settlement in the Weald should not be interpreted as implying that the forest formed an impassable obstacle to passage along the Roman roads that ran through it. Indeed it may well be that the whole complex of fifth-century Saxon settlement south of the Thames in Surrey owed as much to the spread of Ælle's authority northwards from Sussex as to immigration up the Thames Valley itself, a movement that could well have been liable to obstruction as long as sub-Roman London retained any effective power to block traffic on the river.

It is even possible that the concentration of fifth-century Saxon settlement on the upper reaches of the Thames beyond the Goring gap may owe something to the brief bretwaldaship of Ælle at that time. The distribution of the earlier series of Saxon saucer brooches, especially the common Sussex type with five running scrolls and other chip-carved decoration, to which E. T. Leeds first drew attention in 1912, is suggestive in this connection.[2] Their occurrence not only in Sussex and Surrey but in Berkshire, Oxfordshire, Wiltshire, and as far west as Fairford in Gloucestershire and northwards into the valley of the Warwickshire Avon, could be interpreted as indicating a movement of their wearers from the south coast into the Midlands. Such a movement would have bypassed, however temporarily, the more obvious routes into the Midlands by the rivers giving access from the east coast and the Wash. It is remarkable in this connection that among the saucer brooches from Fairford are several which include as a central feature a human mask very similar in style to some of those which form the decoration of the button brooches characteristic of South Saxon fashions at this period.[3] It is difficult to see how these hybrid types

[1] There is a convenient map of early Saxon sites in Surrey related to these Roman roads in *Surrey Archaeological Collections*, 56 (1959), 149.

[2] *Archaeologia*, 68 (1912), 159–202 and fig. 10. Some more sites could now be added to this map, but they would only serve to emphasize the pattern which it displays. Leeds himself does not appear to have noticed the possible relevance of this distribution to the bretwaldaship of Ælle of Sussex.

[3] The whole corpus of button brooches, nearly 120 in all, has been elaborately

came to be produced in Gloucestershire except under the influence of a movement originating in Sussex for which the bretwaldaship of Ælle provides the most likely context. On any showing this can only have been a brief and superficial affair, not apparently outlasting his own lifetime. It was perhaps only in the still highly mobile conditions prevalent in fifth-century Britain that such an ephemeral occurrence as Ælle's temporary supremacy could have left any traces on artistic fashions of this sort at all.[1]

There are several ways in which the late Roman dispositions on the Saxon Shore may have influenced the course and character of the early settlement of Germanic folk upon these coastal regions. They are perhaps best mentioned at this point, since they concern the possible survival into later Saxon times of administrative arrangements whose remote origins may be traceable to the days of the *Litus Saxonicum*.

It is, for example, a remarkable fact that, in addition to the special cases of Kent and Wessex, three other sections of what must have constituted in the late fourth century the command of the *comes Litoris Saxonici* reappear in early Saxon times as the independent coastal kingdoms of Sussex, Essex, and Lindsey, each with one or more ruling families of their own. At least two of these families, in Sussex and Essex, are specifically Saxon in origin and may go back to the last days of the Saxon Shore. It may also be significant that the pedigree of the kings of Lindsey included at least one king

classified by R. Avent and V. I. Evison in *Archaeologia*, 107 (1982), 77–124. As their maps show, the distribution is almost exclusively south and west of the Thames Valley, and there are no grounds for claiming, on the basis of a single stray from Kempston, Beds., that the form developed in Middle Anglia (p. 98). Apart from Class A, which is essentially Kentish, the distribution of the commonest classes B, C, and E, mostly dating between 425 and 500, 'spread to cover the whole periphery of Andredesweald' (p. 100), from the Sussex coast to the upper Thames and westward into Hants., Wilts., and Gloucs. Nothing could be more suggestive in both time and place of a movement related to the bretwaldaship of Ælle. The Fairford brooches are in N. Åberg, *The Anglo-Saxons in England*, figs. 21 and 26. A decadent button brooch with human mask has recently been found as far west as Cadbury, Somerset, a site described as 'the scene of very great activity' in the fifth century: D. Brown, *Anglo-Saxon England* (1978), 46.

[1] Myres, *Anglo-Saxon Pottery*, map 8 facing p. 115, shows the wide distribution of some other objects that could be relevant to the bretwaldaship of Ælle.

with a British name.[1] It is even more remarkable that all
these three kingdoms, when administrative records were
written down in the days of Mercian supremacy in the eighth
century,[2] were each reckoned to comprise the lands of seven
thousand families. For fiscal purposes it was no doubt convenient that such assessments should be expressed in round
numbers, regardless of any more precise estimates of population or economic value. But that the same figure should
have been used for each of these very different and widely
separated regions is at least an odd coincidence. It may of
course originate simply in the rough-and-ready methods
employed by Mercian bureaucracy. But in these early times
such fiscal assessments were subject to very powerful
supporting pressures from ancient custom and could well
survive unaltered in conditions of great political change.
The uniformity of the figures might thus perpetuate a
tradition from far-off Roman times, when perhaps the *Litus
Saxonicum* had been divided into several administrative
sections treated as of equal consequence,[3] which came to be
controlled by prominent families of Saxon or mixed Saxon
and British antecedents.[4]

[1] Caedbaed, third in descent from Winta, the first historical figure in the royal
line of Lindsey, can hardly be dated later than the third quarter of the sixth
century and could well be earlier. For the early history of Lindsey see F. M.
Stenton in H. W. C. Davis (ed.), *Essays in History presented to R. L. Poole* (Oxford,
1927), 136–50, and below pp. 176–7.

[2] In the so-called Tribal Hidage (*CS* 414), on which there has been much discussion: e.g. C. R. Hart in *TRHS* 5th ser., 21 (1971), 133–58, and W. Davies and
H. Vierck in *Frühmittelalterliche Studien*, 8 (1974), 223–93. The reliability of its
figures has been questioned, as e.g. by F. W. Maitland, *Domesday Book and
Beyond*, 506–15.

[3] A hint of such a sub-division of the Saxon Shore into several roughly equal
administrative units may survive in the *Notitia*, where some of the garrisons of
the several fortresses seem to be grouped in equivalent pairs. Thus Brancaster goes
with Burgh Castle in what became East Anglia; Dover with Lympne, and Reculver
with Richborough in Kent; and Pevensey with Portchester in Sussex. The evidence
for linking the garrisons of Bradwell and Walton Castle is not so clear, but they
form a natural pair for the later Essex: M. W. C. Hassall in D. E. Johnston (ed.),
The Saxon Shore, CBA Research Rept. 18 (1977), 8.

[4] It has been noted that the combined hidage of the mysterious folks
recorded in the Tribal Hidage as the *Noxgaga* and the *Ohtgaga* also amounts to
7,000. Their location is unknown, but it has been observed that the Tribal Hidage
does not include any unit which certainly represents Surrey, a region which in the
670s could still be described in a charter (*CS* 34) as a *provincia* with a *subregulus*
of its own. Wherever it was located this might be another 7,000-hide unit derived
originally from the *Litus Saxonicum* (Welch, op. cit., i. 262).

It will be seen in the next chapter that there are grounds for suspecting that an arrangement of this kind may underlie the formation of the West Saxon kingdom on the western boundaries of the Saxon Shore. This was beyond the limits of the special federate arrangements that traditionally determined the origin of the kingdom of Kent. It is thus of great interest to find that there are marked differences between the social structures of Wessex and Kent, about both of which there is unusually detailed information preserved in the seventh-century law codes which have survived for these two kingdoms. The most significant of these differences for the present purpose is that in the earliest laws of Kent provision is made for the rights and duties of what was clearly a large category of persons called *laets*, who were divided into three socially distinct groups. But no such people appear under this name in West Saxon society, although legal arrangements are made for folk of specifically British descent remaining in the lands occupied by the conquering Saxons.

Many changes of status may have overtaken the *laets* of Kent during and after the collapse of the *Litus Saxonicum*, and before the first Anglo-Saxon law codes were written down early in the seventh century. But there can be no doubt that their name derives directly from that of the *laeti*, who in late Roman times formed the bulk of the barbarian settlers planted out with military obligations in the frontier provinces of the Empire. On the Saxon Shore in Britain such *laeti* are likely to have been already thick on the ground well before the collapse of direct Roman rule. They would have preceded the subsequent arrangements for federate settlement by more formally organized barbarian mercenaries, of which Hengist and his Jutes are the best documented example. The great antiquity of the Kentish *laets* is further suggested by the fact that they no longer appear as a distinct social class in the Laws of Hlothere and Eadric (*c*.675 or later). By then they had evidently been merged with the main body of Kentish *ceorls*.

Such arrangements for the earlier settlement of *laeti* may have been made on other parts of the Saxon Shore in addition to Kent. This is suggested, for example, by the persistence in early medieval East Anglia of folk called *lancetti*, evidently successors to the *laten* noted in the Frisian law codes, whose influence on the social structure of East Anglia was wide and profound.[1] On the other hand the presence of people with such an evident background in the *laeti* of late Roman times is not recorded at all in seventh-century Wessex. This can only mean that such a type of land tenure had never been established among the British population beyond the limits of the Saxon Shore although Britons as such soon came to be accorded a recognized status in West Saxon society. How this came about, and how it affected the formation of the West Saxon kingdom, will be considered next.

[1] See G. C. Homans, 'The Frisians in East Anglia', *Econ. Hist. Review* (1957), 189–206.

6

THE FORMATION OF WESSEX

OF much more permanent consequence than the fleeting
victories of Ælle of Sussex were the events which, if
their dating in the *Anglo-Saxon Chronicle* is approximately correct, were taking place, only a few years later than
his time, in southern Hampshire and the Isle of Wight. This
had been the region that covered the western limit of the
Litus Saxonicum in the last days of Roman Britain and
became the heartland of the West Saxon kingdom. There is a
much firmer basis for the elucidation of its story than is
provided in the *Chronicle* for Sussex by the brief notices
relating to Ælle's battles and the information which Bede had
that he was reckoned to be the first bretwalda. The entries
dealing with the establishment of what became the royal
house of Wessex in Hampshire and the Isle of Wight are of
much greater significance. This is because they are based on
traditions related to the family from which Alfred—who was
probably concerned with the circulation of the *Chronicle*,
though perhaps not directly with its textual content—was
himself descended.[1]

This does not mean of course that every recorded incident
must be taken at its face value, or even that they are necessarily reported in the right order or with the correct dates.
It has already been noted,[2] for example, that these West
Saxon annals appear to contain two versions of what is
basically the same story. These tales have been woven
together by Alfred's clerks and provided with two sets of
dates to fit the annalistic structure of the *Chronicle*.[3] This
procedure has to a large extent succeeded in concealing what

---

[1] See Appendix II. There has been much discussion of the part played
by Alfred in the composition and circulation of the *Chronicle* entries before
890. I follow here the conclusions put forward by J. Bately in *PBA* 64 (1978),
93-129.

[2] p. 5, especially n. 1.

[3] K. Harrison, *EHR* 86 (1971), 527-33.

would otherwise be seen as an obvious duplication. Clearly allowance must be made for such understandable consequences of the need to convert into written annalistic form a group of heroic traditions long preserved orally in an illiterate society. When this is done it is reasonable to conclude that underlying the brief entries in the *Chronicle* are memories, some more reliable than others, of the way this western end of the *Litus Saxonicum* became the centre of the kingdom of Wessex.

The annals contain several significant hints that suggest ways in which this may have happened. There are, for example, more or less direct references to the fate of the two major Saxon Shore forts in this region. The most westerly known of the mainland series is probably *Portus Adurni*, Portchester Castle, on the northern shore of what is now Portsmouth harbour. It need therefore cause no surprise to learn from the *Chronicle* that in 501, just ten years after the traditional date for Ælle's sack of *Andredesceaster*, a chieftain appropriately, if suspiciously, named Port came with his sons to *Portesmutha*, and there they killed a young Briton of very high rank. Whatever may be thought of the name Port, which probably signifies no more than that the attacker's real name had been lost, the incident was clearly memorable as the moment when *Portus Adurni* went the way of *Andredesceaster*, and its last sub-Roman commander lost his life in attempting its defence.[1]

Then there is the notice that in 530 Cerdic and Cynric captured the Isle of Wight and killed a few men in *Wihtgarabyrig*. Further references in 534 and 544 to Wihtgar himself, an obvious personification of the *Wihtwara*, the people of the Isle of Wight, and to his burial at *Wihtgarabyrig*, make it clear that this place was thought of as the central stronghold of the island. Though its Romano-British name had been forgotten, it was evidently remembered as the administrative headquarters of the *Wihtwara*, and the death and burial of Wihtgar there in 544 must be intended to indicate the extinction of

[1] It is of some interest that excavation has revealed the presence in Portchester in the late fourth century of what seems to have been a sort of 'peasant militia' accompanied by wives and children; this may have continued far into the fifth century: B. W. Cunliffe in *Excavations at Portchester Castle*, i (1975), especially 429-31, and ii (1976), especially 301-2.

its independent status. In 534 Wihtgar's name is coupled with
that of one Stuf, who could be a genuine participant in these
events since his name does not appear to derive from that of
any known place in the island or the adjoining mainland.
Wihtgarabyrig itself can hardly be anywhere but Carisbrooke
Castle, which is not only centrally sited for the control of the
island but is known to overlie a late Roman military structure
which could well be a Saxon Shore fort, though little is
known of its form.

Both Bede and the archæological remains from the island
agree that its settlers were in some way related to the Jutes
of Kent. It may well be that *Wihtgarabyrig*, whatever its
name had been in Roman days, stood to the island in the
same administrative relationship as the former Roman centres
of what became the lathes of Kent. Thus, for example,
Durovernum, in becoming *Cantwarabyrig*, retained in the
Jutish system the same relationship to its tribal lands that it
had held in Roman times. Although the *Chronicle* does not
explain the relationship of the Isle of Wight to Kent, it is
known not only that the island's early rulers were Jutes but
that there were family links between them and what became
the royal house of Wessex.[1] This is apparent not only from
the *Chronicle* entry for 534 but from Asser's life of Alfred
which records that the king's own mother was descended
from them.[2]

The *Anglo-Saxon Chronicle* is the main source of information for the early history of the West Saxon royal family.
In spite of the brevity of its entries relating to them, and the
chronological confusion which appears to mark them, these
entries convey more detail about their story than is known
for any other ruling family of this time. Several points of
great interest stand out from these notices. One is that when
Cerdic and Cynric, the traditional founders of the dynasty,
make their first appearance in the annals in 495 they are
described as *ealdormen*, and not by any term implying royal
rank or any outstanding military distinction. When the

[1] It has even been suggested that the Victgils, Vitta, and Vecta who figure
among Hengist's mythical ancestors may owe their names to a vaguely hinted
family association with the Jutes of *Vectis*, the Isle of Wight: see P. Sims-Williams,
Anglo-Saxon England, 12 (1983), 25.
[2] Asser, *Life of King Alfred*, ed. W. H. Stevenson (Oxford, 1904), 2.

Chronicle was compiled in Alfred's reign, the term *ealdorman* was normally used for a prominent official having authority, both civil and military, over a specific territory forming part of a kingdom or other major political unit.[1] It is thus odd to find it used here to describe the leaders of what purports to be an independent band of invaders, whose origins and authority are not otherwise specified.[2] It looks very much as if a hint is being conveyed that Cerdic and his people owed their standing to having been already concerned with administrative affairs under Roman authority on this part of the Saxon Shore.

This impression is strengthened by several other pieces of information which this group of annals provides. The most striking is of course that Cerdic himself bore a British, not a Germanic, name. Moreover native names of this kind, such as Caedwalla, occur in later generations of the West Saxon royal family.[3] It is also of interest, and may well be significant of his local consequence in southern Hampshire, that Cerdic's name is associated with place-names mentioned in the *Chronicle*, such as *Cerdicesford* (508), and *Cerdicesleaga* (527). Moreover his traditional burial-place was at *Cerdicesbeorg*, a former barrow at Stoke near Hurstbourne recorded in an eleventh-century charter.[4] These place-names are of course on a totally different footing from those associating Port and Wihtgar with Portsmouth and the Isle of Wight, for there is no reason for thinking that any of the Cerdic names existed long before the traditional date of the events associated in the *Chronicle* with his activities. It is also of great interest

---

[1] H. R. Loyn in *EHR* 68 (1953), 513–25.

[2] In his important article on 'Anglo-Saxon royal genealogies' (*PBA* 39 (1953), 305), K. Sisam points out that Cerdic's pedigree has no independent authority. It has been put together from that of the Bernician kings and his real ancestry is unknown. He evidently could not claim descent from any Germanic family of importance.

[3] They occur also among Cerdic's contemporaries in the West Saxon annals. One of Port's sons mentioned in 501 is given what is probably the Celtic name Maegla: see K. Jackson on names in *maglo-* (*Language and History*, 463–4).

[4] *CD* 1077: *CS* 594. It is of some interest that Hurstbourne was already a possession of the West Saxon kings when Alfred made his will between 873 and 888. See D. Hill, *An Atlas of Anglo-Saxon England* (Oxford, 1981), fig. 148 for the interesting distribution of these royal properties, some of which may go back to very early times. See also the discussion of the name Cerdic and some of the place-names which contain it in E. Ekwall, *English River-Names* (Oxford, 1928), lxviii-lxix.

that in 519 Cerdic and Cynric are recorded as 'beginning to
reign', for this suggests that a moment came when their status
changed, no doubt as a consequence of the conflicts reported
in earlier entries, from that of dependent *ealdormen* to that
of rulers in their own right.

It is thus possible, in the light of the historical situation
that may have given rise to these annals, to think of Cerdic
as the head of a partly British noble family with extensive
territorial interests at the western end of the *Litus Saxonicum*.
As such he may well have been entrusted in the last days of
Roman or sub-Roman authority with its defence. He would
then be what in later Anglo-Saxon terminology could be
described as an *ealdorman*. If his authority as such extended
some way into the country behind the Saxon Shore itself, it
would have been in parallel with the *Andredesweald* to the
east which depended on *Andredesceaster*.

It would also be easier to understand what have always
been puzzling difficulties in relating the West Saxon annals
in the *Chronicle* to the archaeological record of the region in
which the story is set. If such a dominant native family as
that of Cerdic had already developed blood-relationships with
existing Saxon and Jutish settlers at this end of the Saxon
Shore, it could very well be tempted, once effective Roman
authority had faded away, to go further. It might take
matters into its own hands and, after eliminating any surviving
pockets of resistance by competing British chieftains, such as
the mysterious Natanleod of annal 508, it could 'begin to
reign', without recognizing in future any superior authority.

Such a take-over need not have involved any substantial
influx of fresh Germanic settlers. Cerdic's military power
could have rested mainly on those already in occupation
of Saxon Shore lands, and for the most part already culturally assimilated to British ways in the last days of Roman
Britain. This would help to explain the scarcity of archaeological evidence of a specifically Germanic character in
southern Hampshire west of the Meon valley,[1] though there

---

[1] At Droxford in the Meon valley there is not only a cemetery with some
marked Jutish features, but also a manor whose medieval custom 'strikingly
recalls the gavelkind of Kent' (Jolliffe, *Pre-Feudal England*, 88, n. 5). See F.
Aldsworth, 'The Droxford Anglo-Saxon cemetery, Soberton, Hampshire', *Proc.
Hampshire Field Club and Arch. Soc.* 35 (1979), 93–182.

is rather more, with a markedly Jutish flavour, in the Isle of Wight.

Both in the West Saxon annals that follow Cerdic's initial take-over, and in the pattern of the archaeological remains that seem roughly to correspond with his proceedings, there is an unexpected emphasis on a movement westward into the chalk country of south Wiltshire, rather than directly north over the Hampshire uplands to the Enborne and Kennet valleys and so towards the upper Thames basin. Thus, in place of any references to the cantonal capitals of the Belgae at Winchester (*Venta Belgarum*) or of the Atrebates at Silchester (*Calleva Atrebatum*), there are battles recorded at Charford-on-Avon in 519, at *Searoburh* (Old Sarum) in 552, and at *Beranbyrg* (Barbury Castle, on the Ridgeway at the west end of the Vale of the White Horse) in 556. Settlement along such a route is marked archaeologically by several sixth-century Saxon cemeteries, such as those at Harnham Hill and Petersfinger near Salisbury, Black Patch in the Vale of Pewsey, and Wootton Bassett west of Swindon. There are also a considerable number of male burials intrusive in prehistoric round barrows in all this chalk country, suggestive of casualties incurred in military operations.

The contrast which this picture presents with the situation further east in Hampshire and Berkshire, where similar signs of West Saxon intrusion might be expected, is very striking. Apart from a couple of cemeteries in the neighbourhood of Winchester, the material evidence for an Anglo-Saxon presence on any considerable scale over all central and north Hampshire and south Berkshire in the sixth century is surprisingly slight.[1] On the other hand there is in north Hampshire a remarkable group of place-names of British rather than Saxon origin (Micheldever, Andover, Candover, and so on), suggesting an unexpectedly vigorous persistence of pockets of the sub-Roman population in those parts.

The most likely explanation for this contrast is to be found once again in the situation that could have arisen in late Roman and sub-Roman times at the western end of the *Litus Saxonicum*. The hinterland, whose coastal defence had

[1] The Hampshire evidence has been conveniently assembled by M. Biddle in Sieveking, Longworth, and Wilson (eds.), *Problems in Economic and Social Archaeology* (1976), 323–42.

rested in the fourth century on forces, whether naval or
military, based on the Saxon Shore forts, no doubt covered
the tribal lands of the Belgae, centred on Winchester, and
probably also those of the Atrebates further north, based on
Silchester. But there is no reason to suppose that this defensive system extended westward over what is now Wiltshire and
Dorset. That Winchester had some sort of para-military
administrative status at this period is suggested by the
presence of some unusual burials in the Lankhills cemetery,
which show funerary practices that can be paralleled in
military contexts on the Continent.[1] It is relevant to note of
both these groups that the suggestion of their intrusive
character does not rest mainly on the nature of the grave-
goods associated with them, but on their ritual arrangement
in relation to the body. Thus their eccentricity might never
have been recognized had they not presented a contrast
to the standard arrangement of normal Romano-British
interments in a large late cemetery. Perhaps the scarcity of
such para-military burials so far noted over all the country
covered by this western extremity of the *Litus Saxonicum*
may be partly due to similar causes and thus be more
apparent than real.

It may, then, be reasonable to think that the country over
which Cerdic and his family were dominant in the last days
of Roman rule, when they could still be described in Anglo-
Saxon terms as *ealdormen* and had not yet 'begun to reign',
already included Hampshire and much of south Berkshire. If
that was so there may well have been no dramatic incidents
affecting *Venta Belgarum* or *Calleva Atrebatum* to justify
special mention in their family traditions, which underlay
the entries eventually incorporated in the *Anglo-Saxon
Chronicle*. It may never have been obvious to the sub-Roman
inhabitants of either city and their dependent lands at
exactly what point of time they had passed from the jurisdic-
tion of the Cerdicing family as the half-British representatives
of a no longer effective Roman authority, to that of the same

---

[1] M. Biddle (ed.), *Winchester Studies*, 3 (1979), 377–403. The emphasis
originally laid on the Germanic character of such burials has been questioned by
C. J. Simpson (*Brit.* 7 (1976), 204–6), who has pointed out that much of their
accompanying equipment was standard in the late Roman army, whatever the
ethnic origin of its wearers.

family as rulers of a mixed native and Saxon war-band now claiming the prestige of kingship.

That the transition was not altogether without incident is shown by the archaeological rather than literary evidence. At Winchester, for example, the main south gate of the Roman city was so effectively blocked in two stages during the fifth and sixth centuries by walling and a ditch dug across the road, that all traffic from the south had for many years to enter by a minor gate further east, later known as Kingsgate, which may not have been much used until the Old Minster to which it gave direct access was built in the seventh century. It was thus outside this gate that the main extra-mural suburb, along the present Kingsgate Street, developed in the Middle Ages, rather than outside what had been the original south gate of the town. Before it was put out of use in this drastic way the south gate road (Margary 42*b*) would have been the direct route between *Venta* and the late Roman fortress at *Clausentum* (now Bitterne) nine miles away near the mouth of the Itchen. It looks as if there came a moment in these dark centuries when the rulers of *Venta* and *Clausentum* were on opposite sides in some unrecorded sub-Roman conflict.[1]

But to the west in Wiltshire the situation was evidently different. Here the British population had never come under the military tutelage of the Saxon Shore system and may never have been infiltrated, as the Saxon Shore had been, by Germanic folk who, to a large extent, came to adopt late Roman cultural ways.[2] Thus any advance by Cerdic's people westward beyond the limits of the *Litus Saxonicum* may have seemed to the native British chieftains as an invasion to

---

[1] M. Biddle, *Ant. J.* 55 (1975), 117-18 and *PBA* 69 (1984), pl. VI, which shows the blocked gate as excavated. I am greatly indebted to Mr. Biddle for discussing the historical implications with me. It looks very much as if the Cerdicing family had always treated Winchester as a major centre of their authority, a usage which may well have begun in late Roman times as part of the administrative structure of the *Litus Saxonicum*. The richly furnished burial found in an extensive domestic complex with fifth-century Saxon pottery in Lower Brook Street in the centre of the city in 1971 may indicate an establishment belonging to a prominent early member of the Cerdicing ruling family: *PBA* loc. cit. 117-18.

[2] A few pieces of sub-Roman metal-work, notably buckles of Hawkes Types IA and IIA from Roman sites in central Wilts. may come from military equipment appropriate to British participants in such conflicts: *Med. Arch.* 5 (1961), map 9.

be resisted by force in battles which provided memorable incidents that were recorded also in the traditions of the invaders. Archaeologically too, the newcomers would leave more conspicuous traces of their presence in settlements and cemeteries that did not merge culturally, at least to begin with, into the British background, as had happened in Hampshire and south Berkshire, but were obviously recognizable as those of intrusive foreigners. It is entirely consistent with this situation that Wiltshire should retain such a prominent and widespread distribution of British place-names, many being related to natural features in areas where Saxon settlement was at first sparse and separate.[1]

To sum up this first stage in the formation of Wessex, it would seem that quite early in the sixth century a point had been reached at which Cerdic and his relations were establishing their independent authority over the former tribal lands of the Belgae and Atrebates in Hampshire and Berkshire with which they had been concerned hitherto only as *ealdormen* under sub-Roman military rule. In addition, they were engaged in extending their power into the native-held regions to the west in Wiltshire which had never formed part of the *Litus Saxonicum*.

But at about this moment the situation began to change. If the dates in the *Chronicle* are approximately correct, Cerdic himself died in 534, and in the same year he and Cynric are recorded as having handed over the Isle of Wight to their relatives Stuf and Wihtgar. This can only mean that their interests were now extending so far inland, beyond the limits of their original base in the *Litus Saxonicum*, that they were content to leave the island to their Jutish relatives.

This conclusion is greatly reinforced if it can be accepted that the *Cerdicesbeorg*, at Stoke in Hurstbourne, was Cerdic's burial-place.[2] It lies in the north-west corner of Hampshire, only a mile or two east of the main Roman road from Winchester to Cirencester (Margary 43). This road passes through Savernake Forest, on its way to the little Roman town of *Cunetio* at Mildenhall east of Marlborough. It runs very close to the point east of which no certain traces of the Wansdyke have been located. In Cerdic's time, and perhaps

---

[1] See EP-NS *Wilts*, (1939), xv–xvi.   [2] See p. 147.

earlier, this was probably dense woodland. How did it come about that Cerdic was apparently operating in this remote corner of Hampshire when he died? And why was he buried at a spot so accessible by a main Roman road both to his probable base at Winchester and to the eastern termination of Wansdyke? Could this great post-Roman frontier earthwork have served already to protect his territory in Hampshire and south Wiltshire from a major danger to the north? And, if that was its purpose, who posed that danger, and who was first concerned to resist it in this massive manner?

Before attempting to answer these questions it may be as well to note the next stage in the formation of Wessex as it is indicated in the brief entries in the *Anglo-Saxon Chronicle*, and to see whether any plausible link can be suggested between them and the British tradition covering these years as it appears in the pages of Gildas.

Cynric, variously described as the son or grandson of Cerdic in different versions of the West Saxon genealogy,[1] is not a figure in whom historians have felt much confidence. His name is linked with that of Cerdic from the start of these annals in 495, and he is also said to have reigned alone for twenty-six years after Cerdic's death in 534. Under 560 is a notice that Ceawlin began to reign, but he and Cynric had already appeared together at the battle of *Beranbyrg* in 556.[2] These entries thus give Cynric an improbably long run of sixty-five years at the centre of affairs. Moreover the oddity of his name might hint that he was not a real hero at all, but a ghost figure primarily designed to personify the continuity of kingship in the ruling family during the gap of twenty-six years between the known dates of Cerdic's death in 534 and of Ceawlin's accession in 560. In fact the only event in the whole sixty-five years of Cynric's supposed career in which he figures as sole leader is the battle at Old Sarum (*Searoburh*) in 552. This was clearly a memorable event since it would have established West Saxon domination over the chalk

---

[1] A Creoda appears between Cerdic and Cynric in the pedigree of Ina of Wessex and some texts that used it, such as Asser and the *Chronicle* entry for 855. No incident involving him occurs in the annals themselves, but his name may survive in a minor Wiltshire place-name, *Creodanhyll*, noted by Ekwall from CS 390, 566.

[2] See Appendix II.

regions of central Wiltshire which became one of the main
foci of the later kingdom.[1] But whether Cynric himself was a
major figure in these central decades of the sixth century
must remain for the moment an open question.

It is possible that the British story briefly and confusedly
recorded by Gildas may help to resolve this question. According to his account the period of chaos and confusion that
followed the breakdown of the arrangement made by the
'proud tyrant' (Vortigern) with the federate Saxons whose
settlement he had arranged in *orientali parte insulae* lasted
for an unspecified time until the Britons were rallied under
the leadership of Ambrosius Aurelianus and achieved a
notable triumph over the invaders at the siege of Mons
Badonicus.[2] After this decisive event the enemy had made no
further advance, and a period of peace followed which was
still continuing when Gildas was writing his book.

No precise dates are given for these events, but the sometimes conflicting time-signals provided for them by Gildas
and others make it reasonably certain to place Mons
Badonicus between 490 and 516.[3] If Gildas is really trying
to say that he was born at that time, and was forty-four at
the date of writing, that would mean that the period of
relative peace, during which the invaders made no further
progress, must have lasted at least until 534 and perhaps to
around 560. Gildas makes it very plain that in his opinion
this situation was not likely to last much longer. His own
death is noted in the *Annales Cambriae* as occurring in 570.
If he was born in the year of Mons Badonicus, that event is
more likely to have occurred nearer 516, the date given
by the *Annales Cambriae*, than 490, for the latter would
make Gildas around eighty when he died.

In any event, Mons Badonicus must have given a sufficient
check to the revolted Saxon federates who had broken out of
their settlements in *orientali parte insulae* back in the fifth
century, to prevent their power spreading further until at

[1] Within a ten-mile radius of Old Sarum can be found the three largest pagan
Saxon cemeteries in Wiltshire, the royal cenotaph on the Salisbury race course,
and the *villa regalis* of Wilton, later the administrative centre of those *Wilsaetas*
who might have left their name as 'Wilset', in parallel with the *Dorsaetas* and
Sumersaetas who formed Dorset and Somerset further west.

[2] *De Excidio*, xxv-vi.

[3] The essential facts are in Appendix III.

least 534 and perhaps 560. It will not escape notice that these dates correspond almost uncannily to the twenty-six years between the death of Cerdic and the accession of Ceawlin, which are filled in the *Anglo-Saxon Chronicle* by the period of sole rule there attributed to the shadowy figure of Cynric.

It has been noted already that Gildas attributes the British recovery, which culminated in their decisive victory at the *obsessio montis Badonici*, to the leadership of Ambrosius Aurelianus. It has also been noted that if Cerdic was buried in 534 at *Cerdicesbeorg* in Hurstbourne he may well have been engaged at the time of his death in some operations connected with the eastern termination of Wansdyke where it is adjacent to the Roman road from Winchester to Mildenhall on its passage through Savernake Forest.

Now this section of Wansdyke[1] stretches westward for some fifteen miles from Savernake Forest across the open downland that forms the dramatic northern escarpment of the vale of Pewsey, at least as far as the point on Morgan's Hill at which it joins, and in fact destroys, the Roman road (Margary 53) that leads from Mildenhall (*Cunetio*) to Bath (*Aquae Sulis*). It faces north and was so aligned as to give maximum visual command of all traffic on or near the Ridgeway, the prehistoric route which runs westwards along the Berkshire Downs from the upper Thames Valley and turns south near Barbury Castle (the *Beranbyrg* of annal 556) to cross the Vale of Pewsey on to Salisbury Plain.

Whenever this part of Wansdyke was built, the intention of those who constructed it can only have been to block access by this route from the upper Thames basin to the central chalklands of Wiltshire, two regions which must at the time have been under different and potentially hostile political control. East Wansdyke is known, both from sections cut across it at various points adjacent to Roman settlements and from the way that it overlies and puts out of use the Roman road at Morgan's Hill, to be of sub-Roman or post-Roman date.[2] It must however be earlier than the

[1] See Myres, 'Wansdyke and the origin of Wessex' in H. R. Trevor-Roper (ed.), *Essays in British History presented to Sir Keith Feiling* (1964), 1-28.

[2] A. and C. Fox, 'Wansdyke reconsidered', *Arch. J.* 115 (1958), 1-48, and A. Clark, 'The Nature of Wansdyke', *Antiquity*, 32 (1958), 89-96.

consolidation of Wessex in the seventh century. After this
time a massive frontier bisecting this part of the kingdom's
heartlands could never have made political sense. In other
words, East Wansdyke must have been built for a purpose
regarded as justifying such a major engineering effort at some
moment between the breakdown of Roman rule in Britain
and the formation of the West Saxon kingdom with which
this chapter is concerned.

The most likely context for the building of East Wansdyke
is that it was constructed by some sub-Roman authority, still
in control of Wiltshire and the west country, to prevent the
penetration of its territory from the north by early Anglo-
Saxon folk bursting out of the upper Thames basin. It is
known from the archaeology of that area that it was full of
Anglo-Saxon folk from at least the early fifth century
onwards, and it has been suggested above[1] that they may
have been reinforced from the south during the brief
bretwaldaship of Ælle of Sussex. They may equally well have
received further bands of intruders both coming up the
Thames Valley and from the north-east. This would have
happened when any treaty arrangements, of the kind recorded
by Gildas in *orientali parte insulae*, broke down in the way
that he describes, letting loose a flood of mixed Angle and
Saxon former *foederati* into the southern Midlands.

It can indeed be suggested with some plausibility that
whatever sub-Roman authority was in control of Silchester
and the northern part of its tribal lands in Berkshire stretching
up to the Thames Valley in the early fifth century, may itself
have planted out a screen of barbarian *laeti* to assist in the
protection of its northern borders along the Thames.[2]
This could well be the meaning of the presence, in a number
of these Thames-side cemeteries, Abingdon, Dorchester, Long
Wittenham, and further down the river at Reading and several
places in its neighbourhood, of Anglo-Saxon brooches,
buckles, and pottery which belong at latest to the early years
of the fifth century. The settlements at Cassington and
Brighthampton on the north side of the river above Oxford
could well have started in a similar fashion. This very early

---

[1] p. 139.
[2] I have developed the case for this view more fully in *Anglo-Saxon Pottery*,
89-91.

Saxon material is matched, sometimes on the same or adjacent
sites, by late or sub-Roman metal-work. Much was found,
unfortunately without datable contexts, in the nineteenth-
century excavation of Silchester.[1] It includes sub-Roman
military buckles of Hawkes Types I and II which occur also
at Dorchester and other sites on the upper Thames.[2] This
material was probably supplied to those frontier posts from
Calleva, where it appears that in its final phase the basilica
in the town centre was turned into a substantial metal-
working area.[3] Another site which has produced very late
Roman material is Lowbury Hill on the Berkshire Ridgeway
overlooking the upper Thames basin. This apparently started
as a pagan temple in late Roman times, but it probably served
finally as a look-out point related to the outer periphery of
the Silchester defences.[4]

Of the last days of sub-Roman Silchester there is unfortunately no written record. It must have come to a complete
end no later than the last years of the sixth century.[5] Had it
retained any vitality into the first half of the seventh it could
hardly have failed to be revived as a major centre of renewed
Christian activity in the fifty years following the coming of
St. Augustine and the Roman mission in 597. It had, after
all, been the walled capital of one of the major southern
Romano-British tribal cantons, one moreover where the
public buildings in the centre of the town had included a
conspicuously placed Christian church. This must have been
the seat of a bishop in the fourth century. But all memory
of this historic past had clearly been forgotten when Birinus
in 634 chose the much smaller, and less significant, walled
town of Dorchester-on-Thames as the centre of his mission
to the West Saxons.

But in the fifth, and perhaps far into the sixth, century
the continuing vitality of sub-Roman Silchester can be
illustrated, not merely by its substantial output of para-
military metal-work and its probable maintenance of a

[1] G. C. Boon, *Med. Arch.* 3 (1959), 79-88 and pls. III, IV. His comments are
very relevant in this context.
[2] *Med. Arch.* 5 (1961), 21-34 and fig. 9.
[3] M. Fulford, *Guide to the Silchester Excavations 1979-81* (Reading, 1982), 7.
[4] D. Atkinson, *The Romano-British Site on Lowbury Hill in Berkshire*
(Reading, 1916).
[5] Ceolwulf of Wessex, 597-611, could well have been responsible: see pp. 171-2.

defensible river frontier in the Thames Valley. It was also apparently protected by stretches of earthworks related to the Roman roads that led to it from the north and west.[1] This may be the reason why the Thames Valley section of the road that had once linked Silchester and Dorchester (Margary 160c) went entirely out of use, its memory surviving only in the later place-name of Streatley. This is not surprising in view of the obviously hostile relations prevailing at this time between the sub-Roman Atrebates and the Thames Valley Saxons. Equally significant perhaps are the Padworth earthworks, which link the surviving southern section of this Dorchester road, exactly at the point of its disappearance, to the main west road out of *Calleva* (Margary 41a and 53) that went via Speen (itself an almost unaltered Romano-British name) and *Cunetio* (Mildenhall) to Bath (*Aquae Sulis*).

The western section of this road between *Cunetio* and *Aquae Sulis* has already been mentioned in connection with the termination of East Wansdyke, which overlies and destroys it where they meet on Morgan's Hill.[2] It is thus worth considering whether these defensive earthworks on the Silchester section of the road, and indeed the whole complex of sub-Roman works north and west of the city, may be part of the same scheme that led further west to the construction of the main section of Wansdyke itself.

Now Gildas provides two clues to the circumstances in which the unrestrained outbreak of Vortigern's federate Saxons was stopped. He gives the name of the British leader, Ambrosius Aurelianus, and the site of the decisive encounter described as the siege, not the battle, of Mons Badonicus. He also hints indirectly at a date which can hardly be later than 516, but could be up to some twenty years earlier.[3] It is tempting to think of the highly Romanized, and clearly still well organized, canton of *Calleva Atrebatum*, still perhaps to some extent sheltered behind the end of the *Litus Saxonicum*, as the most likely political base for a leader with

---

[1] As was pointed out by B. H. St. J. O'Neil in *Antiquity*, 18 (1944), 113-22. The accompanying map makes the relationship of the various earthworks to the Roman roads around Silchester very clear.

[2] p. 155.

[3] Appendix III.

such a purely Roman name as Ambrosius Aurelianus. But the loss of all records relating to Silchester makes it unwise to indulge such speculations, and, as will be seen shortly, there are good reasons for thinking that Ambrosius' power-base is likely to have been in Wiltshire.[1]

On the other hand there seems no reason to doubt that Gildas' 'Mons Badonicus' must be his latinization of a name later anglicized as Badbury, or, in modern English, Mount Badon. There are several places in Wessex which could have given rise to such names. By far the most probable are two close together on the Wiltshire Downs south-east of Swindon. One is a hill-fort on the escarpment which left its name to the adjacent village of Badbury, though for some centuries the fort itself has been generally known for local tenurial reasons as Liddington Castle. There are several considerations which point strongly to the significance of this Badbury in the geographical context of Gildas' Mons Badonicus. Its situation had obvious strategic importance in the post-Roman age, for it lies just south of the point on the Ridgeway where the Roman road from Winchester (Margary 43) converges with that from Silchester (Margary 416) before they make their way together north-westwards to Cirencester. It must therefore have been in sub-Roman times a place where several roads met, in fact a communications centre of some consequence.

But it is likely that the name Mons Badonicus was intended by Gildas to identify a wider area than that just marked by a hill-fort and a road-centre above modern Badbury. It could mean in more general terms 'the hill-country of Badon'. This more extensive meaning receives strong support from the fact that, some three miles to the south-east on the Roman road from Silchester (Margary 416) is Baydon itself.[2] This place, standing some 760 feet above sea-level, and at the highest point reached by the Roman road, is the most elevated village in Wiltshire. Its position, set high between

---

[1] pp. 160 and 212-13.
[2] Early forms of Baydon do nothing to support Ekwall's derivation from OE beg-dun, 'berry hill'. He does not note its obvious connection with nearby Badbury for which, as for other Badbury hill-forts, he suggests an origin in the name of an unrecorded hero called Badda, who for some unexplained reason specialized in leaving his name to hill-forts.

deep valleys to the north and south, would make Gildas'
use of the word *mons* to describe his Badon quite appropriate
to Baydon. Although it shows no present indication of
defensive earthworks, and is thus less likely than Badbury to
be the actual site of Gildas' *obsessio montis Badonici*, its
presence near Badbury strongly suggests that the name Badon
could be applied in early times to the whole stretch of hilly
country south of the Ridgeway through which the Roman
roads from Cirencester to Silchester and Winchester had to
pass. Gildas must surely have intended to locate his Mons
Badonicus somewhere in the region dominated by these two
very prominent topographical features which still bear its
name.[1]

Any enterprising leader anxious to protect central Wiltshire
from Saxon forces proceeding down the Ridgeway from the
upper Thames basin, and intent on forcing the passage of
Wansdyke, could not do better than anticipate such a move
by using either of these Roman roads to interrupt their
progress at Mons Badonicus. If this is what Ambrosius did,
the various scraps of evidence from both sides that make up
this complicated story fall into a pattern which at least makes
tactical sense.

If the centre of Ambrosius' power was not in the Romanized
tribal lands of the Atrebates, virtually untouched by Saxon
penetration in his time, though increasingly threatened from
the upper Thames basin, it must have lain in central Wiltshire
west of the hinterland of the *Litus Saxonicum*. This was an
area not yet taken over by Cerdic and his people pressing out
from Hampshire. And here, strategically situated in the Avon
valley, almost due south of the central section of East
Wansdyke at *Wodnesgeat*, some fourteen miles away across
the vale of Pewsey, is Amesbury, which in a charter of about
880[2] was spelt *Ambresbyrig*. Place-name scholars in the past
have been strangely reluctant to consider the possibility that
this name may contain a shortened form of that of the
British leader, and so mean 'the stronghold of Ambrosius'.
Neither Ekwall nor the authors of the Wiltshire volume of the
English Place-Name Society mention this as an alternative to

[1] The possible relevance of Baydon to Mons Badonicus has been suggested by
H. M. Porter, *The Saxon Conquest of Somerset and Devon* (Bath, 1967), 58.
[2] *CS* 553.

their derivation from a Germanic name Ambr or Ambre not otherwise recorded in any historical context in this country.[1] But whatever the philologists may think, no place in fact could be better suited to be the focus of Ambrosius' operations as here reconstructed than the neighbourhood of Amesbury itself.[2]

Whether Mons Badonicus was fought as early as 490 or as late as 516, the forty-four years (or more) of peace that followed it will have left the Britons of Wiltshire and south-western Britain in general unmolested. They would have remained under the control of Ambrosius and his unrecorded successors until at least the death of Cerdic in 534 and perhaps as late as the accession of Ceawlin in 560. What the relations between Cerdic and Ambrosius may have been there is no means of knowing. But it is at least possible that at the time of his death, not far from the eastern termination of Wansdyke, Cerdic may have been engaged, with or without British collaboration, in plans to fill the gap between this point and the peripheral defences north and west of Silchester against the risk of further onslaughts from the Thames Valley Saxons.

This area forms, in fact, the central watershed of southern England. The upper reaches of the Kennet to the north flow east to join the Thames at Reading. In the vale of Pewsey, across the chalk barrier to the south are the headwaters of both the Salisbury Avon, which eventually falls into the English Channel, and the Bristol Avon, which runs west towards the Severn.[3] For whatever reason, and it may well have been Cerdic's death that stopped the work, no effective barrier such as Wansdyke was ever built across this strategic watershed. There are a number of disjointed sections of bank-and-ditch in the eastern part of Savernake Forest and a long

[1] Ekwall's *Dictionary* was published in 1936, the *Place-names of Wiltshire* in 1939, both at a period when there was a largely unjustified tendency to rely on unrecorded Germanic personal names to explain difficult elements in English toponymy.

[2] For further development of this argument for the topographical basis of Ambrosius' power see pp. 212-13.

[3] The keen observation of John Aubrey had already noticed in the seventeenth century how these three rivers all rise 'at the foot of Martinsoll-hill' and then 'divide like the parting of the haire on the crowne of the head and take their courses their severall wayes . . . to the east, south and west coasts': see his *Natural History of Wilts.*, ed. J. Britton (1847), 29.

stretch running south from Chisbury Camp and partly blocking the valley north-east of Great Bedwyn.[1] But the impression left is one of incoherence and· incompleteness, quite unlike the purposeful progress of Wansdyke itself, across the open chalklands to the west of *Cerdicesbeorg*.

Writing some forty-four years after Mons Badonicus, Gildas was thoroughly justified in thinking that the precarious peace it had secured for the Britons could not last much longer. It was his professional business to attribute their growing danger to the sins of the British people, and to use it as a powerful inducement to make them mend their ways. But on any showing the signs of renewed peril to the Britons were clear enough. Their hold on the chalklands of central Wiltshire, perhaps still centred on Ambrosius' probable stronghold at *Ambresbyrig*, could hardly have long survived the victory at Old Sarum attributed to Cynric in 552, which probably indicated renewed westward pressure by the Hampshire Saxons. Four years later, in 556, the *Chronicle* records the last appearance of Cynric and, more significantly, the first mention of Ceawlin, in a battle with Britons at *Beranbyrg*. The result is not stated, but a fresh conflict in this area, so close to Mons Badonicus, suggests that the long peace that had followed the earlier struggle hereabouts was wearing thin.

For the next thirty years and more the West Saxon annals are dominated by the doings of Ceawlin and his kinsmen, which introduce a completely new dimension into the formation of the West Saxon kingdom. No longer are the recorded incidents related to events in Hampshire· and Wiltshire. The whole scene has shifted dramatically northwards into the upper Thames region, from which expeditions are mounted, not always successfully, down the Thames

[1] Ekwall derives the name Bedwyn from early English forms of the word for the common wild convolvulus now generally known as bindweed. This seems a very odd way to describe what was certainly an important centre in the early Saxon centuries. One cannot help feeling that it may conceal a much older name very possibly of British origin. EP-NS *Wilts.* agrees that the name is likely to be pre-English. If so, it may be linked with the group of British place-names in north Hampshire noted on p. 149 as indicating strong native survival in these parts. It may be significant of early association with the West Saxon royal family that both Bedwyn and one of these nearby British place-names, Candover, appear among the estates disposed of in King Alfred's will 873–88: D. Hill, *An Atlas of Anglo-Saxon England*, fig. 148.

towards Kent in 568, westwards as far as Cirencester, Gloucester, and Bath in 577, and northwards into the Midlands in 584. Until the last year of his life, when Ceawlin met with disaster in 592, apparently on the Wansdyke itself, there is no reason to believe that he ever operated south of that barrier which had played such an important part as a northward-facing frontier in the earlier stages of the creation of Wessex.

It is clear from the echoes of poetic diction which they contain, notable especially in the annals for 584 and 592, that these entries, dealing with the exploits of Ceawlin and his relatives, are based on a lost saga recalling the more dramatic aspects of his reign. A saga of this kind is not likely to have been provided with exact dates.[1] These would be of little interest to the audiences before which such tales were recited or sung on cold winter evenings around the fire in a lord's hall. But there is no reason to doubt that the story of Ceawlin as a whole belongs to the second half of the sixth century, and thus follows closely upon the forty-four years or more of peace initiated by Mons Badonicus.

The *Anglo-Saxon Chronicle* is almost certainly right to attach the Ceawlin saga chronologically to the last recorded doings of Cerdic's direct successors in the Wansdyke area in the middle of the sixth century. It must however remain very doubtful whether it is correct in attaching Ceawlin himself and his relations, Cuthwine, Cuthwulf, and Cutha (the last probably an abbreviated version of one of the other names), directly to the Cerdicing pedigree. This is doubtless made more plausible by the fact that their names, like those of the early Cerdicings, alliterate in initial C.

But the Ceawlin saga itself clearly relates to the doings of chieftains based topographically not on Hampshire and Wiltshire at all, but on the upper Thames. This, as has been seen, was a region already full of early Saxon folk. Some of

---

[1] See Appendix III. These entries bear clear signs of artificial dating. Except for the battle of Deorham in 577 and the note of his death in 593, both dates that might well be known independently, the annals from the Ceawlin saga are all spaced at multiples of four years, 556, 560, 568, 584, and 592. These are the only instances of such rhythmic dating in the West Saxon annals of this period, except for three earlier and possibly accidental pairs, 519, 527: 530, 534: 552, 556, of which the last has probably been drawn into the Ceawlin sequence, since it includes the first mention of his name.

these people, if the interpretation of Wansdyke and the Silchester dykes here proposed is correct, had been established there in force since quite early in the fifth century. They must have been regarded both by Cerdic and his people, coming up from Hampshire, and by the Britons, whether of *Calleva* or those further west in Wiltshire, as a major menace to their security. Their joint capacity to meet the danger is, indeed, shown by the building of Wansdyke and the Silchester dykes further east, but there are indications of increasing discord between them, and also perhaps among the British leaders themselves.[1] This was no doubt one reason for the alarm felt by Gildas as he was writing the *De Excidio* about the time of Ceawlin's accession.

Ceawlin and his people can thus only be understood as the leaders who had imposed their rule on the Thames Valley Saxons. They were at first quite independent of, and hostile to, the Saxon and British followers of the Cerdicing family as the latter moved up from the western limits of the Saxon Shore. The Wansdyke and Silchester frontiers thus typify the potential conflict between the two groups. The collaboration recorded between Ceawlin and the shadowy Cynric in fighting the Britons at *Beranbyrg* in 556 may well have been designed by the compilers of the *Chronicle* simply to establish a plausible relationship between these two distinct and hostile families on their first contact.[2] But it is significant that there is no further mention of collaboration once Ceawlin is stated to have 'succeeded to the kingdom' in 560, and, as will be seen shortly, it is very likely that his fall in 592 was a direct consequence of conflict between the two families.

[1] Nennius, *Hist. Britt.* 66 preserves a memory of internal dissension between two British leaders called Ambrosius and Guitolin (Vitalinus) with a battle at Gwoloph. If this is one of the Wallops in Hampshire, it could well belong to a time after Mons Badonicus when Ambrosius' authority was in decline. Ekwall suggests a Germanic origin for the name Wallop, but as it does not appear in any written form earlier than Domesday Book, this is clearly no more than an implausible guess. If the conflict was between two British leaders it was most likely in British territory and at a place with a British name.

[2] Ceawlin appears as Cynric's son in the genealogy, but as Cynric's own place in the succession (and indeed his very existence) is so doubtful, this does little to strengthen Ceawlin's links with Cerdic's family. It seems clear from the preface to the *Chronicle* that great pains have been taken, whether in Alfred's time or earlier, to secure that every prominent ruler in West Saxon history can be claimed as a direct descendant of Cerdic.

Between 560 and 593 the main series of events recorded in the careers of Ceawlin and his relations presents a reasonably coherent story. They appear to concern the formation of a power centred on the upper Thames region and to record its expansion therefrom, although both the significance and the dating of some of the incidents may be difficult to fit into a plausible pattern. The initial campaign of 568 in which Ceawlin and Cutha are said to have driven Æthelbert of Kent in flight to his own country after a battle at Wibbandun[1] seems to imply that the West Saxon chieftains were already in firm control of the upper Thames region. They could thus apparently resist with success any attempt at invasion from powerful neighbours downstream.

On the other hand the next entry records that in 571 a certain Cuthwulf fought the Britons at *Biedcanford* and captured four towns, Limbury, Aylesbury, Bensington, and Eynsham; and in the same year he died. This seems to relate to a quite different, and presumably much earlier, situation, in which the establishment of Saxon power both in the upper Thames basin and in the vale of Aylesbury is only just beginning.

It is not certain whether *Biedcanford* can be identified with Bedford; the identification becomes plausible by the simple deletion of what may be the mistaken intrusion of the one letter 'c'. That the name was originally written Bedanford, from which modern Bedford would naturally derive, is strongly suggested by Ethelweard's use of that form in his tenth-century Latin translation of this annal in the *Chronicle*. It is also significant that the name Bieda, giving rise to Bedanford, appears also to underlie Biddenham, a village adjacent to Bedford on the west. The form Bedcanford, if not a simple spelling mistake, could possibly have arisen from the use of Biedca as a pet-form of Bieda when the *Chronicle* was first compiled.[2]

---

[1] The location of Wibbandun is uncertain. It cannot be identified with Wimbledon, but may well have been somewhere nearby.

[2] For this sensible solution to the problem see the letter from K. R. Davis in *Current Archaeology* 92 (1984), 286. In support of this A. Bell has pointed out (ibid. 93, 319) that a similar thematic development may have occurred in the case of another place-name in this group of West Saxon annals, *Feathanleag*, recorded in the *Anglo-Saxon Chronicle* under 584. In all four twelfth-century MSS of Gaimer, *Estorie des Engles*, this name is spelt *Feadecanlee*, a form which Gaimer must have found in a lost MS of the *Chronicle* to which he had access.

But wherever the battle took place, this annal seems to describe quite clearly a movement from Middle Anglia south-westwards through the vale of Aylesbury to the upper Thames. This is, in fact, exactly the movement which success-ive archaeologists from E. T. Leeds to the present day have proposed as the main source of the Saxon concentration in this area from the fifth century onwards. It would be there-fore a natural conclusion from the archaeological evidence that this entry for 571 has simply been dated by the *Chron-icle*'s compilers a century, or a century and a half, too late. There is no reason to suppose that they had any firm basis for the date they attached to a saga story of this kind. If this emendation is accepted most of the difficulties felt by historians in its interpretation can disappear at once.[1]

In fact, there are several good reasons for regarding this entry as a misfit in its present position in the Ceawlin saga. One is, obviously, that it does not relate to Ceawlin at all, for he is not mentioned in it, as he is in all the other entries of this sequence. Moreover its hero Cuthwulf appears nowhere else in the story they tell, and the fact that he is here recorded to have died in the same year as his victory at *Biedcanford* suggests that nothing further was thought memorable about him. In other words, there is every reason to conclude that this 571 entry is the sole survivor from a preface to the Ceawlin saga explaining how his ancestor Cuthwulf came to establish his rule in the Thames Valley. Of this prefatory material no other incidents, even if they had survived to Alfred's time, were felt by the compilers of the *Chronicle* to deserve inclusion in it.

This does not mean that the information contained in the 571 entry is unimportant. It is in fact one of the most interesting of the whole series. Wherever Cuthwulf's victory was won, it must surely have been somewhere in the Bedford/Cambridge area and the consequences are quite clear. Aylesbury and Limbury were key sites in the open country below the Chiltern escarpment that led south-west towards the upper Thames basin, and Bensington (now Benson) and Eynsham are both on the main course of the

[1] The date and significance of this 571 annal have caused much perplexity to historians. The solution here proposed is the simplest way to restore a meaning and context to the events described.

upper Thames, Benson being not far from the downstream
limit of concentrated early Anglo-Saxon settlement above the
Goring gap, while Eynsham could be taken to mark its
approximate upstream limit. It would, no doubt, be possible
to define this upper Thames area of really early Saxon
settlement more exactly. But it looks as if the annalist is
indicating broadly by these markers what he took to be the
consolidation of Cuthwulf's authority over the most densely
populated region in which the Saxon writ was henceforth to
run. The inclusion of Aylesbury and Limbury shows that it
was intended to run also in the country north of the
Chilterns, through which Ceawlin's ancestors and their people
had come from Middle Anglia.

A further consequence follows from this redating. If
Cuthwulf's conquests can be pushed back a century or more
earlier than 571, the difficulty felt by scholars in the notice
that his enemies in this campaign were Britons at once
disappears. In the fifth century, as distinct from the sixth,
there may have been no previous major Anglo-Saxon intrusion
into this British-held country below the Chiltern escarpment.
Indeed, forested Chiltern valleys to the south-east probably
remained in British hands long after,[1] as did the lands of
the Atrebates that bordered them to the south in the middle
Thames Valley, so long as sub-Roman *Calleva* retained any
active life.

What is more surprising is that there is no mention of the
fate of Dorchester-on-Thames in the list of Cuthwulf's
conquests. This little walled town, at the confluence of the
Thames and the Thame, had certainly had some administrative
standing, if only as the *vicus* on which the whole area was
centred in the last days of Roman Britain. This is shown by
the discovery there of a late Roman altar dedicated by a man
holding an official position as *beneficiarius consularis*.[2]
There are also burials, both north and south of the walled
area, of persons equipped with belt-fittings and brooches of
types that were normally used by barbarian *laeti* or native
para-military personnel engaged in official duties of various
kinds. Indications of early Saxon *Grubenhäuser*, and other

---

[1] The evidence is assembled in K. R. Davis, *Britons and Saxons: the Chiltern
Region 400–700* (Chichester, 1982).
[2] *RIB* 235.

post-Roman structures noted at several points within the walls, show that Dorchester retained some form of life well into the fifth century. Though, as has been noted, the road that had linked it through Streatley to Silchester (Margary 160c) went out of use in these troubled years, that which ran north to what may well have been a similar walled *vicus* at Alchester, on Akeman Street near Bicester (Margary 160b), is traceable throughout and probably remained open. The chance discovery at Dorchester of a gold and garnet jewel (now lost), a gold coin of Maurice Tiberius (582-602), and a runic Anglo-Saxon gold coin of 640-50, suggests that it was either the residence or the burial place of an early Saxon chieftain of some standing.[1] That it was not mentioned among Cuthwulf's conquests may mean simply that it had passed, without conflict, from the control of the barbarian *laeti* who still held it early in the fifth century to become the headquarters of Cuthwulf's people some years later.[2] Such a combination of sub-Roman and aristocratic Saxon associations would also explain the choice of Dorchester as the site for Birinus' West Saxon bishopric when the royal family became Christian in 634.

The West Saxon annals relating to Ceawlin himself present fewer chronological and topological problems. The battle of 577 at Dyrham in Gloucestershire shows him striking west into the Avon and Severn valleys, to capture three strategic Roman cities, Gloucester, Cirencester,[3] and Bath, and eliminate the sub-Roman 'tyrants' who had controlled them. Two of these men had Celtic names, Coinmail and Farinmail, and the third, Condidan, a Roman name evidently broken down from something like Candidianus. These names are all preserved in forms which could be derived from a sixth-century written source.[4]

[1] T. M. Dickinson, *Cuddesdon and Dorchester-on-Thames*, BAR 1 (1974), 25-30.
[2] There is a convenient summary of the structural evidence for continuity of occupation in Dorchester from late Roman to early Saxon times in Davis, op. cit. 22-3.
[3] The Roman amphitheatre at Cirencester had been converted into a fortified stronghold in sub-Roman times: J. Wacher, *The Towns of Roman Britain* (1974), 314, and A. McWhirr (ed.), *Studies in the Archaeology and History of Cirencester*, BAR 30 (1976), 15-19.
[4] I have suggested in Trevor-Roper (ed.), op. cit., 25 that the stretch of West Wansdyke which crosses, and was presumably intended to block, the Fosse Way at Odd Down south of Bath may well have been the British answer to the capture

It must surely be significant that Ceawlin's campaign of 577 was directed against what was evidently a major concentration of British power in the lower Severn area. This is certainly suggested by the detail given in the *Chronicle* of the names of the British leaders and of their bases in the surviving Roman walled cities of the region. But it is worth noting that this region has also produced one of the greatest concentrations in southern Britain of sub-Roman metal-work both military and civilian in character. On the military side this comprises the buckles and belt-fittings of Hawkes Types I and II,[1] apparently British-made derivations of more official late Roman equipment, and on the civil side the various forms of contemporary annular and penannular brooches to whose significance attention was first drawn by Savory.[2] It looks therefore as if Ceawlin was striking in 577 against what may have been regarded by the Thames Valley Saxons as a major menace to their security.

Then in 584 is recorded a battle at *Fethanleag*, a place identified by Stenton from charter evidence as near Stoke Lyne in north-east Oxfordshire. In this fight Cutha, whose name is probably a shortened form of the Cuthwine recorded as accompanying Ceawlin in the 577 battle of Dyrham, was killed, and, after capturing many villages and countless spoil, Ceawlin is said to have 'returned in anger to his own'. This entry is of particular interest, not only for its markedly poetic diction, but for the topographical hints it provides on Ceawlin's movements and on the probable centre of his power.

It so happens that Cutteslowe, on the Banbury road three miles north of Oxford, preserves the memory of the *hoga de Cudeslowe*, which could well have been the burial mound of the Cutha killed at *Fethanleag*.[3] Unfortunately the barrow

of Bath by Ceawlin in the course of the Dyrham campaign. Unlike East Wansdyke, this barrier, which seems deliberately to exclude Bath, was clearly sited in conditions which gave its defenders a very poor visual command of the terrain to the north in the Avon valley.

[1] *Med. Arch.* 5 (1961), 21–34 and map fig. 9. These types are described by S. Hawkes as showing 'the last recognizable phase of Roman metal-work in Britain'.

[2] In D. B. Harden (ed.), *Dark-Age Britain*, 40–58 and fig. 10.

[3] *Antiquity*, 9 (1935), 96–8. I suggested this identification in *The Oxford Region* (1954), 100.

itself was demolished by royal orders in 1261 as a haunt of robbers on the Banbury road. It is however very possible that, in returning 'to his own' from what seems to have been a less than wholly successful campaign, Ceawlin buried his dead companion Cutha by the roadside in the *hoga de Cudeslowe* which has preserved his name to the present day. It is, moreover, tempting to think that in returning 'to his own' Ceawlin was in fact travelling towards Cuddesdon, a village a few miles south-east of Oxford, which, like Cutteslowe, contains the name Cutha or Cuthwine. Recent excavations near the front entrance of the bishop of Oxford's former palace at Cuddesdon have confirmed earlier accounts pointing to the existence there of another princely interment of this age. The presence of this rich burial reinforces the evidence of the name that it was in all likelihood a *villa regalis* of the Thames Valley Saxons,[1] perhaps established there since Cuthwulf's conquests following the battle of *Biedcanford*.

Cuddesdon would have been a very suitable centre for such a purpose. It overlooks the valley of the Thame on the last stage of its passage from the Vale of Aylesbury to join the Thames at Dorchester. It also has a fine visual command both of the Chiltern escarpment to the south and, beyond the Goring gap to the west, of the distant line of the Berkshire Downs that carry the Ridgeway past White Horse Hill into Wiltshire.

If Ceawlin returned to Cuddesdon 'in anger', after his not over-successful expedition into north Oxfordshire in 584, one may be tempted to think of him looking out from his hall there at this extensive prospect. It could have led him to contemplate the possibility of further conquests in the lands which the Ridgeway might open up as far as Wansdyke, and beyond it on to Salisbury Plain. He had, after all, already secured the Cotswold country, formerly dependent on the Roman cities of Cirencester, Gloucester, and Bath. He had thus confined the British rulers of south-western Britain, now cut off from their compatriots in Wales, behind their frontier defences of West Wansdyke, south of the Avon gorge that

[1] T. M. Dickinson, op. cit. 3–24 and 31–32. Cuddesdon was still an extensive royal estate, which included Wheatley to the north, in 956: *CS* 945. Wheatley also had an early Saxon cemetery.

leads down to the Severn estuary. To force the passage of East Wansdyke by the Ridgeway route might seem the best way to completing control not only of the Cerdicing family lands in Hampshire and east Wiltshire but of all the country still held by British princes westwards into Dorset and Somerset. It would make possible a move to take West Wansdyke from the rear.

But if this was Ceawlin's plan, it led him in 592 to disaster and in the following year to his death. The *Chronicle* records tersely that in 592 there was a great slaughter at *Wodnesbeorh* and Ceawlin was driven out, and that in 593 Ceawlin, Cwichelm, and Crida—the last two no doubt chieftains associated with him—perished.

There can be no reasonable doubt that the *Wodnesbeorh* near which Ceawlin met his Waterloo was the long barrow, since Christianized under the name of Adam's Grave, that stands dramatically on a hill-top in Alton Priors parish, on the north side of the Vale of Pewsey. It is immediately south of the line along which Wansdyke had been built to block traffic coming down the Ridgeway to cross the Vale on to Salisbury Plain. After crossing Wansdyke, a mile to the north at Raedgeat, the Ridgeway passes close under the west side of the almost isolated summit that carries *Wodnesbeorh*, making this point the strategic centre of the whole defensive system. Having failed to force its passage at this crucial spot, and having apparently lost much of his host in the attempt, Ceawlin's authority was fatally compromised and, though the circumstances of his death a year later are not known, the mention of two other chieftains having perished at the same time suggests that it may well have been as an outcome of internal revolt.

The victor of *Wodnesbeorh* is not directly named by the *Chronicle*, a fact which shows that its source at this point is still essentially the Ceawlin saga, in its final tragic episodes, rather than more official West Saxon annals. But since the *Chronicle* records that Ceol began to reign in 591, he must be credited with this decisive triumph. It is, moreover, highly significant that Ceol's successor, Ceolwulf, who began to reign in Wessex in 597, is given by the chronicler a unique tribute among the rulers of this age. It is stated there that he continually fought against either the Angles or the Britons

or the Picts or the Scots. Of his exploits against the Picts and
Scots nothing is known, and they may be no more than
formal and picturesque attributes appropriate to a more than
normally active military career; but it is surely of the greatest
interest that he was thought memorable for fighting continually against the Angles and the Britons. This may well
mean that, after the collapse of Ceawlin's power-base on the
upper Thames, it was Ceolwulf who incorporated that whole
region, the mixed population of which included folk whose
origins and continuing contacts lay in Middle Anglia, into the
new Wessex. And if he fought also with Britons, that could
mean that he brought about the end of independence for the
surviving Atrebates and the final desolation of Silchester.
Ceolwulf may also have completed the consolidation of
Ceawlin's conquests in the Severn and Avon valleys in the
lands won from the sub-Roman tyrants of Cirencester,
Gloucester, and Bath. The reign of Ceolwulf, between 597
and 611, must thus have been the time when all the various
strains that contributed to the formation of the West Saxon
kingdom were drawn together into a single whole. His wide-
flung ambitions included even the South Saxons. According
to the *Chronicle*, he fought a campaign against them in 607,
though its result is not stated.

There is no need to pursue the fortunes of Wessex further.
Its future story falls in any case beyond the chronological
limits set for this book. But it has been right, in this study of
the English settlements, to bring it this far, in fact to the eve
of the conversion to Christianity. It was Cynigils, Ceolwulf's
successor, who established the first bishopric of the West
Saxons under Birinus at Dorchester-on-Thames.

Wessex is thus the only one of the Anglo-Saxon kingdoms
whose story can be followed, with however many gaps and
uncertainties, right through the darkest centuries between the
collapse of Roman Britain and the emergence of Anglo-Saxon
England into recorded history. It is only here that the literary
record, based on both the British tales told by Gildas and
Nennius and on the traditions of dominant Anglo-Saxon
families that had survived until Alfred's time, can be plausibly
set in the geographical context where they must belong and
with the appropriate archaeological and place-name evidence
to support and explain them.

Even in Kent there is, after the initial phase of federate settlement in the fifth century, virtually no political history to record until the arrival of St. Augustine in 597.[1] During the intervening two centuries scarcely anything is known of the doings of the royal family, or of the relations that developed between the incoming federates, whether Saxons or Jutes, and the British Cantiaci, from which the special culture of the Cantwara with its wealth of art-forms and peculiar institutions sprang.

Even less is known, owing to a total lack of written records, of the political history of the East Saxons, the East and Middle Angles, Lindsey, and Deira. Throughout these regions there must have been developments, dramatic or otherwise, comparable to those of which it is just possible to follow the outline in Wessex. But in the absence of any surviving oral traditions which might have been used later on to form the basis of literary records, comparable to the West Saxon story in the *Anglo-Saxon Chronicle* before the seventh century, the whole early history of eastern and central England in this period has been lost.

That is why the evidence, however fragmentary and confusing, for the formation of Wessex is so precious, and why it has been important to examine it in detail. With all allowance made for variations due to geography, geology, the relative strength at different times and in different places between invaders and invaded, and the infinite variety of personality involved in every situation, something like this story must have been taking place all over eastern and central Britain during these lost centuries.

---

[1] What little can be made of the political history of Kent before the coming of Augustine is conveniently assembled in K. P. Witney, *The Kingdom of Kent* (1982), 9–108.

7

THE HUMBRENSES AND THE NORTH

I N Bede's day, the estuary of the Humber was regarded as a barrier or dividing line between the northern and the southern English, a frontier which held apart the northern peoples whom Bede himself seems to have been among the first to call Northumbrians, from those 'South-umbrians' who were falling in his lifetime under the domination of the Mercian kings. Bede repeatedly speaks of the Humber in this sense. The sway of the early Bretwaldas, he writes, extended over those provinces 'which are separated from the Northerners by the river Humber and boundaries adjacent to it'.[1] The Mercian supremacy, at the end of his life, he describes as covering all southern England 'as far as the limit of the river Humber'.[2]

But there are many reasons for believing that this was not likely to have been the function of the Humber in the earliest period of Anglo-Saxon settlement. Elsewhere in eastern England the river-systems became the centres rather than the boundaries of the first Germanic settlements. On the lower Thames, the name of Surrey, 'the southern region', still bears witness to a primitive political situation in which it was closely linked to the Middle Saxons north of the river, though this association may have been of brief duration and had evidently passed out of memory before the days of written record. The Fenland rivers also formed the natural lines of penetration, which carried peoples of a common cultural equipment ever farther into the southern Midlands. There is every reason to believe that the Humber would have exerted a similar attraction, linking together rather than holding apart the various folk who used it to give access to all the lands drained by the tributaries which formed its basin to the north, west, and south of the main estuary. To appreciate its function in the early days it is thus necessary

[1] *HE* ii. 5.   [2] *HE* v. 23.

to penetrate behind the political conditions of Bede's time, to the more primitive circumstances of the age of settlement.

To do so is not, in fact, so difficult as might at first sight appear. There is clear evidence that as late as the end of the seventh century it was still customary to refer to those who, following the usage adopted by Bede, have since his time been called Northumbrians, as Humbrenses or Hymbronenses, the people of the river itself. This was the more natural because it is clear that the name Humber, now restricted to the lower part of the estuary between Trent Falls and the sea, had once a far wider geographical extension. It could be applied, for example, to the Ouse as far north as York, to the Don, and to at least the lower course of the Trent. It was thus reasonable to use the term Humbrenses to cover in early days most of the folk who came to settle the whole region drained by the tributaries of that river system.[1]

Eventually indeed, as the position and name of the present-day Northumberland indicate, the settlement of folk whose origins sprang mainly from the Humbrenses came to extend northwards, far beyond the limits of the Humber basin, to the lands watered by other rivers of the north-east coast, of which the most important are the Tees, Tyne, and Tweed. The southern connections of some of these people have survived in tell-tale place-names, such as that of Bede's monastery *In Gyrvum* (now Jarrow), derived from the Gyrwe of the northern Fenland, or Lindisfarne off the Northumberland coast, which clearly comes from the Lindiswaras, the people of Lindsey. Thus the beginnings of Bernicia as well as of Deira, Lindsey, and Mercia (Map 6) must be sought, in greater or less degree, among the Humbrenses of the Humber basin.[2]

It is however clear that, if this is so, the earliest of the Humbrensian settlements will be those most closely linked to the Humber estuary itself. There are also likely to be clear signs that, in the earliest days, these basic Humbrensian folk were closely linked to one another. One or two examples

---

[1] For the detailed evidence on which the argument of this and the preceding paragraph is based, see my article 'The Teutonic settlement of northern England', *History*, 20 (1935), 250–62.

[2] Thus Bernician kings as late as the end of the seventh century referred to themselves as kings of the Humbrenses. Ecgfrith, for example, seems to have used this title as an official style.

may be given to suggest that this was so. At the great cremation cemetery at Sancton, on the Roman road (Margary 29) that leads north from the Humber at Brough (*Petuaria*) below the edge of the chalk Wolds towards York, there was a potter in the fifth century whose very distinctive style can be recognized in at least seven urns used for burials in that cemetery. At least two more examples of his work have been found at South Elkington in Lincolnshire, not far from the little Roman walled town of Caistor-on-the-Wolds, which shows that the Humber proved no obstacle to social intercourse between settlers north and south of the estuary at that time.[1]

More remarkable perhaps is the case of a rather later workshop, operating probably in the sixth century, whose simpler, and perhaps earlier, products have come from Newark, where the Fosse Way comes close to the Trent, and from Loveden Hill in south Lincolnshire near Grantham. More sophisticated examples have been found at Baston (Lincs.), and a larger group once again at Sancton north of the Humber. Isolated pieces from this workshop, whose products evidently were widely appreciated, have turned up as far away as Melton Mowbray in Leicestershire and at two cemeteries in East Anglia. But the centre of its activity was evidently based on the Humber basin, and in its last phase almost certainly at Sancton itself.[2]

This conclusion is reinforced by the location of some significant place-names. Hardly any literary record has survived regarding the origin of the kingdom of Lindsey, apart from the pedigree of its early kings. The first of these with a historical basis, free from the misty mythological origins which surround the earliest ancestral figures on most of the Anglo-Saxon king-lists, is called Winta, who can probably be dated in the middle of the fifth century. Stenton, who first pointed out the historical interest of the Lindsey royal pedigree,[3] did not note that this name, or what he regarded as its close cognate Wintra, underlies the names

---

[1] Myres and Southern, *Cremation Cemetery at Sancton*, 19–20: Myres, *Corpus*, i. 82 and ii. figs. 196–7.

[2] Myres, op. cit. i. 59–60.82 and ii. figs. 347–8.

[3] F. M. Stenton, 'Lindsey and its kings', in Davis (ed.), *Essays in History*, (1927) 136–50, especially 137–8 n. 2.

of two Lincolnshire villages, Winteringham and Winterton. Their position in relation to the probable Humbrensian origin for the settlement of Lindsey is highly significant. These two villages lie side by side almost on the bank of the Humber. Winteringham, which is likely on formal grounds to be the earlier of the two settlements, is exactly on the line of the main Roman road from the south (Margary 2d) at the point where its course must have been continued by means of a ferry in Roman times across the river from Winteringham Haven to Brough on the north bank. On any showing, this was strategically the obvious point from which the Humbrensian settlement of Lindsey is likely to have originated. It is of the greatest interest that it should still bear, in these two adjacent villages, the name of one who was in all likelihood its first historic king.

The evidence of these place-names is supported by considerations of a different kind. Recent excavations in and around the important Saxon church at Barton-on-Humber, close by to the east of Winteringham, have provided archaeological indications for a close association of late Roman with fifth-century Anglo-Saxon occupation at this significant point on the south bank of the Humber. Although no Roman or Anglo-Saxon structures have been certainly identified near the church at Barton, the excavator has concluded, from the co-terminous distribution of both kinds of pottery, that 'there is no reason to suggest a break of occupation between the Roman and Saxon periods' on this site.[1] Here too, therefore, as at Winteringham, it looks as if Winta's people may have directly succeeded to an existing Romano-British environment.

From Winteringham Haven the Roman road, described by Margary as 'one of the most magnificent in the whole of Britain', ran, and still runs, almost straight for thirty-two miles southwards to enter Lincoln under the Newport arch. This is the only Roman gateway in this country which, in spite of recent attempted demolition by an errant lorry, continues to span a major Roman road. It is hardly surprising that Winta's people, confronted in this dramatic fashion by such massive survivals of the Imperial past, should have

[1] *Ant. J.* 62 (1982), 307.

adopted the name *Lindum colonia* almost unaltered as
Lincoln. Moreover they extended its use in the form *Lindissi*
or Lindsey to cover the whole of what is now northern and
central Lincolnshire, which had doubtless formed much of
the *territorium* of the Roman colony.[1] The Roman fortifications of *Lindum* certainly survived in what seems to have
been an unusual state of preservation. In addition to the
Newport arch, another gate, which was still standing in
Norman times on the west wall of the upper *colonia*, was
completely buried by the earlier ramparts of the later castle
and thus remained almost intact until it was uncovered, and
unfortunately destroyed, in the nineteenth century.

Whether Lincoln itself remained a centre of population,
either British or Germanic, in early Anglian times is uncertain.
No substantial cremation cemeteries have been located in its
immediate vicinity to suggest the sort of continuity provided
by the nearby settlement of barbarian *laeti*, as in the case of
York, Caistor-by-Norwich, or Cambridge. A small early
Anglian pot was found close at hand in the Roman villa at
Greetwell on the road running east towards the Wolds,[2] and
there are a few other chance finds, but nothing to indicate
that it became a focus for early Germanic occupation. On the
other hand, in the second quarter of the seventh century,
before the coming of Christianity, which seems to have been
necessary as a stimulant to the reawakening of town life on
many Roman sites, there was already an Anglian *praefectus
Lindocolinae civitatis*. His presence in the city seems to imply
some degree of population within the old walls. Bede
mentions his name, Blaecca. As it alliterates suggestively with
the Beda, Bubba and Biscop who were successive kings about
this time, this may indicate that he was a member of the
reigning dynasty.

Blaecca was converted by Paulinus, who built a fine stone

[1] It has been plausibly argued that the regular pattern of parish boundaries
in north Lincolnshire could have arisen from the progressive extension of settlement up the tributary streams of the Humber, giving way southwards to the series
of villages whose lands are carefully aligned upon both sides of the main Roman
road to Lincoln: see W. Page, *Antiquity*, 1 (1927), 454-61. But this clearly
artificial arrangement is not closely datable. It could have originated with the later
Danish settlement, or even perhaps be a relic of the *territorium* of the Roman
colonia.
[2] Myres, *Corpus*, i. 3 and ii. fig. 10.

church for him in the city. This does not seem to have been a successful venture, for Bede mentions that it was roofless and all but deserted in his day.[1] So Lincoln, in spite of its Roman and Christian traditions, had to wait many centuries before it became once more the centre of a Christian bishopric. Recent excavations on the site of the derelict church of St. Paul-in-the-Bail have shown that it probably overlay the remains of Paulinus' church. Conspicuously set in the first Christian building on the site was a disturbed grave, which had been accompanied by a seventh-century enamelled hanging bowl, indicating a burial of a person of consequence, who might even have been Blaecca himself. The position of this very early church is also of some interest, for it was centrally placed in relation to the headquarters buildings of the *colonia*, suggesting that these, whether still in use or not, were at least sufficiently obvious to indicate the main focus of the Roman city.[2]

It is not known whether, towards the end of the Roman period, what became the Lincolnshire coastlands were included in the defensive arrangements of the *Litus Saxonicum*. There are no signs of Saxon Shore forts on the coast north of the Wash, nor have signal stations of the type that line the cliffs of Yorkshire north of Scarborough been located south of the Humber. On the other hand, there are few harbours in Lincolnshire, except Grimsby, on which defensive fortifications could have been based, and much of the coastline was extensively protected against direct settlement by dangerous and obstructive sandbanks. There has also been a good deal of erosion, which could have removed the remains of coastal works. It seems on the whole most likely that defensive arrangements were here based on fortified points set inland on the Wolds from which military operations could readily be mounted against any threat of seaborne invasion. Two such places, Caistor-on-the-Wolds to the north and Horncastle further south, were certainly provided with bastioned walls in the fourth century, and it has been argued that both could have served as the equivalent of small inland

---

[1] *HE* ii. 16.
[2] B. Gilmour in *Med. Arch.* 23 (1979), 214-18, and W. Rodwell, *Archaeology of the English Church* (1981), 144 and fig. 69. See also p. 195 for a possible parallel at York.

Saxon Shore forts.[1] The same could be said of the unexcavated site at Kirmington, north of Caistor-on-the-Wolds,
which, as mentioned earlier,[2] has produced both very early
Saxon and very late Roman material. Although there are no
visible signs of fortification at Kirmington, the early cremation
cemetery at Elsham is close at hand to the west and could
well have started as the burial place of *laeti* settled around
Kirmington.[3]

Both Horncastle and Caistor-on-the-Wolds are similarly
related to nearby cremation cemeteries. A few miles south-
east of Horncastle is that at West Keal. At Caistor-on-the-
Wolds there was a cemetery almost adjacent to its west wall,
and another at Fonaby only a mile to the north-west. These
two are linked by the fact that each has produced a small
early-fifth-century pot, of the type attributed by Werner to
his *Laetenhorizont*, and dated by him around 400; these
two are so alike as to be probably attributable to the same
potter.[4]

It would thus appear that, whether or not Lindsey was
formally included in the command of the *comes Litoris
Saxonici* towards the end of Roman times, steps had certainly
been taken to give it some protection from coastal intrusions.
It may well be that the existence of these defences was
adequate to divert later invaders, either southwards to the
Wash or northwards to the more attractive Humber estuary.
When, therefore, probably around the middle of the fifth
century, Winta and his people entered Lincolnshire from the
Humber, they may have found the eastern Wolds already
occupied by the descendants of *laeti* settled a century
earlier originally as garrisons for such strong points as
Horncastle, Caistor, and whatever gave rise to the discoveries

---

[1] Plans of both are given by P. Corder in *Arch. J.* 112 (1955), figs. 7 and 8,
with discussion 38–40.

[2] p. 82.

[3] Another place with some suggestive late-fourth-century occupation is the
mainly Iron Age and earlier Roman site at Dragonby near Scunthorpe. This has
produced late Roman pottery and coins to the end of the fourth century and a
zoomorphic buckle, nearly all from unstratified contexts apparently associated
with stone and timber structures of uncertain purpose: see J. May, *Ant. J.* 50
(1970), 222–45, and S. C. Hawkes, *Brit.* 5 (1974), 387 and fig. 3.4.

[4] The Fonaby pot is from Grave 34. Both are discussed in *Ant. J.* 53 (1973),
78–81, and illustrated together in Myres, *Corpus*, ii. fig. 271, with comments ibid.
i. 46.

at Kirmington/Elsham. Another large cremation cemetery on the top of the Wolds at South Elkington, north-west of Louth, may have served at first the needs of another settlement of *laeti* established nearer the coast at that point.[1]

But it is likely that the original kingdom of the Lindiswaras did not extend far south of Lincoln. There is a marked scarcity of early settlements both in its immediate neighbourhood and along the whole middle course of the Witham valley. In contrast there is a concentration of such sites further south around Sleaford and Ancaster. Here the river Slea forms the next break on the limestone ridge that separates the marshlands draining into the Wash from the Trent valley to the west. Ancaster itself stands in this gap, where the main Roman road south from Lincoln (Margary 2c) crosses it. Adjacent to the south gate of its late Roman walls was an early Anglian cremation cemetery, suggesting a history similar to that of Caistor-on-the-Wolds. Ancaster may thus have been fortified to form a comparable strong point to cover the south flank of the same defensive system for the *territorium* of *Lindum*. But it is probable that many of the settlers who were buried in the great cemeteries at Sleaford to the east of the gap and Loveden Hill to the west of it, as well as many other sites in what early became a rather densely populated neighbourhood, had a different origin. They had arrived not from Lindsey to the north but from the Wash and the Fenland to the south-east. As such they came to occupy the districts later known as the Parts of Kesteven and Holland, and were in early times quite distinct from the Humbrensian folk who established the kingdom of Lindsey.

It is interesting that the apparent gap that separates these two areas of early settlement in Lincolnshire includes the surroundings of Lincoln itself, which one might expect to have formed, as in Roman times, the focus of the whole region.[2] It is possible that the scarcity of early Anglo-Saxon

---

[1]   Graham Webster in *Arch. J.* 108 (1951), 25-64.

[2]   See my article, 'The Anglo-Saxon pottery of Lincolnshire' in *Arch. J.* 108 (1951), 65-99, especially 65-9. The accompanying map, fig. 13, illustrates the division between north and south Lincolnshire in early Anglo-Saxon times. Although many fresh discoveries have been made in the last thirty years, they do not greatly alter the pattern it presents.

remains around Lincoln may mean that it was taken over more or less intact, along with what remained of its existing sub-Roman population, by the kings of the Lindiswaras.[1] This might help to explain the survival of the name *Lindum* and also of the walls, gates, and some other buildings of the upper *colonia*. It may also be relevant that one of the sixth-century kings of Lindsey was called Caedbaed, a name at least partly of British origin. This suggests the possibility of a marriage link between the new royal house and a prominent native family. For all these reasons it cannot be denied that an unusual degree of Romano-British survival in and around the *colonia*, culiminating perhaps in a more or less peaceful absorption of the whole enclave, with far less disturbance than probably occurred on most major Roman urban sites, possesses an attractive plausibility.

Westward from Lindsey, the marshy country surrounding the lower reaches of the Trent and the Idle was no bar to the progress upstream of those Humbrensian folk who eventually found drier riverside lands in south Nottinghamshire and Leicestershire and laid there the foundations of the Mercian people. At Newark at any rate, where the Fosse Way in its course south-westwards from Lincoln to Leicester touches the south bank of the Trent, an extensive early cremation cemetery has produced very large numbers of urns. Some two hundred of these, excavated from beneath the floors of cottage property demolished in the course of recent re-development, are in the Newark Museum. Many others from the same area are known to have been dispersed or destroyed in the nineteenth century. Among the survivors are several of special interest from their early date or apparent reminiscence of Romano-British styles in form or decoration.[2]

Other cremation cemeteries, mostly on the right bank of the Trent or clearly related, as at Willoughby-on-the-Wolds,

---

[1] The presence of a very early Anglo-Saxon pot in the Roman villa at Greetwell, east of Lincoln (already noted p. 178 and n. 2) is suggestive, in this connection, of possible continuity of occupation there.

[2] See Myres, *Corpus*, i. 2.3 and ii. figs. 7, 8, 9, 11 for a number of early plain biconical urns, several accompanied by combs, and ibid. i. 18 and ii. fig. 92 for the remarkable wheel-made sub-Roman urns 3453 and 3740 from the Newark cemetery. A rather later Newark potter used stamped designs to decorate such urns as 3884, 3910, and possibly 3554 (ii. fig. 96), whose faceted and sharply carinated forms suggest familiarity with styles of much earlier date.

to the course of the Fosse Way running south-west towards
Leicester, indicate an early and substantial settlement up
such southern tributaries of the main river as the Soar.
Throughout this part of Leicestershire and Rutland they
must here have met and mingled with folk from the Fenland
region and other areas of what became Middle Anglia, who
had found their way across the easy watersheds into the
upper valleys of streams that flowed into the Trent.

What happened at Leicester itself is not altogether clear.
The large early cremation cemetery at Thurmaston, near the
Fosse Way, a few miles to the north-east of Leicester, may
well have served at first a settlement of *laeti* in and around
the Roman city, which had been the cantonal capital of an
important east midlands tribe, the *Coritani*. Between
Thurmaston and the outskirts of Leicester is a village with
the significant name Humberstone. While Ekwall derives
this from a personal name Hunbeorht, for which the earliest
form of Humberstone (Domesday Book) provides no convincing evidence, it is far more likely to retain a memory of
the first Humbrensian settlers who, probably as *laeti*, were
charged with the defence of Leicester and started the
adjacent Thurmaston cemetery.[1] There are a few other early
Anglo-Saxon finds nearer to its Roman defences, particularly
in the neighbourhood of the east gate.[2] Moreover the so-
called Jewry Wall, which had formed part of a large Roman
bath complex in the centre of the town, remained, as it still
remains, an upstanding feature sufficiently prominent to be
linked to the west front of the church of St. Nicholas, which
probably marks the first centre of Christian worship. Immediately to the east of St. Nicholas' church there was in
the fifteenth century another building whose two parts,
separated by a row of columns, were dedicated respectively
to St. Augustine and St. Columba. It was known as *le Holy-
bones*, but whether this referred to a pre-existing, perhaps
sub-Roman, cemetery on the site or to its possession of

[1] Another Humberstone, on the south bank of the estuary near Grimsby,
is accepted by Ekwall without question as containing the river-name Humber.
For the detailed topography of north Leicestershire in this period see P. W.
Williams, *An Anglo-Saxon Cemetery at Thurmaston* (1983), especially fig. 1.

[2] Myres, *Corpus*, i. 17 and 47, and ii. figs. 88 and 278; see also T. H. McK.
Clough and others, *Anglo-Saxon and Viking Leicestershire*, Leics. Museums . . .
Service (1975), 54–62.

significant relics is not known. The unusual dedications may well go back to the seventh century when an earlier cult of the Humbrensian Columba could have been combined by Roman missionaries with devotion to Augustine.[1] This would imply the survival of at least an inhabited urban nucleus of some sort remaining in the old town at that time.

On the other hand, Leicester's Roman name *Ratae Coritanorum*, unlike that of *Lindum Colonia*, entirely disappeared. It left no trace whatever in the Latin *Legorensis civitas* of a charter of 803 or the Saxon *Legoraceaster*, which the place had become by the tenth century. The origin of the first element in this name is itself obscure. It may derive either from a lost Celtic river-name, perhaps related to that of the Loire, or possibly from that of a minor community, otherwise unrecorded, among its first Anglo-Saxon settlers.[2] In any case the complete loss of the Roman name must imply that there was a period in which no one, whether native or invader, had occasion to refer to what must have been, for a while, a place of little consequence to either.

This temporary eclipse of Leicester in the later part of the pagan period is one good reason for believing that political cohesion among the incoming settlers was here late in achievement. The first indication of an emerging royal family in Mercia is a reference to the fact that Edwin of Deira married the daughter of a mysterious Mercian king named Cearl.[3] This alliance is mainly of interest as indicating a close link between two branches of the Humbrensian people still persistent early in the seventh century. But Cearl does not appear in the pedigree of the later Mercian dynasty, and there is no other record of a king of Mercia before the accession of Penda in 626.[4] Indeed the close, if hostile, relations between Edwin of Deira and Cuichelm of Wessex, who, according to Bede,[5] was so alarmed by Edwin's growing power that he

[1]   These topographical details are recorded in a Leicester Abbey Rental (now Bodleian MS. Laud Misc. 625 at fol. 54 verso), to which my attention was first drawn in 1954 by Mr. F. Cottrill.

[2]   It has been plausibly suggested that the name may derive from *Lloegrwys*, the Welsh name for Middle Anglia: M. Gwyn Jenkins, *Bull. of the Board of Celtic Studies*, 19 (1960), 8-23; but this may itself derive from *Legoraceaster*.

[3]   Bede, *HE* ii. 14.

[4]   Or 633 if Bede's authority (*HE* ii. 20) be preferred to that of the *Anglo-Saxon Chronicle*.

[5]   *HE* ii. 9.

endeavoured to arrange his assassination, make it difficult to
believe that a people of any political consequence existed in
the country between them much before this date.

The Mercian dynasty of Penda is known to have claimed
descent from the royal family of the continental Angles.
They were later called the Iclingas, which may imply that
Icel, who appears in the pedigree five generations—say,
about a century and a half—earlier than Penda, was the first
of the line to achieve prominence in Britain, probably around
450. There are a number of place-names in eastern England
such as Ickleton (Cambridge), Ickleford (Herts.), and probably Icklingham (Suffolk), whose early forms appear to
contain the name of Icel or his people, the Iclingas. These
may imply that Penda's ancestors first made a name for
themselves in Middle Anglia before penetrating to the heartlands of the later Mercia. Indeed it may well be that Penda
himself was the first of his line to consolidate this movement,
for in the *Historia Brittonum*[1] he is described as the king who
first separated the Mercians from the *Regnum Nordorum*.
Until his day, it would appear that earlier rulers of Mercia,
such as Edwin's father-in-law Cearl, had remained politically
dependent on the Humbrenses, the Men of the North.

There is, furthermore, a duality in the settlement of Mercia
which suggests that its eventual unity was not achieved until
a comparatively late date. The earliest Mercian people are
represented archaeologically by the cremation cemeteries on
the right bank of the middle Trent and on its southern
tributaries. In Bede's day the Trent itself separated the five
thousand families of these southern Mercians from the seven
thousand families of the northern Mercians beyond the
river.[2] There is a marked archaeological contrast between the
two areas. North of the river cremation cemeteries, so
common to the south, are conspicuously absent. In their
place are found poorly-furnished inhumation cemeteries and
many secondary burials in prehistoric barrows which suggest,
as in Wiltshire, that a long period of raiding and sporadic war-
fare may have preceded and delayed the final occupation.

It is probable that it was in this phase of Mercian history

[1] *Hist. Britt.* 65.
[2] *HE* iii. 24. For these Pecsaetan or Peak Dwellers of northern Mercia see
A. Ozanne, *Med. Arch.* 6-7 (1962-3), 15-52.

that the term Mercia itself — the land of the frontier or march—may have first come into use, thus pointing to a time when the Trent marked the boundary between the settled lands to the south and east and the insecurely held country stretching north and west towards the foothills of the Peak. That the districts south and east of the Trent were the earliest focus of Mercia is suggested further by the fact that, when the land was Christianized in the seventh century, both its main religious centres (at Repton and Lichfield) and the most important *villa regalis* of its kings (at Tamworth) were all in this part of the kingdom.

The rapid rise of Mercia to political dominance in the seventh and eighth centuries, after this somewhat unpromising start, is of the greatest interest from an economic point of view. Much of the Trent basin and of the northern Midlands as a whole had been heavily forested in prehistoric times. It seems to have still supported only a scanty population in the Roman period in spite of the clearances effected in some places by the development of villa estates. With the collapse of Romano-British agricultural exploitation in the fifth century, it is likely that much of the woodland brought into cultivation at that time will have reverted to a tangle of dense scrub. This might be supposed to have proved even less attractive to Saxon agricultural pioneers than the more open ground cover normally to be found before the high canopy provided by long-established natural forest had been cleared. It is therefore remarkable that the Mercians seem to have been among the first of the Anglo-Saxon peoples to cope effectively with the systematic exploitation of the heavy clay-lands of the Midlands, characterized even in the nineteenth century, by Hilaire Belloc, as 'sodden and unkind'. Only so could have been brought about that evolution in political and economic geography on which the dominance of the eighth-century Mercian kings must have been based.

Northwards, beyond the Humber, the line of the Lincolnshire Wolds is picked up and emphasized by the wolds of east Yorkshire, which, sweeping on towards the Malton gap and then eastwards along the south side of the Vale of Pickering, finally plunge into the sea at Flamborough Head. These chalk hills, with their escarpments to west and north and their gentler slopes and fertile valleys south-eastwards to the low-lying and forested Holderness, constitute another natural and clearly demarcated region, even more obviously attractive than Lindsey to the earliest Humbrensian settlers.

In Roman times this had been the land of the Parisii, whose cantonal capital at Brough (*Petuaria Parisiorum*) has been mentioned already as the northern end of the ferry crossing the Humber from Winteringham Haven, and so from the main road south to Lincoln. Excavations at Brough have shown that it possessed a complex system of Roman fortifications, suggesting that it may long have retained some of the military significance which it had originally possessed in the earlier Roman centuries. But in fact the place apparently played little or no part in coastal defence after the middle of the fourth century. By the time of the *Notitia Dignitatum* what was probably the remains of its garrison had been moved to Malton, under the title of a *Numerus supervenientium Petuarensium*.[1]

There is little evidence, apart from a few pieces of Germanic pottery, for the continued occupation of Brough in the post-Roman period. But it must always have remained the natural landfall for traffic crossing the Humber from Winteringham on its passage northwards from Lindsey whether to York or to Malton. Both had been key points in the last days of Roman rule when York was the headquarters of the *Dux Britanniarum* and Malton had probably become the supply base for the line of coastal signal-stations on the north Yorkshire cliffs between Flamborough Head and the Tees.

Little is known of the early history of the kingdom of Deira, centred on the chalk wolds of east Yorkshire. Even the origin and meaning of its name are obscure. It has been suggested earlier[2] that this part of north eastern England had probably been heavily infiltrated by barbarian *laeti*, partly at least of Alemannic origin, from the fourth century,

---

[1] J. Wacher suggests (*Excavations at Brough-on-Humber*, Soc. Ant. of Lond. Research Ctee. Report 25 (1969), 4) that this evident demilitarization of *Petuaria* in the late fourth century was due to its harbour becoming silted up and unsuitable as a naval base for Roman warships. The much lighter craft of the Anglo-Saxons would not have been so much troubled by this difficulty, for they were accustomed to being drawn up in shallow water or on shelving beaches when not in use.

[2] p. 81.

if not earlier. But beyond the Vale of Pickering and the northern parts of the plain of York, the civilian aspects of Romano-British life become progressively less easy to recognize. There are few signs of agricultural estates centred on country houses of the villa type in Durham or Northumberland, and there is no walled town as the civic centre of a major British tribe north of Aldborough (*Isurium Brigantum*), close to Boroughbridge on the Ure.

It would thus appear that already in the Roman period there was a marked cultural and political contrast between what became Yorkshire and the lands to the north of it which remained a militarized frontier zone. The social consequences, following the use made of barbarian *laeti*, may well have taken different forms in the two areas. In the north they may soon have become indistinguishable from other irregular bodies of military auxiliaries, making little social contact with the native population and no attempts to strike permanent economic roots in the countryside. In Yorkshire, on the other hand, they are likely to have settled under their own leaders on lands allotted to them on a more regular basis, and often within the structure of existing estates. This could have led, as it seems certainly to have done further south on the *Litus Saxonicum*, to the eventual creation of a barbarian kingdom.

The traditional pedigree of the Deiran royal family suggests that something of this kind may have happened in Yorkshire. In one version of this pedigree there is a note against the name of a king Soemil to the effect that 'he first separated Deira from Bernicia'.[1] Soemil appears in the list six generations above Edwin who was killed in 635. He could therefore have been a prominent figure among the Yorkshire *laeti* in the early years of the fifth century. It looks as if he was remembered for the leading part he played in making his people independent of whatever sub-Roman authority had succeeded to the military command once held

---

[1] *Hist. Britt.* 61, and my earlier comment on this passage in *Anglo-Saxon Pottery*, 99 n. 2. The pedigree of the kings of Deira given in the *Anglo-Saxon Chronicle*, on the accession of Ælle in 560, lists five successive generations of the family with names alliterating in S who are likely to have flourished in the fourth and early fifth centuries. None of them can be certainly identified with Soemil, whom *Hist. Britt.* inserts in the middle of this list.

by the *Dux Britanniarum* in the northern frontier lands that were eventually to become Bernicia.[1]

The country of the Parisii in east Yorkshire may thus have passed into the political control of Soemil and his *laeti* quite early in the fifth century. If this happened as the culmination of a gradual process of settlement, it would help to explain the apparent decline in the fortunes of *Petuaria* as a centre of local administration in the later years of Roman rule. It was in fact replaced in early Anglo-Saxon times by a concentration of activities on the line of the Roman trunk road that led north from *Petuaria* (Margary 2e), along and below the escarpment of the Wolds. This road divided at South Newbald, with one branch leading north-west across the vale to York, and the other (Margary 2g) continuing north to Malton.[2] In this area are to be found, within a few miles of each other, the major burial-ground at Sancton, of which more must be said shortly, other cemeteries to the north at Londesborough and to the south at North Newbald, and the main pagan sanctuary of the Deiran people at Goodmanham, whose dramatic overthrow in 627 is described by Bede.[3]

Outside Malton, the late Roman fortress at the south-west corner of the Vale of Pickering, there seems to have been another cremation cemetery, almost at its gates, and somewhere nearby on the Derwent was an administrative centre, a *villa regalis*, frequented by Edwin of Deira early in the seventh century.[4] Malton, indeed, seems to symbolize the continuity that connects late Roman to early Anglo-Saxon times in Deira. It has already been suggested that the *supervenientes Petuarenses*, who formed the final Roman garrison at Malton, had been recruited from the *laeti* originally based on Brough. They may have been connected both with those Germanic folk who deposited their dead in cremation urns at its gates, and with the establishment nearby of what became a *villa regalis* of the Deiran kings.

[1] The suggestion that the settlement of Deira began with a deliberate portation of Germanic mercenaries by Roman authority in the early fifth cen' was put forward by P. Hunter Blair in *Arch. Ael.* 4th ser. 25 (1947), 1-51.

[2] It is of great interest that where this road passes close to Market Weig it is still known as Humber Street, a remarkable reminiscence of its early the Humbrenses of Deira: Margary, *Roman Roads in Britain* (2nd edn., 1967)

[3] *HE* ii. 13.

[4] *HE* ii. 9.

The great cemetery at Sancton is remarkable in many respects. It clearly indicates the religious focus, along with nearby Goodmanham, of the kingdom of Deira in its pagan phase.[1] It is even possible that its name reflects the veneration in which the place was long held in early times. No forms of the word are on written record before the 'Santon' of Domesday Book. But Ekwall, who does not seem to have been aware of the cemetery's importance, notes that the form Sancton was in use at least by 1200, and he suggests that it could have arisen by deliberate association with Latin *sanctus*. If so, it would imply that the place was always thought to possess a special sanctity. This would not be at all surprising, for not only is the cemetery, or cemeteries, among the most extensive in the country, but their significance has always been well recognized in the neighbourhood. Objects from them, including complete pots as well as small objects, were still in common use in the village in the nineteenth century.[2]

It is impossible to estimate the total number of interments made at Sancton in the pagan period, or even to indicate with any precision the whole area which the burials originally covered. They should probably be reckoned in thousands, and must have been spread over at least thirty acres. The earliest group of cremations seems to have been placed high on the chalk escarpment about a mile north-east of the village. From there the cemetery spread downhill, not necessarily continuously but in related sections including an increasing proportion of inhumations. It extended right down to and across the Roman road, where a final group, apparently all inhumations, immediately adjoins the northern boundary of the medieval churchyard. It seems very likely that the latter came into use soon after the conversion of the Deirans and the destruction of their pagan temple at

[1] The cemetery is fully described, and its surviving contents illustrated and discussed, by Myres and Southern, op. cit.; some further information is given by M. L. Faull in *Ant. J.* 56 (1976), 227-33. More recent excavations in 1976-8 are briefly described in N. Reynolds, *Sancton* (1979), who records that 'no limit to the cemetery has been found in any direction within the excavated area'.

[2] G. Rolleston writes that Anglo-Saxon pots 'were quite common things in the village and I was told that one woman used to keep her whitening in one of the urns': Myres and Southern, op. cit. 6.

Goodmanham following the crucial debate in 627 recorded by Bede.[1]

The use of the Sancton cemetery should thus provide a cross-section of the whole history of the Deiran people throughout its pagan phase. Its sheer size indicates that it must have served as a major central burial-ground for a considerable part of these people over a period of at least two hundred and fifty years. But unfortunately, while much very informative material is preserved from it, many of the earlier discoveries have been lost, and others are widely scattered and without known associations or exact provenance.

The first systematic work on the site was carried out in 1873 by an excavator, George Rolleston of Oxford, who, as a distinguished professional anatomist, was primarily interested in the skeletal remains from inhumations. But he was soon confronted with quantities of cremation urns and their contents. Unfortunately he took to publicizing his discoveries by distributing many of his finds, particularly complete pots in relatively good condition, among his wide circle of academic colleagues and other friends not only in this country and Europe, but in America, Australia, and New Zealand. Pottery from Sancton has thus been traced, in addition to the main collections now at Hull and Oxford, to other English museums such as Birmingham and Nottingham, to the Smithsonian Institution at Washington, D.C., to the Canterbury Museum at Christchurch and the Otago Museum at Dunedin, New Zealand, and elsewhere. Other pots which have not been traced are known from Rolleston's correspondence to have gone to Max Müller at Dresden, to friends at Hamburg and elsewhere in Germany, as well as to Cardinal Wiseman at Westminster, and to Canon Greenwell of Durham, who is known to have 'procured about twenty'. So far as is known, none of these far-flung finds have been properly published, nor did Rolleston leave any site plan to show the position or arrangement of his discoveries.

---

[1] *HE* ii. 13. The medieval church at Sancton was largely rebuilt in the nineteenth century and now retains no certain evidence of pre-Norman date. A water-colour of *c*.1770 showing its dilapidated state before these alterations, indicates that there was then a large round-headed arch in the south wall of the thirteenth-century chancel, which appears out of place in that position and could have survived from an earlier Saxon church. *Ant. J.* 56 (1976), pl. XXXVII.

In spite of all these losses and the dispersion around the world of what remains of the cemetery's contents, much can still be learned from the two hundred and fifty or so surviving cremation urns and the miscellaneous small objects once associated both with them and with some of the inhumations. More may still remain to be discovered in parts of this very extensive burial-ground that have never been systematically explored.

With all allowance made for these uncertainties, it is possible to draw from Sancton some tentative conclusions on the early history of Deira. The surviving pottery includes a considerable number of pieces which can be closely paralleled in the cemeteries of the continental Angles in Schleswig and Fyn, where they are mostly dated no later than the fourth or early fifth centuries. Genrich has published a type series of some thirty forms which the pottery of the continental Angles took at this time.[1] At least a dozen of these can be exactly matched among the surviving Sancton urns. It is even more remarkable that in two-thirds of these cases the urns used by Genrich to illustrate the continental types should come from the great cemetery at Borgstedt, centrally situated in southern Schleswig. It was evidently with the communities that used this cemetery that the Sancton Angles were most closely related in their early days, very possibly as *laeti*, in Britain.

This intimate connection with the heartland of the continental Angles was evidently well-remembered at the time of Gregory the Great's famous interview with the English boys whom he found on sale in the Roman slave market. Not only were they well aware of their own Angle origin, but they recalled the name, Ælle, of the king of Deira from whose land they had come. It was their clear memory on these matters which enabled Gregory to make the celebrated puns which, according to Bede's story, led some years later to his promotion of the Augustinian mission.[2]

But the early cremation urns from Sancton are by no means confined to types whose continental distribution lies

---

[1] A. Genrich, *Formenkreise und Stammesgruppen in Schleswig-Holstein*, Abb. 2. Details of the links between these types and the Sancton urns are in Myres and Southern, op. cit. 15-16.

[2] *HE* ii. 1. The *Anglo-Saxon Chronicle* dates the reign of Ælle 560-588.

mainly in Schleswig and Fyn, though it was no doubt
primarily of these parts that Bede was thinking when he
reported that the Anglian homelands had been largely
deserted in consequence of the migration to Britain.[1] There
are many others whose continental parallels are to be found
further south and west towards and beyond the lands around
the lower Elbe. Here German scholars have located what they
term a *Nordseekustengruppe* of folk, whose characteristics
spring as much from Saxon as from Angle antecedents.
Closely similar in form and decoration to a number of the
early Sancton pieces are thus pots from such Saxon cemeteries
at Westerwanna, Wehden, Altenwalde, Gudendorf, and the
Galgenberg near Cuxhaven.[2]

All these types of pottery, whether of Angle or Saxon
origin, mingled at Sancton as in other parts of eastern
England to produce during the following century a wide
range of mixed Anglo-Saxon styles in form and decoration.
That Sancton was itself an influential centre of this cultural
development is shown by the fact that, throughout the
Humbrensian area and beyond it in East and Middle Anglia,
products of one or other of the Sancton pottery workshops
have been identified. Other cases have been noted where
designs typical of Sancton workshops seem to have influenced
the work of potters based elsewhere. Such links occur in the
output of the Sancton/Elkington potter, who made rather
ill-formed *Buckelurnen* decorated with a variety of free-hand
linear designs in the fifth century.[3] They are also found in
the work of the Sancton/Baston potter, who, perhaps a
century later, used complex patterns of hanging swags filled
with stamped ornament to produce sophisticated and almost
three-dimensional effects.[4]

But other influences besides those from the Angle and
Saxon coastlands bordering the North Sea can be traced
among the Germanic pottery from Sancton. It has been
suggested earlier, on literary and place-name evidence,[5]

---

[1] *HE* i. 15.
[2] Details of these parallels are given in Myres and Southern, op. cit., 16–18.
[3] Ibid. figs. 16–18.
[4] Ibid. figs. 36 and 40 include three Sancton pieces from this workshop;
others are illustrated in Myres, *Corpus*, ii. figs. 347 and 348.
[5] p. 81.

that *laeti* from the Alemannic areas of central and south Germany are likely to have been among those settled in Yorkshire in the last century of Roman rule. A number of the Sancton urns show signs in form and decoration that their potters were familiar with fashions prevalent both among the Alemanni[1] and among the Franks of the middle Rhineland. Most remarkable among the latter is the so-called *biconus* potter, who produced at Sancton a number of hand-made vessels more or less closely modelled in form on the wheel-made biconical pottery of the Rhineland. That these pots are not themselves imports from the Continent is suggested by the fact that, unlike their Frankish wheel-made models, they are all hand-made. Moreover they are mostly decorated with stylized zoomorphic designs clearly more Anglo-Saxon than Frankish in inspiration.[2]

It would seem, therefore, that the Sancton cemetery came to be used not only by communities of Angle and Saxon origin but also by others from parts of central and southern Germany that are now included in Sachsen-Anhalt, Mittelfranken, and Nord-Baden as well as the Rhineland. Some of these groups which seem to have maintained cultural links with their homelands can be plausibly associated with folk such as the Alemanni originally settled in Yorkshire as *laeti* in late Roman times. Whether the Angle and Saxon people who came eventually to dominate the affairs of Deira were first introduced into the country in the same way is uncertain, but there are two considerations which suggest that this may have been so. One is their common use of the Sancton cemetery, which might imply that the conditions of their settlement were similar. The other is the very early date which the continental parallels to some of their cremation pottery seem to indicate. If they were already burying their cremated dead at Sancton in urns of late-fourth- or early-fifth-century types, the probability is that their settlements had taken place, most likely in controlled

---

[1] Myres and Southern, 20–1; the large urns of globular or rounded form such as 2017 on fig. 14 and all those on fig. 19 can be most readily matched in central and south Germany.

[2] Ibid. 23–4 and figs. 37 and 38; the discussion includes a table of identical decorative motifs used on eleven of the Sancton urns attributable to the *biconus* potter: see also Myres, *Corpus*, i. 26 and ii. fig. 152.

conditions, before the final collapse of Roman rule in northern Britain.

The legionary fortress at York (*Eboracum*), headquarters of the *Dux Britanniarum*, must have been the military base from which the last phases of the occupation of the north by Rome were controlled. It would be very interesting to know how the early Germanic settlements along the western margins of the chalk wolds, between Brough and Malton, were related to the last days of Roman York. Recent excavations within the legionary fortress, including those resulting from the need to strengthen the foundations of the Minster, have shown that the structural weakness of the building beneath both its central tower and its west front was largely due to the fact that it overlies upstanding remains of the legionary headquarters. Parts of this must still have survived to some height amongst the accumulations of Roman rubble and rubbish through which the medieval foundations of the church were laid.[1] Elsewhere in the city it has been found that Roman property boundaries were often used to demarcate later structures, and that walls and floors of Roman date were sometimes incorporated in the lower parts of medieval buildings.

The alignment of the Norman Minster itself does not correspond with that of the Roman street grid. But it is quite possible that the church of St. Michael-le-Belfry, just outside its south-west angle, which, though of late medieval date in its present form, is on the Roman alignment, may overlie the church which Paulinus was allowed by Edwin to build in York after the Deirans had accepted Christianity in 627. This is rendered more likely by the fact that, like Paulinus' church underlying St. Paul-in-the-Bail at Lincoln,[2] it occupies a prominent central situation in relation to the Roman headquarters buildings. These were evidently still recognizable, however ruinous, when it was first built.

All this evidence for some degree of continuity between

---

[1] A nearly complete column from the basilica is shown where it fell, apparently in the ninth century, in J. Campbell and others (eds.), *The Anglo-Saxons* (1982), fig. 38. Destruction levels covering the ruined Roman buildings under the crossing included some Middle Saxon potsherds probably of the seventh century: RCHM York Minster Excavation negs. YM 680–3.

[2] See p. 179.

Roman *Eboracum* and Dark Age *Eoforwic* must be interpreted in the context of the early Anglo-Saxon cemeteries
which lie close at hand outside its walls. The neighbourhood
of that at the Mount, where at least seven cremation urns
have been found in disturbed conditions, has also produced
a number of pieces of Roman-Saxon pottery, suggesting that
folk with barbarian tastes in decoration were already settled
nearby in late Roman times. From another cemetery, at
Heworth just across the river Foss, which joins the Ouse
from the north-east immediately south of the city, have come
at least forty-five cremation urns, found during railway
construction in the nineteenth century. Several of these are
of types that could have been in vogue in the early fifth
century.[1]

Although there are no certain potter-links between these
Heworth urns and the products of the workshops that
supplied the Sancton cemetery, the two series have many
similarities. They must be roughly contemporary and belong
to folk of similar Saxon background. York was, after all,
directly accessible from the Humber estuary by the main
stream of the Ouse, itself known as the Humber in early
times. It could be reached equally by the Roman roads that
led from Brough through the Sancton/Goodmanham concentration of early Anglian settlement, and from what seems to
have been a similar concentration on the Derwent around
Malton. From what Bede says[2] of the regal style adopted by
Edwin of Deira in the early seventh century, it looks as if
he may have thought of himself and his people as the direct
heirs to the Imperial authority once wielded by the *Dux
Britanniarum* at York, and maintained by the settlement of
Germanic *laeti*, of whatever tribal origin, around the main
strategic centres of the region that became Deira.[3]

[1] e.g. Myres, *Corpus*, ii. fig. 162.89 with simple *stehende Bogen* design;
fig. 178.105 a Group I Buckelurne; figs. 262.98 and 268.4017 with simple
chevron designs; and most notably fig. 271.93, a large vessel of Plettke A6 type
dated by him in the fourth century but associated by Werner and Tischler with
their *Laetenhorizont* c.400; fig. 265.87 is very like Westerwanna 1342 with
fourth-century brooch. For discussion of these parallels see ibid. i. 46-7.

[2] *HE* ii. 16.

[3] It is worth noting that the *Dux Britanniarum* killed during the *barbarica
conspiratio* of 367 was himself apparently of Germanic origin, to judge from his
name Fullofaudes. Perhaps he owed his position to being leader of the local
laeti, and lost his life when they joined the revolt.

How far north from York and Malton this pattern of settlement extended in the early days must remain uncertain. Further sporadic finds at the Roman centres of Aldborough (*Isurium Brigantum*) and Catterick (*Cataractonium*), a small early cemetery at Darlington, and another ill-explored site at Norton near Billingham[1] would suggest a northward movement up the Roman roads. They show that the neighbourhood of what had once been important Roman centres remained in the sixth century the more obvious points from which the agricultural development of a naturally forested region could most easily radiate.

It is likely that this increasing takeover by Germanic settlers may have met with British resistance, some of it based on native kingdoms far to the north. The Gododdin poems, attributed to the near-contemporary poet Aneirin, contain an account of a disaster at *Catraeth* (Catterick) which befell a British expedition apparently originating near Edinburgh. There has been much debate over the date and circumstances of this campaign.[2] On the one hand it would seem that the historical situation implied in the poem is unlikely to have prevailed after the consolidation of Anglian Bernicia in the country between Edinburgh and Catterick under Æthelfrith between 592 and 617. That the campaign did not take place later than the early years of the seventh century is also suggested by the mention of Catraeth as a past event in the panegyric on Cadwallon which, if genuine, must antedate his death in 633. On the other hand, if the siege recorded as the *obsessio Etin* in the *Annals of Ulster* in 637 (638) and the *obsessio Etain* in the *Annals of Tigernach* in

---

[1] That *Cataractonium* was still occupied by Roman military or paramilitary forces as late as the early fifth century is suggested by the presence of two zoomorphic buckles of Hawkes Types IA and IVB stratified under a floor from which came a coin of that date: *Med. Arch.* 5 (1961), 20, 43, 62. For the Norton site, which has produced an early sixth-century cruciform brooch, see *Med. Arch.* 28 (1984), 173–5, and for early Anglo-Saxon settlement in Bernicia generally R. Miket in *Anglo-Saxon Cemeteries*, ed. P. Rahtz, T. Dickinson, and L. Watts, BAR 82 (1980), 289–305, and R. Cramp in *Settlement in North Britain 1000BC–AD1000*, ed. J. C. Chapman and H. Mytum, BAR 118 (1983), 263–97.

[2] e.g. K. Jackson in *Antiquity*, 13 (1939), 25–34; I. Ll. Foster in Foster and G. Daniel (eds.), *Prehistoric and Early Wales* (1963), 231; and my comment in *EHR* 71 (1955), 92. There is a summary by C. A. Gresham in *Antiquity*, 16 (1942), 237 of Ifor Williams' argument in *Canu Aneirin* (Cardiff, 1938) dating Catraeth about 600.

635 is rightly placed by Jackson at Edinburgh,[1] it was
apparently still in British hands, if under, probably Anglian,
threat in the 630s. Perhaps its *obsessio* at that time was a
direct or indirect consequence of the earlier failure by
the Britons to check the Anglian advance at Catraeth.

But the Tees valley, as has already been noted, seems to
have marked the limits to which Roman civilian culture had
penetrated. Beyond it, in what became Bernicia, it would
seem that the main impact of Germanic settlement took a
different form. Here it fell upon a land of native Celtic
traditions, whose scanty pastoral population still lived largely
in the moorland fastnesses from which the Roman armies and
the irregular para-military forces of *laeti* had but temporarily
and partially dislodged them. Such a countryside, poor by
nature, and poorer still after the destructive raids of Picts and
Scots had repeatedly passed over it, was not one to attract
early Germanic settlement within the framework of the
existing society. Thus when invasion came, it came late, and
seems to have taken the form of a seaborne assault on the
Northumbrian coast, apparently by-passing most of what is
now the countryside of Durham.[2] The traditional date, 547,
for the beginning of the reign of Ida, 'from whom the royal
stock of the Northumbrians claims descent', may well mark
the winning of the earliest effective Anglian foothold in
Bernicia.

The coastal distribution of such pagan archaeological
remains as have been recognized in Bernicia suggests penetration from two main points of entry. One was the estuary
of the Tyne, from which raiding parties, followed by more
permanent conquest, passed easily westward along the river
valley and the line of the Roman Wall. They left sixth-
century brooches and other signs of their presence in the
Roman supply base of Corbridge (*Corstopitum*) and in
several Wall forts such as Birdoswald (*Camboglanna*). By
the seventh century there was somewhere already established

---

[1] P. Clemoes (ed.), *The Anglo-Saxons, Studies . . . presented to Bruce Dickins*
(1959), 35–42.
[2] In the twelfth-century Life of St. Oswald, the early boundary between
Bernicia and Deira is said to have been uncertain, because the whole country
between Tees and Tyne had been 'a deserted waste and was thus nothing but a
hiding-place and home for wild and woodland beasts' (*Symeon of Durham*,
Rolls Series (1882), i. 339).

a *villa regalis Ad Murum*, whose site is not certainly identified.

The other main area of penetration from the coast lay
further north, between the Coquet and the Tweed, with a
focus behind Lindisfarne and Bamborough. The promontory
fortress of Bamborough, a natural stronghold for sea-faring
invaders, became an early political centre as an *urbs regia* of
the Bernician kings. Lindisfarne, whose name echoes that of
those elements of the Lindiswaras from south of the Humber
who must have taken a prominent part among Ida's followers,
was the first centre of Bernician Christianity in the seventh
century. Inland, at Yeavering in Glendale, was another early
centre of royal authority, a *villa regalis* recorded by Bede
with the Celtic name *Ad Gefrin*.[1] This site was already
marked in British times by a large hill-fort. Under extensive
and meticulous excavation by Hope-Taylor[2] it has revealed
many traces of elaborate timber halls and other buildings,
apparently of Edwin's time. These include a unique example
of what appears to have been a structure for public assem-
blies, whose roughly semicircular plan seems to be based on
that of a Roman theatre. If this analogy is correct, it provides
another very striking example of the deliberate adoption by
the early Northumbrian kings of a public image designed to
emphasize their claim to be the true heirs of the Roman
imperial tradition in northern Britain.

It is clear that for twenty or thirty years after the arrival
of Ida and his people from the south in 547, their penetration
inland from the Northumberland coast was strenuously con-
tested by the untamed British kings. Some of the names and
exploits of these warriors are preserved in the *Historia
Brittonum*. They became the subjects for native sagas and
elegies, partly still preserved, if often in garbled form, in later
collections of Welsh traditional poetry. At one time there
is a tale of four kings—Urien, Ridderch, Guallanc, and
Morcant—who fought against Hussa; at another, of Hussa's
successor, Theodoric, besieged by Urien for three days and
nights in Lindisfarne.[3]

---

[1] *HE* ii. 14.
[2] B. Hope-Taylor, *Yeavering: an Anglo-British Centre of Early Northumbria*
(1977), *passim.*
[3] *Hist. Britt.* 63.

It would seem that it was hardly before the days of
Æthelfrith, in the last quarter of the sixth century, that the
Bernician warriors were able to turn a struggle for bare
existence on the Northumbrian coast into a political supremacy. Eventually however Æthelfrith could make his
power felt alike by the Picts of Scotland, the Britons of
Cumbria and North Wales, and the parent stock of the Angles
in Deira. He was still remembered in Bede's day as the king
who above all others 'had laid waste the nation of the
Britons . . . for no one before him had rendered more of their
lands either habitable for the English by the extermination
of the natives or tributary by their conquest'.[1]

Bede's characteristically forthright statement throws a
penetrating light on the methods of settlement adopted by
Æthelfrith and his people. It also illuminates the whole
question of British survival in Northumbria, and the mutual
relations of invaders and invaded during the centuries of
conflict.[2] The process seems to have taken the form mainly
of a military conquest by a numerically inferior, but more
vigorous and better equipped body of aristocratic invaders.
It does not resemble a mass movement of settlers primarily
interested in their own exploitation of the best tracts of
agricultural land.

If this interpretation is correct it would help to explain
some features of later Northumbrian society. Here many
Celtic institutions persisted, as did strong traces of the Celtic
language and many Celtic place-names. The peculiarities of
the later Northumbrian agricultural system have also been
claimed as due to direct Celtic influence. There are strong
traces of a system of local organization which probably goes
back to British times. In many parts of Bernicia the countryside seems to have been grouped into substantial regions
each dependent on a royal *vill* to which taxes and dues were
paid and from which local justice was administered in the
pre-feudal age. This arrangement is closely similar to that
which prevailed in Kent where each province or lathe was
centred in the same way on a *villa regalis*. There are also
traces of a system of this kind surviving on the medieval

---

[1] *HE* i. 34.
[2] M. Faull in L. Laing (ed.), *Studies in Celtic Survival*, BAR 37 (1977), 1-56.

estates of the bishop of Durham further south. Here some customary dues were described in terms clearly derived from Celtic words, themselves of Latin origin. Thus the annual payment in livestock made by some villages was known as *metreth*, from Welsh *treth*, and ultimately from Latin *tributum*.

Such survivals clearly indicate that in much of Bernicia a substantial quantity of the native lands was probably left in the occupation of tributary British subjects under the new military aristocracy. The situation was thus quite different from what happened in those parts of Britain where the invaders were rather seeking habitable lands for their own exploitation than to live on rents extracted from a dependent native population. Northumberland can indeed be properly described as 'a county of villages rather than hamlets'.[1] Most of these villages have Germanic or hybrid names and must have grown up round the residences of the new Anglian aristocracy and their followers. But between and around them the countryside long retained elements both of language and of local customs which perpetuate arrangements that go back to Celtic times.

[1] H. L. Gray, *English Field Systems* (Cambridge, Mass., 1915), 153 and 189. See also F. W. Dendy, 'The ancient farms of Northumberland', *Arch. Ael.* n.s. 16 (1894), 121-56.

8

CHANGE AND DECAY

R EADERS of this book will probably have noted in passing
many of the more obvious factors, operating at various
times and in different parts of the country, which combined to transform the late Roman provinces of Britain in
the fourth century into the still very confused and chaotic
mosaic of Anglo-Saxon and British kingdoms which were
taking shape at the end of the sixth. It may be convenient if
an attempt is made in conclusion to draw together into a
more coherent pattern the most significant strands which
form what must always remain a somewhat tangled skein.
Although it has inevitably to involve some reiteration of
points already made in earlier chapters, an attempt at clarifi-
cation will be the purpose of this final summary.

The basis for any sound understanding of the complex
forces which converted Roman Britain into Christian England
can only be a clear appreciation of the changes which over-
took the native population of the country during these two
centuries. These changes profoundly, if patchily, affected
both its numbers and its nature. The first point to grasp is
that during the centuries of Roman rule, and as a direct
consequence of it, there had been overall a massive increase
both in the numbers and in the material prosperity of the
population. Many factors had contributed to bring about this
result. On the political side the mere imposition of the *pax
Romana* on what had been a large number of mutually
hostile tribes, which had for centuries been engaged in in-
effective but destructive internal struggles for supremacy,
must have provided for the first time more or less stable
conditions to encourage a rising population. On the economic
side there were soon many new forces at work to make
profitable employment for increasing numbers. Rome had
greatly developed the money economy, whose tentative
beginnings were already appearing among the more advanced
British tribes in the century before the conquest. Moreover

the new ruling classes, both civilian and military, encouraged expanding markets both for the profitable disposal of agricultural produce, especially corn for the armies, and for the exploitation of other natural resources derived from forestry, mining, quarrying, and so on.

For the first time, therefore, there was in Britain a substantial body of well-heeled consumers, mostly engaged in the defence, administration, and development of the country. Many of them were accustomed to a much higher and more civilized standard of living and accommodation than had been known here before. The expanding money economy provided the means which enabled them to gratify their tastes for the comforts, conveniences, and amenities of life on a scale quite unprecedented in pre-Roman times. One has only to consider the expenditure involved in the building, equipment, and maintenance of the new towns, country houses, roads, forts, and port facilities to appreciate the scale of the economic revolution that transformed British society in the earlier centuries of the Roman occupation. These developments must have had profound effects on the numbers and the prosperity of the native population. As time went on conditions changed. Both political and economic instability increased, and eventually proved uncontrollable; but it may well be that in its earlier stages the growing pressure of inflation rather stimulated than restrained the initial boom conditions for industrial development.

Thus in Britain, perhaps more than in those parts of the western Empire that suffered continuously from political disturbances, a generally prosperous economy seems to have persisted, with only temporary set-backs, well into the fourth century.[1] There were indeed continually increasing signs of internal political weakness and of growing barbarian pressure on the frontiers. But these conditions did not immediately spell disaster. It may well be that the military build-up around the south and east coasts of Britain resulting from the fortification of the Saxon Shore, and its administrative consequences, may have contributed to the increase of economic prosperity in the countryside of southern Britain.

[1] More detailed evidence for this conclusion can be found in C. Taylor, *Village and Farmstead* (1983), 47-106.

Here the widespread rebuilding and enlargement of villas and rural industrial establishments led Haverfield long ago to refer to the fourth century as the Golden Age of Roman Britain.[1] While such indications of well-being are less evident in the towns, some of which had clearly been planned on too ambitious a scale, both economic and political factors may have contributed to a genuine shift in the balance of prosperity from town to country at this time.

There are certainly many signs of a rising population in the countryside of lowland Britain. On the Saxon Shore itself and its immediate hinterland there will have been, in addition to the increased military presence, some immigration of Germanic folk. This could have arisen either by unregulated infiltration from the continental coastlands or by the deliberate settlement of *laeti* with or without para-military obligations to the authorities of the *Litus Saxonicum*.[2] The development in the fourth century of such rural industries as the potteries in the New Forest or on the margins of the Fens, around Water Newton (*Durobrivae*), and in the lower Trent valley, may have been largely due to increasing demand from immigrant communities of this kind. Certainly it is very likely that those potteries which specialized, as at Much Hadham, Essex, in the production of the so-called Romano-Saxon wares, decorated in ways designed to appeal to barbarian taste, were stimulated by demand from newly settled Germanic immigrants on the Saxon Shore. (See Fig. 7).

It is only in recent years that the full extent and depth of this population explosion in the countryside of fourth-century Britain has been appreciated.[3] The environmental

[1] F. J. Haverfield, *Roman Occupation of Britain*, revised by G. Macdonald (Oxford, 1924), 265.

[2] The distribution of the so-called Marbled Ware flagons imported from the Rhineland in the third and fourth centuries is very suggestive of immigration to the Kentish section of the *Litus Saxonicum* at that time. They occur in the Saxon Shore forts of Richborough, Dover, and Lympne, as well as in London, Southwark, Canterbury, and elsewhere in coastal Kent, but not apparently further inland: *Brit.* 14 (1983), 247–52 and fig. 3. A similar concentration in Kent, Essex, and around London is shown by the distribution of fourth-century Argonne ware, though this extends into coastal Sussex and Hampshire and is occasionally found further afield. See M. Fulford, 'Pottery and Britain's foreign trade in the later Roman period', in D. Peacock (ed.), *Pottery and Early Commerce* (1977), 40, fig. 1.

[3] C. Taylor, op. cit., especially ch. 8, 'A crowded country'.

evidence for it is particularly striking. It has come very largely from the widespread discovery of rural settlements in what appear at first sight to be areas of untouched ancient woodland. The .known number and extent of such settlements has been very greatly increased in recent years by the clearance of woodland for agriculture, quarrying, and housing schemes. Much information has come from the building of new motorways, which have provided illuminating thin sections across many parts of lowland Britain.

It had been generally supposed that conditions of deep natural forest would have inhibited such settlement until the late Saxon period, or at least confined it, as in the Weald, to the immediate vicinity of Roman trunk roads. But it would now appear that by the fourth century much of Britain's natural woodlands had already been cleared. Partly no doubt this was to provide timber for building and other industrial purposes,[1] but partly also to supply fuel for the innumerable furnaces required not only for all kinds of manufacturing industry, but for the domestic heating which was so novel and so universal a feature of the new architecture in town and country alike. Whatever the reason, there was evidently much more cleared land becoming available for agricultural exploitation and rural settlement than had ever been the case in earlier times.

The fact that so much of lowland Britain was becoming both well-populated and prosperous in the fourth century helps to explain some otherwise puzzling references in contemporary and later literature. Thus Britain became well-known as a plentiful source of exports of all kinds, whether agricultural, such as corn for the armies on the Rhine frontier, or raw materials especially lead and tin, or such manufactured goods as the textiles whose price required regulation by Imperial Edict. As late as 429 Germanus could be greeted, apparently at Verulamium, by a gathering of wealthy landowners luxuriously attired and accompanied by their supporting tenantry. Nearly a century later Gildas still looked back with nostalgia to an age of unparalleled prosperity that

[1] The very large quantities of heavy timber used by the Roman army in building forts have been well illustrated from recent excavations in water-logged deposits at Carlisle (*Luguvallium*): see M. R. McCarthy, *Ant. J.* 63 (1983), 124-30.

had left vivid memories to the generation of his parents.[1] During the fourth century and at least the earlier years of the fifth, the literary and the archaeological evidence are thus in apparent accord. They both suggest that, at any rate over much of lowland Britain, the rural economy displayed a surprising resilience in the face of Rome's increasing political weakness.

But of course these adventitiously favourable conditions could not long survive the political collapse of the western Empire. Before the middle of the fifth century both military and civilian administration had disappeared from Britain. With them had gone the money economy which had supported them and the associated spending power which had maintained the internal markets for food and manufactured goods. At the same time what remained of the profitable export trade was disrupted and eventually brought to an end by the barbarian pirate fleets that increasingly infested the coasts and harbours on both sides of the Channel. When Gildas complains that a time came when 'the whole province was deprived of its food supply except for the resources of hunting', this is precisely the economic situation that he must have had in mind.[2]

It was also the situation which led to the breakdown of good relations between the British authorities and the barbarian *laeti* and other Germanic immigrants now thickly settled on the Saxon Shore. Gildas is quite clear that this breakdown arose directly from the failure to maintain the promised supplies on which these folk depended. It was this situation that sparked off the uncontrollable outbreak which soon put an end to what was left of Romano-British prosperity. The departure of the army and the civilian administration had in any case left a power-vacuum at the centre of affairs. Procopius was no doubt right in saying a century later that this had only been filled by what he termed 'tyrants', the normal word in use to describe self-styled local emperors at this time. The type is of course personified in Britain by Vortigern, a figure who has always been known by this title rather than by a personal name. It was almost exactly the

---

[1] Constantius, *Vita Germani*, 14 and 18 where Britain is called *opulentissima insula*; Gildas, *De Excidio*, 21.
[2] De Excidio, 19.

verbal equivalent of the *superbus tyrannus*, to whose unhappy dealings with the revolted *laeti* Gildas, perhaps rather unfairly, attributes the whole collapse of Roman civilization in Britain.[1]

It is easy to see how vulnerable sub-Roman civilization had become to an outbreak originating in this way. The very circumstances which had led to the exceptional prosperity of rural Britain in the fourth century left it peculiarly exposed to hostile action. It was especially open to assault from those who, especially after the withdrawal of the regular garrisons, were primarily responsible for the security of the Saxon Shore. It is probable that many of these irregular forces, however long they had been settled on the east and south coasts, were only superficially assimilated to provincial life, though they had become dependent on it for both the necessities and many of the amenities of that life. When times turned sour with the progressive breakdown of the money economy, they might well come to view with envy and dislike the apparently continuing prosperity of the upper classes still largely self-supporting on their rich but unprotected villa estates. At the same time, as Gildas makes clear and the archaeological evidence confirms, these Germanic immigrants remained in touch with friends and relations among the footloose tribes beyond the North Sea. Many of these were only too ready to take advantage of invitations, whether official or not, to come over and join ostensibly in the defence of coastal Britain, whether it was supposedly threatened by Picts and Scots, or by attempts at reconquest from the authorities of Roman Gaul.

All the surviving evidence, whether from literary, archaeological, or environmental sources, combines to emphasize the appalling consequences of the breakdown of relations. On one side were the 'tyrants' of the *civitates* and the villa-owning notables, while on the other were the *laeti* of the Saxon Shore supported, and perhaps soon dominated, by unknown numbers of much less civilized barbarian intruders. The so-called 'Groans of the Britons' was an appeal from some still coherent sub-Roman authority in Britain, whose text is briefly summarized by Gildas.[2] It was addressed to

[1] Ibid. 23. [2] Ibid. 20.

Aetius in Gaul during his third consulship, and thus dates what was evidently a very serious phase of the rebellion between 449 and 453.

Gildas himself emphasizes the destruction of the towns, which must have been the main power-bases of the sub-Roman 'tyrants' at this time. His witness on this point is most important, and is borne out in many ways. A general cessation of town life at this moment helps to explain the total disappearance of the urban episcopate, a fact of the utmost consequence for the future.[1] In Gaul at this period, it was the persistence in many cities of a more or less continuous succession of bishops that guaranteed the survival, not only of the Christian organization with all its religious implications, but of a language based on Latin, many Roman principles of law and custom, and some appreciation of the classical tradition in art and culture.

All this seems to have disappeared in Britain with the total destruction of Romanized life in the cities soon after the central years of the fifth century. Where any archaeological evidence for continued habitation has been noticed, it generally consists of apparent attempts to maintain or refurbish the defences. This included significantly the blocking of gates, and occasional signs of Germanic mercenaries occupying huts and *Grubenhäuser* inserted among ruined buildings and accompanied by pottery and other domestic rubbish, as often of barbarian as of sub-Roman types. Nowhere in the towns of Britain have any convincing signs been found of civilian life continuing on any level but that of bare subsistence even as late as the end of the fifth century.

The disappearance of town life and all that it implied had profound effects on the whole structure of society. It led directly to the disappearance of the old tribal divisions on which, since pre-Roman times, the pattern of local loyalties and administration had rested. This dramatic change can best be appreciated once again by pointing to the contrast with Gaul. There most of the main cities, which, as in Britain, had been the centres of local government, continued after the Frankish conquest to be called by abbreviated forms of the names of the tribal *civitates* of which they had been the

---

[1] Ibid. 24. Gildas particularly emphasizes the destruction of churches and the whole Christian organization on which the towns depended so heavily at this time.

administrative centres.[1] In Britain the only apparent case of this practice is in Kent where the British *Cantuarii*, in the Germanic form *Cantware*, replaced with their own name any version of *Durovernum* at Canterbury. But elsewhere in Britain the names of the tribal cantons which had been joined with those of their administrative centres passed entirely out of memory during the transition to Anglo-Saxon society. Where the towns retained any nominal reminiscence from Roman times (and this was by no means everywhere[2]) it took the form of a bungled abbreviation of the town name itself. This was generally attached to the Germanic loan word *ceaster* (*castra*) in recognition of the appearance of the place as a former fortified stronghold.[3] Nowhere but at Canterbury was the old tribal name thought to be worthy of retention in any recognizable form. This can only mean that the tribes themselves had ceased to exist for any purpose which required the retention of their names.

Thus the structure of rural society must have suffered as disastrously as that of the towns. The town councils, or *ordines*, that had managed the local affairs of the tribes and had formed their link with the Roman provincial administration, must have been largely composed of the principal villa owners of the neighbourhood. These were men whose authority and wealth were still apparent at the time of the visit of Germanus to Verulamium in 429. But by then their position was no longer supported by any form of military organization. While themselves Christian, and interested to debate the current doctrinal controversies over Pelagianism with visiting ecclesiastics from Gaul, it would appear that they had little or no contact with, or control over, the outlook of their own tenantry. Germanus, at any rate, found it necessary to baptize the local forces, hastily assembled to cope with the immediate menace of a Saxon raid, before organizing them into a ramshackle army. He was moreover careful to avoid committing them to actual combat, and achieved the Alleluia victory by an ingenious ruse which did not involve much fighting.[4]

[1] p. 31.
[2] e.g. *Ratae Coritanorum*, which turned into Leicester: see p. 184.
[3] p. 31.
[4] *Vita Germani*, 17-18.

The picture of a still rich but quite defenceless society which is revealed by this story, makes it very easy to understand how swiftly and completely it could fall victim to barbarian intrusion. If Germanus had not chanced to be at Verulamium in 429, and capable, with his military and administrative experience in Gaul, of rapidly organizing effective resistance, those passing Saxon raiders might have put a permanent end not only to the wealthy villas in their path across the countryside but to the very existence of Verulamium, once the second city of Roman Britain and the resting-place of its most famous Christian martyr.

Sooner or later destruction must thus have been the fate of the villas as well as the cities of Britain. The archaeological evidence suggests that few villas lasted as local centres of Romanized life far into the fifth century. Clear signs of physical destruction are uncommon and in any case difficult to identify or date at all closely. But the effects of economic decay, and a reduced or sometimes completely altered lifestyle, are often obvious. Thus bath-buildings and hypocausted living-quarters are found abandoned or put to more squalid uses; rubbish from collapsed roofs or the camp fires of squatters overlies worn or damaged mosaic pavements; and, here and there, timber barns or halls have been found built into or against earlier rooms, suggesting the deliberate replacement of what had been a Romanized by a barbarian way of life.

But the great majority of Roman country houses and working farms seem to have gone completely out of use. Early Anglo-Saxon pottery or metal objects are very rarely found on their sites, and hardly ever in stratified contexts which make continuity of occupation certain.[1] Where, as sometimes happens, a later Saxon or medieval village is found to overlie Roman buildings, there is seldom any reason to believe that the one directly succeeded to the other.[2]

[1] Three certain cases of rather different kinds are summarily described and illustrated in C. J. Arnold, *Roman Britain to Saxon England* (1984), 62-5, from Rivenhall (Essex), Orton Hall (Northants.), and Barton Court, Abingdon (Oxon.). Saxon pottery from the Rivenhall villa included a fifth-century bowl with linear decoration. See Myres, *Corpus*, ii. fig. 212.

[2] There are no certain cases in this country, as there are many in France, of the gradual conversion of villas into early medieval fortified houses or monasteries, or of their partial survival in the fabric of parish churches: J. Percival, *The Roman*

The coincidence of site is often more readily explained by the convenience of its position in relation to natural features, such as water supply or lines of communication, or even the mere availability of building materials from deserted Roman structures. Place-names such as Cold Harbour are sometimes quoted as indications of continuous occupation. But they are more likely to indicate the presence of abandoned buildings than any significant continuity. In any case such names provide no certain clues to the date or the circumstances in which they were first thought to be appropriate.

Much more significant of a real institutional break in the occupation of the Romanized countryside is the total disappearance of villa names. Not one of the many hundreds, if not thousands, of rural estates that dotted the countryside of lowland Britain in the later Roman centuries can be certainly shown to have left any trace of its name in recognizable form on the modern map.[1] Once again, the contrast presented with the situation in Roman Gaul is most remarkable. There the family names of countless Gallo-Roman proprietors have survived all over France, in abbreviated adjectival forms which must originally have been attached to such terms as *ager* or *fundus*, signifying the ownership of a rural property whether big or small. Most of the very large numbers of French place-names ending in -*ac*, -*ecque*, -*nan*, -*gny*, -*at*, etc. are derived from the names of Gallo-Roman landowners or farmers cut down in this way.

This can only mean one thing. In Gaul the Frankish settlement took place very largely within the framework of existing estates, whose identity was preserved to facilitate their partition, in accordance with the legal principles of *tertiatio* and *hospitalitas*, between the old proprietors and the incoming Franks. But in Britain it would appear that no arrangements of this type, if they were ever made, for example, in such regions of early settlement as the Saxon Shore, survived to leave memories of the Roman estate names. There was thus apparently no formal reason requiring

---

Villa (1976), 183-99. Nor are there more than a dozen cases in Britain of villa sites being used for later cemeteries, against several hundreds in France and Belgium. The British examples, few, if any, of which can be shown to indicate any significant continuity, are listed by Percival, 217.

[1] The most likely case is Amesbury: see pp. 160-1.

the retention of these names, which no longer served any practical purpose. There could hardly be a clearer indication of the complete breakdown in Britain of the basic pattern of Romanized land tenure than this almost total disappearance of the names of villas and their owners.

The fact that Gildas, while deploring in melodramatic terms the destruction of towns, makes no direct reference to the fate of the villas, suggests that they had mostly been destroyed or abandoned at least a generation earlier than the time when the same fate befell the towns.[1] The whole structure of Romanized country house life, and the rural economy on which it rested, had thus virtually passed out of memory by the time he was writing around the middle of the sixth century.

The only figure from the villa-owning class of rural landowners to whom Gildas makes a brief reference is Ambrosius Aurelianus. He was remembered for the part he had played in the last memorable victory achieved by sub-Roman forces over the barbarians towards the end of the fifth century.[2] But Gildas makes no attempt to localize his activities, and may indeed have been unaware of the circumstances in which this decisive event took place, or the resources which had enabled the Britons under Ambrosius to achieve it. It has been suggested earlier[3] that that struggle can be plausibly related to Saxon attempts to break out, either from the upper Thames Valley or the western end of the *Litus Saxonicum*, into what is now Wiltshire. That region might well have been one of the last areas of southern Britain, apart from the far west, in which some coherent survivals of Romanized villa estates still remained as a base from which landowners like Ambrosius could recruit their tenantry for

---

[1] Numismatic evidence in support of this conclusion must be used with care. Thus it has been stated that of 135 villas with coin series adequate to be significant, 65 have produced no coins later than 360: J. Campbell and others (eds.), *The Anglo-Saxons*, 19. No source for these figures is quoted, nor any indication given of the topographical distribution of the villas which do not have any coins later than 360. Negative evidence of this kind could be due to other causes than complete abandonment, such as a change of site for the main buildings, inadequate excavation, alteration of agricultural methods, or mere accident.

[2] *De Excidio*, 25. Bede in his *Chron. Min.* dates the British recovery under Ambrosius between 474 and 491.

[3] pp. 155-7.

battle with the intruders. And if, as suggested above,[1] it is
not too fanciful to guess that Amesbury may contain a
shortened form of Ambrosius' own name, then it might
provide a unique example in Britain of the possible survival
of an estate name from late Roman times in parallel with
what happened all over Gaul. But this can be no more than
an attractive speculation.[2]

There can be little doubt that the disastrous events that
destroyed the main features of Romano-British society
between 450 and 600 brought about a very drastic reduction
in the numbers of the population. Anything approaching
precise figures are unobtainable. But it is highly likely that
over lowland Britain as a whole the numbers of surviving
natives around the end of the sixth century amounted to
only a small fraction of those that had composed the
flourishing communities of the Golden Age in the fourth
century. Some of these communities had almost entirely disappeared. Urban society had collapsed completely, and with
it had gone all those concerned with local administration,
nearly all manufacturers and traders, and the whole apparatus
of the Christian church. Here and there a local 'tyrant' might
still be using the old fortifications as a military base, and as
a centre for refugees from the countryside, but his effective
manpower was as likely to be composed of Germanic *laeti*
and other barbarian adventurers as of survivors from the
Romano-British townsfolk.

Winchester, Canterbury and perhaps London (see p. 129)
are the most likely of the larger towns to have maintained a
precarious existence in this way. All were closely associated

[1] p. 160.
[2] Both Glanville Jones (*Antiquity*, 35 (1961), 230 and fig. 4) and S.
Applebaum (*Brit.* 14 (1983), 245-6) have called attention to tenurial links
between Amesbury, Lyndhurst, and Bowcombe (close to Carisbrooke, I.o.W.).
These suggest the possibility of a large sub-Roman estate in these parts, whose
connection with Ambrosius might be further evidenced in such names as Amber-
wood, attached to an enclosure connected with one of the late Roman pottery
sites near the northern edge of the New Forest. See also J. Morris, *Age of Arthur*,
100 and map 5, who plots other places in southern Britain whose names may
derive from that of Ambrosius, and perhaps hint at the wide extent of his estates
or reputation. But by no means all of these are convincing derivations and for
most of them there are no early forms. Amesbury, however, certainly had early
links with the West Saxon royal family who may have been in some sense
successors in title to Ambrosius' authority in these parts. It is included among
estates mentioned in King Alfred's will of 873-88: D. Hill, op. cit. fig. 148.

with the Saxon Shore, and all became centres of the Saxon kingdoms that grew out of it. There is evidence for some continuity also at Colchester at least until the sixth century. Late Roman belt-fittings and Romano-Saxon pottery come from several sites and both fifth- and sixth-century *Grubenhäuser* are known within the walls. The nearby cemeteries on the Mersea Road and Butt Road have both produced post-Roman as well as late Roman burials, and the former seems to have had a sub-Roman church. But Colchester cannot have survived into the seventh century. It has no early associations with the East Saxon kings and it never became the site of their bishopric which, under strong Kentish influence, was in London.[1]

In the countryside, the landowning classes mostly lost their homes and their estates and were either dead or had fled. Their tenantry will have taken early opportunities of political and social confusion to escape both their legal obligations to their lords and the unwelcome attentions of barbarian raiders. Many of those who survived these experiences may have sought precarious refuge in the towns. Others, particularly in the south-west, will have joined the considerable numbers of displaced persons who made their way overseas to seek a new life in what soon came to be called Brittany. Some farmers, especially those with small properties less dependent on semi-servile labour, may have sought to maintain the cultivation of enough land to provide a subsistence livelihood. Others will have come to terms, probably involving labour services, with neighbouring barbarian chieftains who were engaged in carving up derelict estates and might be glad to obtain help in their cultivation. But there is plenty of evidence to show that wide areas of lowland Britain which had been cleared of forest and brought into cultivation in the later Roman centuries reverted at this time to wilderness, waste, and scrub. This fact by itself is enough to show how very sharply the British population must have declined during these years. It must also have taken a long time before the Anglo-Saxons, with their comparatively small initial numbers, were able to reverse this

---

[1] P. Crummy, *Aspects of Anglo-Saxon and Norman Colchester*, CBA Research Rept. 39 (1981), 22, summarizes the archaeological evidence.

decline and arrest the relentless advance of the wilderness over what had been the cultivated fields of lowland Britain.

It is only in the far south-west that a somewhat more coherent picture of British survival can be seen. Beyond the chalklands of Wiltshire and Dorset there is little sign of massive Saxon settlement before the seventh century. Here British society persisted under the rule of native chieftains thrown up by the confusion of the times to become some of the 'tyrants' mentioned by Procopius, and described in more personal detail by Gildas.[1] The latter complains that although they were nominally Christian, their behaviour, whether at the political or social level, did not conform to the standards of conduct which the Church still endeavoured to maintain. It was however no longer able to rely on a civilized urban background, but had been largely reduced to a vagrant rural monasticism, retaining only the little authority that could be based merely on a nostalgic and fading memory of the Roman past.

Gildas, indeed, in his severely critical attitude to the moral shortcomings of these rulers, may have done less than justice to their economic strength and political effectiveness, certainly in south-western Britain. The archaeological evidence from these parts presents a striking contrast to the almost completely negative showing of British material remains in the central and eastern parts of the country. Thus several of the numerous pre-Roman hill-forts in Somerset and Devon have produced late Roman and native pottery to suggest re-occupation at this time.[2] Perhaps more significantly there are also on several sites fragments of vessels of east Mediterranean and south-western Gaulish origin which indicate the existence of a surprisingly far-flung overseas trade persisting from Roman times. It is particularly interesting that much of this trade seems to have been in luxury goods, the import of which must have been balanced in some way by a corresponding flow of British exports.[3]

Moreover some of these hill-forts, which had gone out of use in the earlier Roman centuries, seem to have been

---

[1] *De Excidio*, 27.

[2] I. Burrow in P. J. Casey (ed.), *The End of Roman Britain*, 212-29; id., *Hillfort and Hill-top Settlement in Somerset*, BAR 91 (1981).

[3] Cornish tin and Mendip lead are the most likely.

elaborately refortified at this time, no doubt as a counter to the threatened advance of Saxon invaders from Wessex. The most striking instance at present known is the great fortress at South Cadbury, Somerset.[1] Here, apparently, the whole innermost line of the multiple Early Iron Age ramparts was strengthened around AD 500 with a massive timber-framed superstructure of rubble stone incorporating a quantity of re-used Roman material from deserted buildings. It has been calculated that the framing which held this construction together would have required at least 10,000 metres of heavy dressed timber for the upright and transverse beams, and a further quantity of the same order in stout planking for the longitudinal walling between them. In addition the structure must have been surmounted by a substantial breastwork requiring an incalculable amount of slighter planking or wickerwork to protect the defenders from hostile assault. There was also some evidence at South Cadbury for at least one large timber hall inside the ramparts at this time, together with some other less determinate wooden buildings.

This massive use of timber for buildings and fortifications shows that in the south-west the forests had been far less affected by clearance for agriculture and industry in the Roman centuries than was the case further east. It also implies that the British rulers in those parts were sufficiently powerful to command the services of a considerable labour force, including craftsmen skilled in handling both masonry and heavy timber.

As Alcock has pointed out,[2] there is a remarkable reference to the attempted construction of a hill-top fortress in precisely this manner in the *Historia Brittonum*.[3] It is there stated that Vortigern had been advised to construct a citadel for himself on a mountainous site somewhere in the west country. To this end he assembled a force of craftsmen to build it from a quantity of timber and stone (*ligna et lapides*) which he had collected on site. It is particularly interesting that the story includes details, however fanciful, illustrating the problems encountered in the construction of such works.

---

[1] The results of the excavations by L. Alcock between 1966 and 1970 have been conveniently summarized by him in *PBA* 68 (1982), 355–88.

[2] Ibid. 365.

[3] *Hist. Britt.* 40.

Eventually these difficulties are said to have prevented Vortigern from completing his fortress. Although the *Historia Brittonum* in its present form is no earlier than the ninth century, this story may well contain matter which goes back to a near-contemporary account of a British tyrant's activities in the fifth.

It is no part of the purpose of this book to discuss the implications of this or other evidence for the political and economic condition of the emerging British kingdoms, beyond the western or northern limits of Anglo-Saxon penetration at the end of the sixth century. But it is relevant to any discussion of the English settlements to point out the remarkable contrast which developed at this time between the fate of the British people in the eastern and central parts of the country and that of their compatriots in the west and the north. In what had been the wealthiest, most densely populated, and most highly civilized parts of Roman Britain, the Anglo-Saxon invasions involved the all but total destruction of the old way of life. The language, institutions, culture, and material resources of the Romanized population virtually disappeared and their actual numbers must have been drastically reduced by war, flight, disease, and economic disaster.[1]

In the west and north, on the other hand, beyond the reach of direct Anglo-Saxon penetration at this time, the British people, whose native culture and institutions had been far less effectively softened by the influence of Rome, developed a remarkable resilience in the face of the dramatic changes taking place in the east and south. Not only did they retain their own languages and much of their pre-Roman social structure, but they took over Christianity, however modified in organization to fit their own cultural needs, and used it both as a powerful unifying force and as a continuing reminder of their spiritual links with Gaul, Rome, and the

[1] It has been estimated that the administrative structure envisaged in the *Notitia Dignitatum* for the British provinces would have involved about a thousand minor officials employed in the various central offices. With their wives and families this would probably mean at least five thousand persons directly dependent on the civilian government for their livelihood before its collapse. Indirectly of course their disappearance would have had wide economic consequences especially in the major centres of urban life: see Goodburn and Bartholomew (eds.), *Aspects of the Notitia Dignitatum*, 104.

Mediterranean world. In later centuries, of course, political
authority over the British lands of the south-west, the nearer
parts of Wales, and most of Cumbria did pass into Anglo-
Saxon hands, with the consolidation of powerful new kingdoms in Northumbria, Mercia, and Wessex. But the British
population in all these western regions managed for long to
retain their cultural individuality, their social organization
and settlement patterns, even their legal systems and the
language used to express them. In Wales, to a large extent,
they retain them to this day.

*

Nearly fifty years ago, when writing the final paragraphs
on *The English Settlements* in the first volume of this *Oxford
History*, I was concerned to emphasize both the complexity
and the inadequacy of the sources which could be used to
produce even the very imperfect account that was then
possible of the transition from Roman Britain to Anglo-
Saxon England. There was a real danger of stressing too
heavily information derived from one or other of a multiplicity of unreliable types of evidence, and so creating a
spurious appearance of certainty without a sound basis of
historical fact. To illustrate the difficulty I borrowed a
sentence from the pagan Roman aristocrat Symmachus, a
contemporary commentator on the religious conflicts of the
late fourth century. He summed up that matter, as he saw it,
in the sentence *Uno itinere non potest perveniri ad tam
grande secretum.*[1] These words are as appropriate to my
purpose now as they were to his purpose then. They epitomize
very neatly the confusing dilemmas constantly presented
to historians by these dark centuries of English history.
On most of these problems it then seemed impossible to
reach, or even hope for, final answers, and the consequent
uncertainties, if inevitable, were depressing for conscientious
historians.

But in the light of the immense increase in the varied
sources of our knowledge over the last half century, and the
great progress which has been made on all sides in their
elucidation, I would now prefer to alter the concluding

---

[1] 'It is impossible to solve so great a puzzle by using one route only.'

emphasis of this book from the persistent darkness of the tunnel to the growing signs of light at the end of it. By the doorway into Arts End at the head of the old main staircase in the Bodleian Library at Oxford, where it was my privilege to serve the cause of learning for eighteen happy years, the attentive student may notice some words from the Vulgate written on the Benefactors' Tablet. They read *Plurimi pertransibunt et multiplex erit scientia.*[1] This book will have served its purpose well enough if it makes a contribution, however small, to the ever-growing multiplicity of knowledge on the English settlement of Britain, as the passing generations come and go.[2]

[1] 'Many shall pass by and knowledge shall be multiplied.'

[2] For a balanced summary of recent advances in the archaeological understanding of these centuries, and of the many uncertainties which still remain, see C. Hills, 'The archaeology of Anglo-Saxon England in the pagan period', *Anglo-Saxon England*, 8 (1979), 297–329.

APPENDIX I

(a) *The Conquest of Kent, as recorded in the Anglo-Saxon Chronicle* [A]

449 Mauricius [for Marcianus, as corrected by MS E] and Valentines [for Valentinianus] obtained the kingdom; and reigned seven winters. In their days Hengist and Horsa, invited by Wyrtgeorn, king of the Britons, sought Britain at a place called Ypwines fleot, at first to help the Britons but later they fought against them.

445 Hengist and Horsa fought King Wyrtgeorn in the place called Agæles threp, and Horsa his brother was killed. After that Hengist took the kingdom and Æsc his son.

457 Hengist and Æsc fought the Britons at a place called Crecganford and slew there four thousand men, and the Britons left Kent and fled to London in great terror.

465 Hengist and Æsc fought the Welsh near Wippedes fleot, and there slew twelve leaders of the Welsh, and one of their own thanes was slain whose name was Wipped.

473 Hengist and Æsc fought the Welsh and took countless spoil; and the Welsh fled from the English like fire.

488 Æsc succeeded to the kingdom and was king of the Cantware for twenty-four winters.

There are no further Kentish entries until 565 [E]

(b) *The Conquest of Sussex, as recorded in the Anglo-Saxon Chronicle*

477 Ælle came to Britain and his three sons Cymen, Wlencing, and Cissa with three ships at the place called Cymenes ora and there they slew many Welsh and drove some to flight in the wood that is called Andredes leag.

485 Ælle fought the Welsh near Mearc rædesburna.

491 Ælle and Cissa beset Andredes cester, and slew all who dwelt in it, nor was there one Briton left.

There are no further South Saxon entries in this period.

APPENDIX II

The West Saxon Annals from the Anglo-Saxon Chronicle

495 Two chieftains came to Britain, Cerdic and Cynric his son, with five ships at the place called Cerdices ora and the same day they fought the Welsh.

501 Port came to Britain and his two sons Bieda and Mægla with two ships at the place called Portes mutha and slew a young Briton, a very noble man.

508 Cerdic and Cynric slew a British king whose name was Natanleod and five thousand men with him. Afterwards the land was called Natan leag as far as Cerdices ford.

514 [E] The West Saxons came to Britain with three ships at the place called Cerdices ora. And Stuf and Wihtgar fought the Britons and put them to flight.[1]

519 Cerdic and Cynric took the kingdom, and the same year they fought with Britons where it is now called Cerdices ford.

527 Cerdic and Cynric fought with Britons at the place called Cerdices leaga.

530 Cerdic and Cynric took the Isle of Wight and slew a few men at Wihtgaræsbyrg.

534 Cerdic died: and his son Cynric reigned on for twenty-six winters, and they gave the Isle of Wight to their kinsfolk Stuf and Wihtgar.

544 Wihtgar died and was buried at Wihtgara byrg.

552 Cynric fought with Britons at the place called Searo byrg and put the Brit-Welsh to flight.

556 Cynric and Ceawlin fought with Britons at Beran byrg.

560 Ceawlin began to reign in Wessex.

568 Ceawlin and Cutha fought with Æthelberht and drove him into Kent, and they slew two chieftains Oslaf and Cnebba at Wibbandun.

571 Cuthwulf fought with Brit-Welsh at Bedcanford and took four townships, Lygeanburg and Ægelesburg, Benesington and Egonesham, and the same year he died.

577 Cuthwine and Ceawlin fought with Britons and slew three kings, Coinmail and Condidan and Farinmail at the place called Deorham, and they took three 'chesters', Gleawanceaster and Cirenceaster and Bathanceaster.

584 Ceawlin and Cutha fought with Britons at the place called Fethanleag and Cutha was killed, and Ceawlin took many townships and countless spoil and returned in anger to his own.

592 There was a great slaughter at Wodnesbeorg and Ceawlin was driven out.

593 Ceawlin and Cwichelm and Crida perished.

[1] In MS A this entry reads: 'The West Saxons ... place called Cerdices ora, Stuf and Wihtgar: and they fought the Britons ...', &c.

APPENDIX III

The date of the 'Obsessio Montis Badonici'

It may be worth while briefly setting out the evidence which enables
one to date this important event between 490 and 516, and at the same
time makes it impossible to tie it down much more closely. The
relevant facts are as follows.

Gildas (ch. 26) says of it: *quique quadragesimus quartus ut novi
orditur annus mense iam uno emenso qui et meae nativitatis est.* The
wording is obscure, but it will perhaps just translate intelligibly as it
stands, in some such way as this: 'and this begins the forty-fourth year
as I know with one month elapsed and it is also that of my birth'.
Gildas is thus apparently trying to say that Mons Badonicus occurred
nearly forty-four years ago, and he knows that this is so because it was
in the same year as his birth, and he is now nearly forty-four. Mommsen
proposed to read *est ab eo qui* for *ut novi*, an emendation which would
greatly simplify the construction of the sentence but is too remote
from the text to carry immediate conviction. A simpler change would
be to read *quia* for *qui*, and some support for this may be derived from
a manuscript reading *qui iam*: Gildas would then definitely be explaining that his knowledge that Mons Badonicus was nearly forty-four years
ago is derived from the fact that he is himself now nearly forty-four.
This is, on the whole, the best and most usually accepted interpretation
of the passage, though it is not, as will be shown later, the only one.

But even this interpretation does not give us a close date for Mons
Badonicus, for we do not know in what year Gildas wrote this book.
It is, however, often assumed that he must have written it before 547,
for Maglocunus, the king of North Wales who is amongst the British
princes whom he attacks by name, is credibly reported by the tenth-
century *Annales Cambriae* to have died of the great pestilence in that
year. This should give us a date some time before 503 for Mons
Badonicus. Unfortunately, however, the *Annales Cambriae* also have a
direct date, 516, for Mons Badonicus itself, and we are thus faced with
a contradiction, insoluble on the sources we possess, between the
chronology of Gildas as interpreted above and the two dates in the
Annales Cambriae, one of which, if we have correctly interpreted
Gildas, must be wrong. It may also be noted that if the death of Gildas
is rightly dated by the *Annales* to 570, and if he was born in the year of
Mons Badonicus, we can be fairly certain that that event did not take
place more than ten or fifteen years before 503 at the earliest.

There is, however, a further difficulty in the interpretation of
Gildas's text. Bede, who used the passage in *HE* i. 16, either had a text
before him which read *XLmo. circiter et IIIIto anno adventus eorum in
Brittaniam* in place of the whole or some part of the phrase *ut novi*

orditur annus mense iam uno emenso, or else he interpreted the text as we have it as meaning that the forty-four years were to be reckoned not backwards from the time of writing but forwards from the *Adventus Saxonicum*.[1] Bede may, of course, be simply misreading an admittedly obscure text, but since the manuscript of Gildas which he used must have been at least three hundred years nearer to Gildas' *ipsissima verba* than any we now possess, we cannot help taking his view into serious consideration, for it is possible that he has preserved what is really the correct phrasing of the original.

Now Bede never gives an exact year for the *Adventus Saxonum*. It lies for him between the extremes of 446 and 455, and Mons Badonicus would therefore have taken place some time between 490 and 499. This in itself is in no way improbable, for both dates fall within the limits set by the earlier line of inquiry: but it does not bring us much nearer to a definite year or even a definite decade in which we can be quite certain that the siege of Mons Badonicus occurred. All that we can say is that it did occur; and that a date either earlier than 490 or later than 516 seems to be excluded by the available evidence.[2]

---

[1] I cannot agree with Plummer's view (see his note on *HE* i. 16) that Bede's authority for the forty-four years may be entirely distinct from Gildas. If we reject the *Annales* it is indeed quite possible, as he points out, that Mons Badonicus may have lain both forty-four years after the *Adventus* and forty-four years before the date of Gildas' book, which would thus have been written between 534 and 543. But Bede is following Gildas much too closely in this passage for it to be the least probable that he has suddenly switched over to another authority, and to one which by an extraordinary coincidence was using the same number of years to date the same event from a totally different angle.

[2] A number of other interpretations of the passage in Gildas could be mentioned, but most of them do not materially advance our knowledge and have little but ingenuity to recommend them.

BIBLIOGRAPHY

TO compile a bibliography for the period of English history surveyed in this book presents unusual difficulties. The student of this age must be prepared to find significant material in a very great variety of different and often unexpected places, and to become familiar with the techniques employed in several different branches of learning. But many of the works which will help him to achieve that familiarity contain in themselves little or nothing that is directly relevant to the present purpose. It is a subject touched marginally by many others, and much of the light by which it is illuminated is derived from the friction generated by these marginal contacts.

Moreover much of the evidence comes from sources that are primarily concerned with the periods before and after these dark centuries, and deal only incidentally or at one or more removes with matters directly relevant to them. Some of the original sources coincide with those for Roman and sub-Roman Britain, while others belong to the later Anglo-Saxon centuries. Nearly all the topographical and much of the periodical literature surveyed in the bibliographies that accompanied Collingwood's and Salway's volumes on Roman Britain in this series is as relevant to this period as to that. Nor is there much point in partially repeating here the much fuller survey of the older literature for early Anglo-Saxon social, legal, cultural, and economic history provided by Stenton in volume II of this *Oxford History*. There are in fact even now very few important works dealing with these topics in the pagan Anglo-Saxon period which do not do so in all essentials as a preface or introduction to their fuller treatment in the Christian centuries that followed. Thus some subjects will be discussed here more thoroughly than others, not because they are in themselves of greater importance but because this is the appropriate place for their discussion.

To revise and bring up to date a bibliography originally put together nearly fifty years ago is a task of some delicacy. Some of what were then standard works, carrying the authority of scholars generally recognized at that time for their erudition and judgement, have worn a good deal better than others. Some of what were then the latest revolutionary projects designed to provide quick solutions to old problems, or to create what appeared to be new patterns for future research, have themselves been outdated by the passage of time and are now no longer worth reading. The proliferation of new sources of evidence, documentary, archaeological, linguistic, or toponymic, has shown that many historical judgements regarded in their day as of basic importance are no longer tenable and that the systems based upon them are at best questionable and at worst wrong. None the less, much of the older literature contains basic information still of fundamental importance even if the conclusions originally drawn from it can no longer be sustained. For this reason I have continued the practice first adopted in the bibliographies compiled for 'Collingwood and Myres' over fifty years ago of treating some sections essentially as brief histories of the subject matter under discussion, in which some of the older books appear rather as landmarks in the growth of knowledge than as recommended current reading. For the same reason, and to facilitate comparison with the bibliography in 'Collingwood and Myres', itself an exercise of some historical interest, I have retained the main sub-divisions which were then adopted, even though the differential rate of progress in different areas of the subject over the past half-century may make this arrangement appear less appropriate now than it was then.

ANCIENT TEXTS, INSCRIPTIONS, AND DOCUMENTS

Mommsen's edition of Gildas, *De Excidio*, and Nennius, *Historia Brittonum* (MGH (AA) XIII, *Chron. Min.* III. pt. i. (1894)) remains the standard text for these authors, though it has been subject to a good deal of criticism, some of it misplaced, in recent years. All writers on this period have to decide for themselves the value to be placed on these works, and it would be impossible to attempt a survey of the various views taken by reputable authorities. My own appraisal of them will be apparent mainly from chapter 1 of this book. Among the older commentaries, F. Lot, *Nennius et l'Historia Brittonum* (Paris, 1934), and H. Zimmer, *Nennius vindicatus* (Berlin, 1893), are worth a mention, if only as period pieces. In the series *Arthurian Period Sources* there are editions of Gildas by M. Winterbottom (1978), and of Nennius by J. Morris (1980). Important articles by D.N. Dumville on many aspects of the British and Anglo-Saxon sources have appeared in various periodicals between 1972 and 1979.

An important account of a situation somewhat similar to that portrayed by Gildas in Britain can be found for the Danubian frontier provinces of the Empire in Eugippius' *Vita Severini* (Latin text with German translation and commentary *Das Leben des heiligen Severin*, ed. R. Noll (Berlin, 1963)).

For the *Notitia Dignitatum* the standard text is still that edited by O. Seeck (Berlin, 1876). There is a useful volume of studies on the *Notitia* and its problems, *Aspects of the Notitia Dignitatum*, ed. R. Goodburn and P. Bartholomew, BAR Suppl. Series 15 (Oxford, 1976), by a group of scholars who took part in a conference on the subject at Oxford in 1974. Some useful points are made by D. A. White in his doctoral thesis on the *Litus Saxonicum* (Madison, Wisconsin, 1961), and by S. Johnson, *The Roman Forts of the Saxon Shore* (1976), especially for the structural evidence. More valuable on many aspects are the essays in *The Saxon Shore*, ed. B. E. Johnston, CBA Research Report 18 (1977). The older collections of the inscribed Dark-Age tombstones of Wales and Cornwall (E.Hübner, *Inscriptiones Britanniae Christianae* (1876) and J.O. Westwood, *Lapidarium Walliae* (Oxford, 1876-9)) are obsolete. The latter has been replaced by V. E. Nash-Williams, *The Early Christian Monuments of Wales* (Cardiff, 1950).

The standard edition of Bede's *Ecclesiastical History* is still that of C. Plummer (Oxford, 1896), with a commentary which, though now inevitably outdated in parts, remains of value for its wide range of learning and consistent good sense. For many purposes it has been superseded by the admirable edition with translation and up-to-date commentary, *Bede's Ecclesiastical History of the English People*, edited by B. Colgrave and R. A. B. Mynors (Oxford, 1969) which has an excellent bibliography. The historical and chronological aspects of Bede's scholarship have been extensively studied in recent years and this is not the place to attempt a comprehensive survey of the resulting literature, much of which is to be found in periodicals. Mention may be made of the volume of essays issued to commemorate the twelve-hundredth anniversary of his death, *Bede, His Life, Times, and Writings*, ed. A. H. Thompson (Oxford, 1935), with a select bibliography of the older literature; *Famulus Christi: essays in commemoration of the 13th centenary of the birth of . . . Bede*, ed. G. Bonner (1976); *Bede and Anglo-Saxon England*, ed. R. T. Farrell (Oxford, 1978). The annual series of Jarrow lectures (1958-) also contains matter dealing directly or indirectly with Bedan studies.

For the *Anglo-Saxon Chronicle*, the edition of *Two of the Saxon Chronicles Parallel*, with commentary by J. Earle and C. Plummer (Oxford, 1892-9, reprinted 1952), remains basic for the texts concerned. But the revised translation with extensive commentary, *The Anglo-Saxon Chronicle*, edited by D. Whitelock, D. C. Douglas, and S. I. Tucker (1961), makes easier reading and is especially valuable for its elucidation of the complex textual problems and for its select bibliography. For dating problems mainly connected with the *Chronicle* see K. Harrison, *Framework of Anglo-Saxon History* (Cambridge, 1976).

The older collections of texts bearing on the earliest stages of English legal, social, economic, and constitutional history can be found in F. Liebermann, *Die Gesetze der Angelsachsen* Halle-a.-S., 1898-1916), A. W. Haddan and W. Stubbs, *Councils* etc. (Oxford, 1869-78), J. M. Kemble, *Codex Diplomaticus Aevi Saxonici* (1839-48), and W. de G. Birch, *Cartularium Saxonicum* (1885-93), together with many publications of the Early English Text Society (1864-). Most of those directly or indirectly relevant to this period have been conveniently assembled, with commentary and bibliography, in the earlier sections of *English Historical Documents*, I, 500-1042, ed. D. Whitelock (1955).

The editions by R. W. Chambers of *Widsith* (Cambridge, 1912) and *Beowulf* (Cambridge, 1914, revised 1932) remain valuable, although both need to be supplemented by the results of more recent work on their historical and archaeological setting. Still useful in this context is M. G. Clarke, *Sidelights on Teutonic History during the Migration Period* (Cambridge, 1911), who developed some lines of thought first propounded by H. M. Chadwick in *The Origin of the English Nation* (Cambridge, 1907), a seminal work which remains of great interest especially for its original use of early Germanic literature in the historic context of this period.

BIBLIOGRAPHIES, BOOKS OF REFERENCE, AND PERIODICALS

Surveys of the earlier literature for the period can be found in most of the standard works on English history and there is little point in referring readers to a multiplicity of what tend to become largely repetitive lists. Some of the more useful select bibliographies on the historical side have been noted in the previous section in connection with recent editions of the principal texts and documents. J. F. Kenney's useful *Sources for the Early History of Ireland*, I (New York, 1929) includes much bibliographical material bearing on the British sources, especially on Germanus, Patrick, Gildas, and Nennius. The older continental reference books such as M. Ebert, *Reallexikon der Vorgeschichte* (Berlin, 1924–32), Pauly-Wissowa, *Real-Enzyclopädie der classischen Altertumswissenschaft* (Stuttgart, 1904–), and J. Hoops, *Reallexikon der germanischen Altertumskunde* (Strassburg, 1911–19), contain articles bearing on early Saxon history and cognate subjects, but the recent rapid advances in the study of Germanic antiquities make these more useful as basic background than reliable as up-to-date assessments of current knowledge.

Much of the best work on every aspect of the period is to be found in periodicals, but in accordance with the general practice of this series no attempt to list individual articles is here made (save for a few outstanding items). Many of the more important are referred to in footnotes to the text. Most of the general and many of the local historical and archaeological periodicals are provided with indexes, or occasional index volumes, from which articles relevant to the subject matter of this book can be identified. But students should be warned that many of the earlier discoveries of Anglo-Saxon antiquities were described on publication as either Roman or British. A comprehensive list of the local journals mostly issued by county and other regional archaeological and historical societies, with the date of first publication in each case, can be found in 'Collingwood and Myres' (1936), 472–3, and, with the addition of *Oxoniensia* (1936), need not be repeated here: in nearly all these series, it is only in the issues dated after about 1900 that significant material for this period is likely to be found.

The following are among the more general English historical and archaeological periodicals (with dates of first issue) that contain material relevant to this period: *Archaeologia* (1804), *Proceedings of the Society of Antiquaries* (1843–1920), *Antiquaries Journal* (1921), *Archaeological Journal* (1844), *Journal of the British Archaeological Association* (1862), *Antiquity* (1927), *Medieval Archaeology* (1957), *Current Archaeology* (1967), *English Historical Review* (1886), *Transactions of the Royal Historical Society* (1871), *History* (1916), *Proceedings of the British Academy* (1904), *Essays and Studies by Members of the English Association* (1910), *English Studies* (1919), *Anglo-Saxon England* (1974).

Some of the more important continental periodicals are mentioned below in the section on the continental background. Access to a large number of Danish, German, Dutch, and Belgian local publications is necessary for an adequate study of many aspects of the subject, but these cannot be listed here.

An indispensable guide to the location and bibliography of the cemeteries is A. L. Meaney, *A Gazetteer of Early Anglo-Saxon Burial Sites* (1964), and mention should be made of W. Bonser, *An Anglo-Saxon and Celtic Bibliography* (1957), now inevitably becoming out-of-date. The early chapters of A. Gransden, *Historical Writing in England 550-1307* (1974) contain comprehensive discussions of the sources and their bibligraphy. *Onoma* (Louvain, 1950-), published by the International Committee of Onomastic Sciences, is a specialized bibliography and information bulletin.

GENERAL WORKS ON EARLY SAXON ENGLAND

Nearly all historians of medieval England have included some account of the pagan Saxon period, often written without much study of the original sources and displaying little first-hand knowledge of their range and complexity. It is only necessary to mention here a few of those whose scale of treatment or specialized interests enabled them to make contributions of permanent value to this part of their subject.

In anything approaching its modern form early English historical study can be said to have begun with the first two volumes of J. M. Lappenberg's *Geschichte von England* (Hamburg, 1834), translated by B. Thorpe as *History of England under the Anglo-Saxon Kings* (1845). This had much influence on historical thought before W. Stubbs, in his *Constitutional History of England*, I (Oxford, 1874), diverted attention from the purely literary sources to the institutional problems at which those sources also hinted, and to the documentary material, much of it only recently published or still awaiting publication, which could assist their understanding. In so doing, however, Stubbs had been to some extent anticipated by J. M. Kemble, who in his *Saxons in England* (1849, best edition 1876) had begun to pioneer the application of extraordinarily modern methods of enquiry to the elucidation of the Saxon settlement. Kemble's work, containing as it did many over-statements and some perversities, was easy to criticize, but his remarkable anticipation of modern methods and lines of enquiry deserves more recognition than it has obtained. He was the first to see the institutional importance of Saxon land charters, a corpus of which he published in his *Codex Diplomaticus Aevi Saxonici* (already cited on p. 226). He pointed out the significance of early place-names as a guide to patterns of settlement. He was an appreciative student of Teutonic philology and mythology and edited *Beowulf* (1833). He demonstrated for the first time the similarities between the Dark-Age antiquities of north Germany and those of England in an epoch-making paper 'On mortuary urns found at Stade-on-the-Elbe, and other parts of North Germany' in *Archaeologia*, 36 (1856), reprinted in *Horae Ferales*, ed. by R. G. Latham and A. W. Franks (1863), and he even conducted excavations in Hanover with the express purpose of throwing light on the settlement of Britain. But he died in 1857 and had no immediate successors in this versatility. The

criticism which some aspects of his work incurred—particularly his
'mark' theory of the early process of settlement, which arose from over-
emphasis on the conclusions he had drawn from place-name study—led
the next generation of historians to under-value the importance and
originality of his outlook. During the next half-century, and more,
scholars tended to concentrate on legal and constitutional problems
arising from the work of Stubbs, F. W. Maitland (*Domesday Book and
Beyond* (Cambridge, 1897)), and their followers, whose primary sources
belonged mainly to the age of Anglo-Saxon literacy following the
seventh century. Such compilations as C. Elton, *Origins of English
History* (1882), the relevant parts of J. H. Ramsay, *Foundations of
England* (1898), J. R. Green, *Making of England* (1881), best edition
1897), and even T. Hodgkin's opening volume in *The Political History
of England*, ed. W. Hunt and R. L. Poole (1906), and C. W. C. Oman,
England before the Norman Conquest (1910) paid little attention to
the evidence which the auxiliary sciences, especially archaeology and
place-names, were capable of contributing. Thus over-reliance on inadequate literary sources produced some one-sided and often uncritical
work, so that, for example, J. R. Green could be described as writing 'as
if he had been present at the landing of the Saxons and had watched
every step of their subsequent progress'.[1] Although great strides were
being made in assembling the evidence available from archaeology, topography, and place-names, as discussed below, it was not until the publication of R. H. Hodgkin, *History of the Anglo-Saxons* (Oxford, 1935)
that a large-scale attempt was made to incorporate the results of these
new studies in a general historical survey. Since then, however, it has
become impossible for historians to write balanced accounts of this
period without assessing the contribution that can be made to its understanding by the auxiliary sciences. D. Whitelock, *The Beginning of
English Society* (1952) is an early example of what can now be achieved
in this way. See also P. H. Sawyer, *From Roman Britain to Norman
England* (1978).

ARCHAEOLOGY AND TOPOGRAPHY

The earliest work dealing directly, if unconsciously, with Anglo-Saxon
antiquities is the charming *Hydriotaphia, Urne-Buriall* (1658) of Sir
Thomas Browne, to the composition of which he was moved by the
discovery of 'sad sepulchral pitchers' in what was clearly an Anglian
cremation cemetery at Walsingham, Norfolk. As Leeds has observed, one
of these urns may have survived as the specimen once in 'Tradescant's
Ark' which formed the nucleus of the Ashmolean collections and is still
preserved at Oxford.[2] Browne, however, thought that they were Roman,
and B. Faussett a century later still held the same view of the objects
unearthed by him in various Kentish cemeteries between 1757 and

---

[1] Plummer's note on Bede, *HE* i. 15.
[2] E. T. Leeds, *Anglo-Saxon Settlements*, 38 and fig. 5. See below for detailed
mention of this work.

1773, which were eventually published, with Faussett's careful notes, by C. Roach Smith in his *Inventorium sepulchrale* (1856). By then, however, such discoveries had been correctly attributed to the Anglo-Saxons, for example by J. Douglas, who carried out systematic excavations in Kent from 1779 and published his discoveries, rightly described, in the stately folio *Nenia Britannica* in 1793. Apart from the inclusion of some Anglo-Saxon material in R. Colt Hoare, *The Ancient History of . . . Wiltshire* (1812-21) little further progress was made until the middle of the nineteenth century when, in addition to Kemble's work, noted above, both general compilations, such as J. Y. Akerman, *An Archaeological Index to Remains of Antiquity* (1847) and his important *Remains of Pagan Saxondom* (1855), a valuable work with beautiful plates, and many topographical studies based on local archaeological remains began to appear. These included G. Hillier, *History and Antiquities of the Isle of Wight* (1855), important for the Chessel Down cemetery, W. M. Wylie, *Fairford Graves* (Oxford, 1852), R. C. Neville, *Saxon Obsequies* (1852), a sumptuous book based on the author's excavation of the Little Wilbraham cemetery, and T. Bateman, *Ten Years' Diggings in Celtic and Saxon Grave Hills* (1861), for Derbyshire. Much Anglo-Saxon material appeared in C. Roach Smith, *Collectanea Antiqua* (7 vols., 1848-80), and J. R. Mortimer, *Forty Years' Researches in British and Saxon Burial Mounds of East Yorkshire* (1905). A general synthesis of the archaeological material was attempted by J. de Baye in his *Industrie anglo-saxonne* (tr. T. B. Harbottle, *The Industrial Arts of the Anglo-Saxons* (1893)), but this has been long out of date. Much more valuable is the comprehensive and detailed account of every class of Anglo-Saxon material of this age contained in G. Baldwin Brown, *The Arts in Early England*, III and IV (1915). These volumes included maps showing the principal cemeteries known at that time, and much photographic illustration, though no detailed drawings. They summarize much of the information which had been appearing since 1900 in the descriptive articles contributed by R. A. Smith to the *Victoria County History*, which by then had covered some twenty of the counties that contain significant quantities of early Anglo-Saxon material. Much more easy to handle and, partly for that reason, more influential on historical thought, was E. T. Leeds' pioneer study, *The Archaeology of the Anglo-Saxon Settlements* (Oxford, 1913). He attempted for the first time to relate the material remains of this age directly to the historical record, and pointed out with some force the main problems raised by apparent conflicts between them.[1] This may be a convenient point at which to draw attention to Leeds' important typological studies of the artefacts, notably his article on saucer brooches, 'The distribution of the Anglo-Saxon saucer brooch in relation to the battle of Bedford, AD 571', in *Archaeologia*, 63 (1912), *Early Anglo-Saxon Art and Archaeology* (Oxford, 1936), and *Corpus of Early Anglo-Saxon Great Square-headed*

[1] For a critical appreciation of Leeds' book see my introduction to the reprint of 1970.

Brooches (Oxford, 1949). Leeds had a blind spot for Anglo-Saxon pottery and never paid it much attention. Attempts were made to fill this gap by the present writer in his *Anglo-Saxon Pottery and the Settlement of England* (Oxford, 1969) and *Corpus of Anglo-Saxon Pottery of the Pagan Period* (2 vols., Cambridge, 1977), with which should also be noted V. I. Evison, *A Corpus of Wheel-thrown Pottery in Anglo-Saxon Graves* (1979). Among other recent studies of archaeological material are R. Avent, *Anglo-Saxon Garnet Inlaid Disc and Composite Brooches*, BAR 11 (1975); G. Speake, *Anglo-Saxon Animal Art* (Oxford, 1980); W. Holmqvist, *Germanic Art during the First Millenium AD* (Stockholm, 1955); M. Swanton, *The Spearheads of the Anglo-Saxon Settlements* (1973); E. Bakka, *On the Beginning of Salin's Style I in England* (Bergen, 1959); J. Reichstein, *Die kreuzförmige Fibel* (Neumünster, 1975).

The irrational, and now obsolete, fragmentation by the old county divisions of the archaeological records, which makes the *Victoria County History* difficult to use for this period, was followed in the County Archaeologies of which six volumes appeared between 1930 and 1933: they are mainly useful for the gazetteer and bibliography of the older local finds which each contains. With them may be mentioned the Anglo-Saxon chapters in F. Elgee, *Early Man in North-East Yorkshire* (Gloucester, 1930) and M. E. Cunnington, *Introduction to the Archaeology of Wiltshire* (2nd. ed., Devizes, 1934). A more sensible regional approach was marked by C. Fox, *The Archaeology of the Cambridge Region* (Cambridge, 1923), since followed by e.g. *The Oxford Region*, ed. A. F. Martin and R. W. Steel (1954). A number of recent regional studies, though not all of the highest quality, mostly contain local information and detail significant in a wider context that may not be easily accessible elsewhere. Among these may be noted:— T. J. George, *An Archaeological Survey of Northants.* (1904); J E. A. Jolliffe, *Prefeudal England: the Jutes* (1933); V. I. Evison, *The Fifth-century Invasions south of the Thames* (1965); E. Blank, *A Guide to Leicestershire Archaeology* (Leicester, 1970); some of the articles in *Anglo-Saxon Settlement and Landscape*, ed. T. Rowley (Oxford, 1974); T. H. McK. Clough and others, *Anglo-Saxon and Viking Leicestershire* (Leicester, 1975); S. M. Pearce, *The Kingdom of Dumnonia* (Padstow, 1978); B. N. Eagles, *The Anglo-Saxon Settlement of Humberside*, BAR 68 (1979); K. R. Davis, *Britons and Saxons: the Chiltern Region 400–700* (Chichester, 1982); *Archaeology in Kent to AD 1500*, ed. P. E. Leach. CBA Research Report 48 (1982); K. P. Witney, *The Kingdom of Kent* (Chichester, 1982); M. G. Welch, *Early Anglo-Saxon Sussex*, BAR 112 (1983).

The Ordnance Survey *Map of Britain in the Dark Ages* (ed. 2, 1966) is essential, and the early chapters of D. Hill, *Atlas of Anglo-Saxon England* (Oxford, 1981) are very useful. In a class by itself is R. L. S. Bruce-Mitford's detailed publication, *The Sutton Hoo Ship Burial* (3 vols., 1975–83).

A number of *Festschriften* include useful articles relating to this period. They also often contain bibliographies of the scholars so honoured, which may sometimes prove the only way to trace minor but significant pieces of their work. Among such are:— *The Early Cultures of North-West Europe*, ed. C. Fox and B. Dickins (Cambridge, 1950), in memory of H. M. Chadwick; *Aspects of Archaeology in Britain and beyond*, ed. W. F. Grimes (1951), for O. G. S. Crawford; *Dark-Age Britain*, ed. D. B. Harden (1956), for E. T. Leeds; *The Anglo-Saxons*, ed. P. Clemoes (1959), for B. Dickins; *Culture and Environment*, ed. I. Ll. Foster and L. Alcock (1963), for Sir C. Fox; *Archaeology and the Landscape*, ed. P. J. Fowler (1972), for L. V. Grinsell; *England before the Conquest*, ed. P. Clemoes and K. Hughes (1973), for D. Whitelock; *Studien zur Sachsenforschung*, ed. H.-J. Hässler (Hildesheim, 1977), for A. Genrich; *Angles, Saxons, and Jutes*, ed. V. I. Evison (Oxford, 1981), for J. N. L. Myres.

The series British Archaeological Reports (BAR) includes a number of volumes which contain material relevant to this period. Among those not noted elsewhere in this book are:
Anglo-Saxon Studies in Archaeology and History, ed. D. Brown, J. Campbell, and S. C. Hawkes, 2pt., BAR 72 and 92 (1979–81).
Anglo-Saxon Cemeteries, ed. P. Rahtz, T. Dickinson, and L. Watts, BAR 82 (1980).
D. Longley, *Hanging-Bowls, Penannular Brooches and the Anglo-Saxon Connexion*, BAR 22 (1975).

LANGUAGE AND PLACE-NAMES

It is one of the major deficiencies in the structure of British education that no provision is made even for the most elementary instruction in the origin and historical development of the English language. Anglo-Saxon is a closed book to all but a minority of specialists, most of whom have only become acquainted with it at an advanced stage of their training. They thus tend to lack the natural linguistic facility which is most easily obtained from early and thorough acquaintance, as was formerly the case with Latin, and sometimes with Greek and even Hebrew, in the age-old curricula of the grammar schools. What is true of Old English is even more true of the general lack of appreciation among scholars of the historical development of the Celtic tongues, except of course in Ireland, Wales, and those parts of Scotland where a continuing tradition of the living language survives. Linguistic studies have in consequence tended to develop in some isolation from other aspects of the broader historical scene, and to concentrate on esoteric minutiae in the interpretation of phonological change over the centuries, or the detailed investigation of dialectal peculiarities in different parts of the country.

Yet all these matters are obviously relevant to an understanding of the English settlements, however difficult for the non-linguist to appreciate in historical terms. An important attempt to bring these studies together can be found in K. H. Jackson, *Language and History in Early Britain* (Edinburgh, 1953), who uses his extensive linguistic expertise to illuminate the historical background, especially in the interpretation of place-names. No subject has attracted more misguided enthusiasts and ignorant amateurs than the study of place-names, and it is essential to beware of any suggested etymologies that are not securely based on the informed collation of all available early forms. This is being made much easier not only by the county surveys issued by the English Place-Name Society since 1925, which now cover most parts of the country affected by primary Anglo-Saxon settlement, but also by such convenient summaries as E. Ekwall, *English River-Names* (Oxford, 1928) and his *Concise Oxford Dictionary of English Place-Names* (1936; 4th ed., 1960). These give easy access to the most significant early forms, although not necessarily providing acceptable interpretations of them. Among earlier county surveys, the following are still useful, if used with care, especially for parts of the country not yet covered by the English Place-Name Society:— E. Ekwall, *The Place-names of Lancashire* (Manchester, 1922); A. Mawer, *The Place-names of Northumberland and Durham* (Cambridge, 1920); J. E. B. Gover, *The Place-names of Middlesex* (1922); A. Fägersten, *The Place-names of Dorset* (Uppsala, 1933); J. K. Wallenberg, *Kentish Place-Names* (Uppsala, 1931) and *The Place-Names of Kent* (Uppsala, 1934), who reacts against the tendency of some scholars to explain doubtful elements by invoking the use of unrecorded personal names. W. J. Watson, *The History of the Celtic Place-names of Scotland* (Edinburgh, 1926) contains interesting material bearing on the early history of Bernicia, but this is not the place to enter more deeply into the complex problems presented by the toponymy of those parts of Britain where English settlement in this period was negligible or non-existent.

As explained in chapter 2 above (pp. 37–43), there have recently been developments in the study of English place-names which throw· doubt on the validity of some basic assumptions on their relative chronology that have hitherto been generally accepted. These particularly concern the dating and significance of names in *-ingas* and related forms, and compounds such as *-ingaham*, *-ingatun*, and so on. These new ideas may affect the reliance that should be placed on such basic works as E. Ekwall, *English Place-Names in -ing* (Lund, 1923) and on some doctrines long enshrined, for example, in A. H. Smith, *English Place-Name Elements* (Cambridge, 1956), in the very important introductions prefixed to most of the earlier county volumes of the English Place-Name Society, and in many works of Sir Frank Stenton, especially his presidential addresses to the Royal Historical Society between 1938 and 1940 (published in *TRHS* 4th ser., 21–3). Much of this new work appeared first in periodicals, but some of the more significant pieces have been reprinted in *Place-name Evidence for the Anglo-Saxon Invasion and Scandinavian Settlements*, ed. K. Cameron, EP-NS (1975), and in M. Gelling, *Signposts to the Past* (1978), which has a good bibliography. *Nomina* (Hull, 1977–), published by English Name-Studies, is a more recent journal in the field. There are some useful essays on place-name evidence for early medieval settlement patterns in *Names, Words, and Graves*, ed. P. H. Sawyer (Leeds, 1979).

THE CONTINENTAL BACKGROUND

There is an enormous literature bearing on all aspects of Germanic *Frühgeschichte* which it would be beyond the scope of this volume to discuss in the present context. Most of it deals only marginally with the settlement of England, and while the older books, though full of basic source-material, have become increasingly out of date, many of those written later, in Germany particularly between 1930 and 1945, are vitiated by racial and cultural doctrines that are no longer acceptable. Of the older books more or less free from such bias, L. Schmidt, *Geschichte der deutschen Stämme* (Berlin, 1904–18) and K. Rhamm, *Die Grosshufen der Nordgermanen* (Braunschweig, 1905) are still useful. Valuable modern surveys are J. M. Wallace-Hadrill, *Early Germanic Kingship* (Oxford, 1971), L. Musset, *The Germanic Invasions*, tr. by E. and C. James (1975), and E. Demougeot, *La Formation de l'Europe et les invasions barbares* (2 vols., Paris, 1969–79). The student of agrarian history must still start with A. Meitzen, *Siedelung und Agrarwesen der Westgermanen* (Berlin, 1895), and follow the Franks westward with G. des Marez, *Le Problème de la colonisation franque* (Brussels, 1926), and M. Bloch, *Les Caractères originaux de l'histoire rurale française* (Oslo, 1931). For the Frisians, J. H. Holwerda, *Nederlands vroegste geschiedenis* (Amsterdam, 1925), P. C. J. A. Boeles, *Friesland tot de elfde eeuw* (The Hague, 1927), and P. Zylmann, *Ostfriesische Urgeschichte* Hildesheim, 1933) contain much background information, and this is perhaps the best point to mention H. Halbertsma, *Terpen tussen Vlie en Ems* (Groningen, 1963), and the other publications of the Dutch Vereniging voor Terpenonderzoek for studies of the coastal mound-settlements, and also G. Faider-Feytmans, *La Belgique à l'époque mérovingienne* (Brussels, 1964). For the Alemanni, W. Veeck, *Die Alamannen in Württemberg* (Berlin, 1931) is basic, and can be supplemented by F. Garscha, *Die Alamannen in Südbaden* (Berlin, 1970). For comparative material from Scandinavia H. Schetelig, *The Cruciform Brooches of Norway* (Bergen, 1906), and B. Hougen, *The Migration Style of Ornament in Norway* (Oslo, 1936) are still significant for metal-work, and E. Albrectsen, *Fynske jernaldergrave*, III–V (Copenhagen, 1968–73) is fundamental for pottery.

Some typological studies of German antiquities directly related to the settlement of England appeared in the inter-war years, such as F. Roeder, *Die sächsische Schalenfibel der Völkerwanderungszeit als Kunstgegenstand und siedlungsarchäologisches Leitfossil* (Göttingen, 1927) for saucer brooches, his *Typologisch-chronologische Studien zu Metallsachen der Völkerwanderungszeit* (Hildesheim, 1930), and *Neue Funde* (Halle, 1933). The first serious study of the pottery was made by A. Plettke, *Ursprung und Ausbreitung der Angeln und Sachsen* (Hanover, 1921), a pioneer thesis by a scholar killed in the 1914 war and posthumously published in his memory. As such it had great influence in spite of the fact that it does not adequately cover material from Schleswig or Friesland, much of the dating is about fifty years too high, and he was not acquainted with the English evidence at first hand.

Apart from the appearance of M. B. Mackeprang, *Kulturbeziehungen im nordischen Raum des 3–5 Jahrhunderts : keramische Studien* (Leipzig, 1943), little progress occurred until 1945. When the war ended a great effort was made, as noted on pp. xx–xxi, largely on the initiative of K. Waller of Cuxhaven, to re-establish cultural relations between the North Sea countries on the basis of a common approach to their archaeological problems. He had already published an important cemetery at the Galgenberg bei Cuxhaven (Leipzig, 1938), and he now set about organizing the informal and loosely knit *Sachsensymposion* as a focus for such studies. He also continued publishing important cemeteries, the last being Wehden: *Der Urnenfriedhof in Wehden* (Hildesheim, 1961). Among early participants in the *Sachsensymposion* were scholars who had already begun making important contributions to the archaeological background, such as F. Tischler (*Fuhlsbüttel, ein Beitrag zur Sachsenfrage* (Neumünster, 1937), 'Der Stand der Sachsenforschung archäologisch gesehen', *Bericht der Römisch-Germanischen Kommission* 35 (1956), 21–215, and *Das Gräberfeld Oberjersdal* (Hamburg, 1955)), A. Genrich, (*Formenkreise und Stammesgruppen in Schleswig-Holstein* (Neumünster, 1954)), J. Werner ('Kriegergräber aus der ersten Hälfte des 5. Jahrhunderts zwischen Schelde und Weser', *Bonner Jahrbücher*, 158 (1958), 372–413), and many others. The proceedings of the *Sachsensymposion* are generally reported in *Die Kunde, Mitteilungen des Niedersächsischen Landesverein für Urgeschichte*, (Hanover, 1949-), which also contains summaries of some of the papers read. So does the *Nachrichten des Marschenrates . . . im Kustengebiet der Nordsee* (Wilhelmshaven, 1963-). Although E. Grohne's *Mahndorf* (Bremen, 1953) is essentially an account of a single excavated site, it includes so much comparative archaeological material as to deserve separate mention here. The same is true of a number of the volumes in *MGH* and other continental series, such as K. Zimmer-Linnfeld and others, *Westerwanna*, I (Hamburg, 1960) and W. Janssen, *Issendorf; ein Urnenfriedhof* (Hildesheim, 1972).

The series *Archaeologia Belgica* (Brussels, 1950-), in which are reprinted many important excavation reports, is very convenient in making access to long runs of local periodicals unnecessary. *Sachsen und Angelsachsen*, ed. C. Ahrens (Hamburg, 1978), and *Siedlung, Sprache und Bevölkerung*, ed. F. Petri (Darmstadt, 1973), are valuable symposia.

Other important recent works which, though mainly of a more general nature, are nevertheless often concerned with particular regions, include:

E. Salin, *La Civilisation mérovingienne* (Paris, 1949–59).
R. Latouche, *Les Origines de l'économie occidentale* (Paris, 1956).
H. Dannheimer, *Die germanischen Funde der späten Kaiserzeit und des frühen Mittelalters in Mittelfranken* (Berlin, 1962).
R. Koch, *Bodenfunde der Völkerwanderungszeit aus dem Main-Tauber-Gebiet* (Berlin, 1967).
V. Koch, *Die Grabfunde der Merowingerzeit aus dem Donautal um Regensburg* (Berlin, 1968).

E. Gamillscheg, *Romania Germanica*, I (ed. 2, Berlin, 1970).

K. Godlowski, *The Chronology of the Late Roman and Early Migration Periods in Central Europe*, tr. by M. Walęga (Krakow, 1970).

A. Schach-Dorges, *Die Bodenfunde des 3. bis 6. Jahrhunderts nach Chr. zwischen unterer Elbe und Oder* (Neumünster, 1970).

G. Clauss, *Reihengräberfelder von Heidelberg-Kirchheim* (Karlsruhe, 1971).

G. Fingerlin, *Die alamannischen Gräberfelder von Güttingen und Merdingen in Südbaden* (Berlin, 1971).

H. W. Böhme, *Germanische Grabfunde des 4 bis 5 Jahrhunderts zwischen unterer Elbe und Loire* (Munich, 1974).

A. Lohaus, *Die Merowinger und England* (Munich, 1974).

M. Fleury and P. Périn, *Problèmes de chronologie concernant les cimetières entre Loire et Rhin* (Paris, 1978).

INDEX

victory at Mons Badonicus 14–15,
162
Pelagian controversy 20
scarcity of archaeological evidence
for 21–3
scarcity of surviving place-names
30–2
appeal to the Angles 109–10
personal names: Caedbaed 140–1,
182; Cerdic and Caedwalla 147;
Natanleod 148
concentration in lower Severn area
169
Brittany (*Armorica*) 8, 18
Brixworth: map 2
brooches:
applied 59, 61–2, 133
button 59, 138, fig. 2
cruciform 57, 59, 115, fig. 1
equal-armed 59, 61–2
long 56–7
Quoit fig. 10; *and see* Quoit
Brooch Style
round 59
saucer 59, 61–2, 86–7, 138–9,
fig. 2
square-headed 56–7, 116
Stützarmfibel 61
style 1 animal ornament on 57, 61,
116–17
tutulus 82
Brooke fig. 1
Brough-by-Sands 77
Brough-on-Humber (*Petuaria Parisiorum*): map 4, map 6, xxvi,
176–7, 187, 189, 195
Brown, Baldwin xx
Bruce-Mitford, R. L. S. xxii
Bubba 178
Buckelurnen 69, 72, 193, fig. 6
Bulmer: map 5
Burgh Castle (*Gariannorum*): map 2,
map 6, 89, 97
Burgundians 79, 81 n., 117
burial customs:
grave goods as dating evidence 25–
8
meaning of 'heathen burials' 38 n.
cremation superseded by inhumation 93
practices of continental Angles 108,
110–11
mixed cemeteries 111–12
significance of cremation 112

inhumation areas in south-east 112–
13
scarcity of cremation in Kent 122
male burials in prehistoric round
barrows 149
Lankhills cemetery 150
practices in Mercia 185

Cadbury 140 n.
Cadwallon 197
Caedbaed 141 n., 182
Caedwalla 147
Caerleon 121
Caesar, Julius 3
Caister-by-Yarmouth: map 2, map 6,
xxvii, 89, 97
Caistor-by-Norwich (*Venta Icenorum*):
map 2, map 5, map 6, xix, xxvii,
72, 87, 89, 96–101, 110, 178,
fig. 3, fig. 5
Caistor-on-the-Wolds: map 4, map 6,
89, 176, 179–81
Calleva Atrebatum see Silchester
Cam (river): map 2
Camboglanna see Birdoswald
Cambridge: map 2, map 5, 87, 101,
166, 178
Cambridge region 38–9, 87, 112
Camulodunum see Colchester
canabae 76
Candover: map 3, 149, 162 n.
Canterbury (*Cantwarabyrig/burh*): map
2, map 5, xxvi, 9, 31, 66,
99, 122–5, 146, 204 n., 209,
213
Cantware (Cantiaci, Cantii) 115, 122–
3, 126 n., 173, 209
Carausius 53, 79, 83–4, 91
Carisbrooke (*Wihtgarabyrig*): map 2,
map 3, map 6, 145–6, 213 n.
Carlisle (*Luguvallium*): map 4, 18,
205 n.
Carrawburgh (*Procolitia*): map 4, 75,
79
Carvoran: map 4
Cassington: map 3, 102, 156
Castlesteads (*Uxellodunum*): map 4,
75
Catterick (*Cataractonium, Catreath*):
map 4, 197
Cawfields 78
Cearl 184
ceaster as place-name element 31–2
Ceasterware see Cesterwara